The Road to Lonergan's
Method in Theology

The Ordering of Theological Ideas

Craig S. Boly S.J.
Gonzaga University

UNIVERSITY
PRESS OF
AMERICA

Lanham • New York • London

Copyright © 1991 by
University Press of America®, Inc.
4720 Boston Way
Lanham, Maryland 20706

3 Henrietta Street
London WC2E 8LU England

Library of Congress Cataloging-in-Publication Data

Boly, Craig S., 1944-
The road to Lonergan's method in theology : the ordering of
theological ideas / Craig S. Boly.
p.   cm.
Includes bibliographical references and indexes.
1. Lonergan, Bernard J. F. Method in theology.
2. Theology—Methodology.   3. Theology, Doctrinal.
4. Catholic Church—Doctrines.   I. Title.
BR118.L653   1990   230'.2'01—dc20   90–46070 CIP

ISBN 0–8191–7741–5 (alk. paper)

The paper used in this publication meets the minimum requirements of
American National Standard for Information Sciences—Permanence
of Paper for Printed Library Materials, ANSI Z39.48–1984.

To my father and mother -- Elwyn and Frances Boly

where my learning began

Tell me and I will forget.
Show me, and I may remember.
Help me do it, and it is mine forever.

Chinese proverb

TABLE OF CONTENTS

Page

PREFACE xiv

INTRODUCTION

The State of the Question 1

The Method of this Study 6

Division of the Development 8

CHAPTER I

THE PRELIMINARY CONTEXT
FOR LONERGAN'S ORDERING OF IDEAS

A Biographical Note 15

A Schematic Outline of the Twofold Way's Development 16

The Introduction to the *Gratia Operans* Dissertation 18

The Early Latin Writings 19

The *De Ente Supernaturali* and the *Via Compositionis* 22

CHAPTER II

RECOVERING THE MIND OF AQUINAS

Resolution to Principles 31

The *Via Doctrinae* 34
    A. The *Crux Trinitatis* 36
    B. The *Imago Dei* 37
    C. Theology as Science 38

The *De Scientia Atque Voluntate Dei* 41

Insight: The Appropriation of One's Own Mind 44

Concluding Overview 48

CHAPTER III

A THEMATIC STATEMENT OF
THE *VIA INVENTIONIS* AND THE *VIA DOCTRINAE*

"Theology and Understanding" 53
    A. Lonergan's Review of Beumer 55
    B. Lonergan's Objections to Beumer 57
    C. The Importance for St. Thomas of the *Via Doctrinae* 59

"Theology and Understanding": Old Problems 63
    A. Speculative Theology and the Truths of Revelation 63
    B. Speculative Theology and the Illumination of Reason by
        Faith 64
    C. Speculative Theology and the Teaching of the Church ... 65

"Theology and Understanding": New Problems 68
    A. Methodological Issues: The Problem of Patterns of Human
        Experience 68
    B. Methodological Issues: The Problem of the Relation
        Between Speculative and Positive Theology 69

Five Observations on the Method of Synthesis 69
C. Methodological Issues: The Relation Between Speculative
    Theology and the Empirical Human Sciences 71
D. Methodological Issues: The Critical Problem and Historical
    Interpretation 71

De Constitutione Christi 72

On Theological Understanding 73

Concluding Overview 77

CHAPTER IV

THREE PROCESSES IN SPECULATIVE THEOLOGY:
ANALYSIS, SYNTHESIS, AND THE HISTORICAL EVOLUTION
OF UNDERSTANDING

The First Chapter of *Divinarum Personarum*: Theological
    Understanding 84

The Threefold Process by Which We Attain the End of Theological
    Understanding 87
    A. Analysis 87
    B. Synthesis 88
    C. The Historical Evolution of Understanding 88
    D. A Comparison Between Natural Science and Theology . . . 89
    E. A Comparison Between the Analytic and Synthetic
        Processes 91
    F. A Summary of the Analytic and Synthetic Processes in
        Comparison with One Another 95

The Historical Dimension of Theological Understanding 96
    A. General Outlines of the Historical Dimension of Theological
        Understanding 96

B. The Historical Development of Theological Understanding and the Transcultural Problem 99

C. A Systematic Treatment of the *Via Analytica* and the *Via Synthetica* in Light of the Transcultural Problem 99

D. The Historical Process Considered in Its Own Right: The Evolution of Dogma and the Development of Theological Understanding 102

E. Examples of the Historical Process of the Evolution of Dogma Theological Understanding 102

   1. The Use of *Homoousion* 102

   2. The Two Natures of Chalcedon That Abandons the *Prius Patristicum* 103

   3. The Discovery of the Systematic *Prius Quoad Se* . . 104

   4. Methodological Uncertainty 105

The Object of Theology 106

Concluding Overview 107

CHAPTER V

PROBLEMS DERIVING FROM THE EVOLUTION OF THEOLOGICAL UNDERSTANDING

The *"De Intellectu et Methodo"* 116

A. On the Question, the Series of Questions, and the Ordering of Responses 117

   1. The Ordering is Logical 118

   2. The Ordering is Coherent 118

   3. Ordered Propositions Ought to Have a Reference to Reality 119

   4. The Same Totality Can be Ordered in Diverse Ways in Equivalent Systems 119

B. On the Series of Orderings of Responses 122

C. On the Criteria for a New Ordering 124

D. On the Threefold Problem: Of Foundations, of Historicity, of the Chasm 124

1. The Problem of Foundations   125
2. The Problem of Historicity   126
3. The Problem of the Chasm   128
4. On the Possibility of the Solution   129
    (a) The Solution to the Foundational Problem .   130
    (b) About the Problem of the Chasm   132
    (c) About the Problem of Historicity   134
5. On the Unity of the Solution   135

On The Notion Of Science   136
    A. Illustrations from Different Notions of Science   137
    B. The Conclusion Concerning the Notion of Science   138

On Method and Its Precepts   139
    A. A Theological Illustration of the First Rule: Understand . . .   141
    B. A Theological Illustration of the Second Rule: Understand
        Systematically   142
    C. A Theological Illustration of the Third Rule: Reverse
        Counterpositions   143
    D. A Theological Illustration of the Fourth Rule: Develop
        Positions   145
    E. A Theological Illustration of the Fifth Rule: Accept Respon-
        sibility for Making a Judgment   155

Lonergan's Concluding Section   156

Concluding Overview   157

CHAPTER VI

THE CONCERN FOR THE PLACE OF HISTORY
IN THEOLOGICAL DEVELOPMENT AND THE TURN
TO THE SUBJECT IN "DE METHODO THEOLOGIAE"

"The Philosophy of History"   165

The De Deo Trino: Pars Analytica of 1961.   171

"*De Methodo Theologiae*" 175
   A. The Transition from Faith to Theology 180
   B. The Transition from the Exegete's Method to the Dogmatic
      Theologian's Method 181
   C. The Dogmatic Theologian's Use of Scripture 182
   D. New Material in the 1962 Regis College Lectures 182
   E. The Methodical Classification of Historical Studies 184

CHAPTER VII

THE 1964 REVISION OF THE *DE DEO TRINO: PARS ANALYTICA* THAT BECOMES THE *DE DEO TRINO I: PARS DOGMATICA*

The 1964 *De Deo Trino I: Pars Dogmatica* 197
   A. The Aim of Dogmatic Theology 198
   B. The Aim of Positive Theology 200
   C. Difference Between the Methods of Positive and Dogmatic
      Theology 203
   D. Dogmatic Development 207

Concluding Overview 211

CHAPTER VIII

THE 1964 REVISION OF THE INTRODUCTION TO THE 1957 *DIVINARUM PERSONARUM CONCEPTIO ANALOGICA*

De Deo Trino II: Pars Systematica, Chapter I, Section 3: "On the Question or Problem" 218

De Deo Trino II: Pars Systematica, Chapter I, Section 4: "The Truth of Understanding" 222
   A. 1964, Section 4: Part ii -- How is Theological Understand-
      ing to be Compared to Antecedent Truth? 223
   B. 1964, Section 4: Part iii -- How is Theological Understand-
      ing to be Compared to Consequent Truth? 225

De Deo Trino II: Pars Systematica, Chapter I, Section 5: "On the Twofold Process by Which the Goal is Attained" 234

De Deo Trino II: Pars Systematica, Chapter I, Section 6: "A Comparison Between Dogmatics and Systematics" 238

De Deo Trino II: Pars Systematica, Chapter I, Sections 7 and 8: "A Consideration of the Historical Movement; A Further Consideration of the Historical Movement" 239

Concluding Overview 239

CHAPTER IX

A CRITICAL REVIEW OF
THE EVOLUTION OF THE TWOFOLD PROCESS

Elements of the Problematic 245
    A. The Medieval Horizon 246
    B. The Thomist Horizon of Wisdom 249
    C. Theology as Analogously a Science 254
    D. The Role of History in Theology -- Accounting for the Development of Dogma 257
    E. Methodical Theology's Shift to the Subject 260

Concluding Remarks 262

BIBLIOGRAPHY OF WORKS CITED 270

INDEX
INDEX OF AUTHORS

PREFACE

This book is an exposition of the theological method practiced by Bernard Lonergan from 1940-1964. At first, he used the procedures of analysis and synthesis borrowed from natural science as the way of accomplishing the work of theology. These procedures, however, are mentioned only in passing in his 1972 *Method in Theology* and subsequent writings. What follows is the mapping of what became of his early theological procedures.

Lonergan's work on the analytic/synthetic processes is divided into three periods. The first period of 1940-1954 reveals him reacting to the manualist aim of establishing proofs of faith. He took as his goal the Thomist speculative ideal of *understanding* the truths of faith. It was in the context of his treatment of grace that he first borrowed from Aquinas the terms for arranging ideas according to a "way of resolution" and a "way of composition" (chapter 1). In the *Verbum* articles, he noted the historical way of studying a science (*via inventionis*), but he was more interested in the Thomist speculative procedure named the "way of teaching" (*via doctrinae*), although at this early stage of his thought he did not distinguish between the dogmatic and speculative elements of a development (chapter 2).

A second period began from the 1954 article, "Theology and Understanding," when he thematized his use of analysis and synthesis. Here he still embraced the Thomist procedures for pursuing speculative theology, but now he admitted four methodological issues when one tries to relate speculative theology and the positive procedures of historical scholarship (chapter 3). In the 1957 *Divinarum personarum conceptio analogica*, he theorized about a "third, historical process" to complement the analytic/synthetic pair (chapter 4). In the 1959 graduate course, "*De intellectu et methodo*," he noted three aspects of the single methodological problem that arose when the historical perspective, introduced by positive studies, compelled a rethinking of the procedures of speculative and dogmatic theology (chapters 5 and 6).

A third period began in 1960 when Lonergan continued to account for theology's historical dimension, but now as performed within the context of methodological theology. In the 1962 graduate course, "*De methodo theologiae*," he turned to the subject and to questions of historicity that spawned terms for establishing what eventually became functional specialization (chapter 6). The conclusion of his development of the analytic/synthetic procedures is depicted in the 1964 revisions of his twin trinitarian volumes, on dogmatics (chapter 7), and on systematics (chapter 8).

The concluding chapter looks at five elements that comprise the problematic connected with Lonergan's development of the twofold way of ordering ideas according to analysis and synthesis (chapter 9). The first element is a weakness in the medieval world view. The second concerns medieval theology's notion of philosophy and its approach to systems. The third is the movement from one notion of science to another. The fourth revolves around the need to account for development. And the fifth and last element centers on methodological theology's shift to the subject. Analysis and synthesis were adequate as one classification of development, as long as the development did not require a shift from one historical context to another. But with the emergence of the historical exigence, a new, more flexible classification of development required theology's procedures to include more than what analysis/synthesis could achieve.

While attempting to appropriate Lonergan's development, I have come to appreciate how rigorous is the achievement of intellectual conversion which is described in *Method in Theology*. I salute my professors and students who have accompanied me on the intellectual journey that this study represents, and acknowledge with equal appreciation those who seek to understand the origins of the thought of Bernard Lonergan.

INTRODUCTION

With the 1972 publication of *Method in Theology*, Bernard Lonergan completed the expression, begun in 1940 with the Introduction of his doctoral dissertation, of a lifelong interest in the various aims and ways of performing the tasks that constitute contemporary theology. While some may argue that Lonergan's contribution to the advancement of the field of theology itself has been curtailed by his preoccupation with accounting for theology's method, few will claim that his thought on method does not warrant serious consideration. In light of his stature as a methodologist of theology, especially in view of his conclusion that eight functional specialties make up the ongoing, collaborative venture of theology today, a significant question arises. What happened to his own early procedures for doing theology according to analysis and synthesis?

The State of the Question

A survey of Lonergan's theological work from 1940 till 1964 shows that the analytic and synthetic procedures dominate his thinking on theological method. A survey of his *Method in Theology* and subsequent writings shows only brief mention of the two ways of doing theology. What happened to them? Did Lonergan abandon them, and if so, why? And if he abandoned them, do they have any interest today? Or did he retain them? And if so, in what form, and with what relation to the new interests of *Method in Theology*?

The question about his early procedures and what became of them is significant. If it is granted that Lonergan is a methodologist of sufficient stature to warrant serious attention, then it follows that knowing where he came from and how he got there will shed light on his ultimate conclusions. A study to answer the question about his early analytic/synthetic procedure and its subsequent development is important because it reproduces the steps he took in getting to what eventually becomes functional specializa-

1

tion in *Method in Theology*. Furthermore, such a study can recreate in the reader the same development Lonergan underwent in the evolution of his theological procedure from the relatively ahistorical Thomist horizon to the world view of intentionality analysis that includes history.

In *The Achievement of Bernard Lonergan*, David Tracy wrote that Lonergan made an important methodological breakthrough for contemporary theology. This breakthrough was the awareness that theology must differentiate the various functions of positive, dogmatic, and systematic methods and then integrate them by means of a transcendental method equal to that task.[1] Tracy pointed out that Lonergan was content in his early theological work, *De ente supernaturali*, with the traditional distinction between doing theology according to the analytic way and the synthetic way. In *De ente supernaturali*, Lonergan was not interested in distinguishing further the two tasks proper to the analytic way, namely, positive and dogmatic theology.[2] It was only later, in the 1964 revised volumes of his trinitarian texts, that he differentiated positive and dogmatic theology and created a genetic-dialectic method to account for the historical facts.

Tracy situated the topic of Lonergan's use of analysis and synthesis in the changed context of Catholic theology subsequent to the biblical, patristical, and liturgical revivals. He adverted to the relationship of Lonergan's early theological procedures and the importance of differentiating a strictly positive theology, and of distinguishing doctrinal development on dogmatic theology from the goal of speculative theology strictly speaking.[3] But it is one thing to see that Lonergan's problematic was how dogmatic and speculative theologies could use the results of positive theology without abandoning their own goals and methods. It is another thing to follow Lonergan's development of his early theological procedures to discover what were the issues that brought about the differentiation of analysis and synthesis into what eventually becomes the dynamic structure elaborated in *Method in Theology* as functional specialization. While Tracy sketched the results of Lonergan's differentiations of positive, dogmatic, and systematic theology, he only noted the presence of the analytic way and the synthetic way as Lonergan's theological procedures without examining how

2

these procedures operated, evolved, met obstacles, and eventually became further differentiated.

By noting Lonergan's use of analysis and synthesis, Tracy provided a valuable service to those who want to understand Lonergan's development of theological method. But he did not demonstrate how Lonergan's use of the twofold way came about. As we shall see, a key element in accounting for the further differentiation of the twofold procedures was Lonergan's understanding of the notion of history. Tracy again made an important contribution to the interpretation of Lonergan's early method by distinguishing the two meanings of the notion of historical consciousness. The first was the "historical sense" needed to realize that, for example, Nicea must be interpreted in its own context and terms. A second, more radical meaning of historical consciousness recognized the need for the historian to ask "what was going forward" according to the canons of contemporary hermeneutics and critical history -- in short, to perform the task envisioned later in "History", the third functional specialty of *Method in Theology*.[4] Tracy saw that Lonergan in his own theological work in the period from 1940 to 1964 used the first kind of historical sense, although not explicitly.[5] While these points are correct, still they need to be elaborated.

Further investigation is needed to substantiate the development in Lonergan's use of synthesis and analysis, first, in the speculative context -- since, following Aquinas, Lonergan held that the proper role of theology was to seek understanding; and later, in response to the crisis in dogmatic theology generated by positive scholarship, when he unpacked the possible uses of the *via analytica*. Moreover, in his article commenting on *Method in Theology*, Frederick Crowe, S.J. gave a list of headings to indicate Lonergan's stages of development, but warned that "there is enormous amount of work to be done on these preliminary efforts, of the sort that David Tracy has initiated in his book on Lonergan if we are to understand and evaluate the final product".[6] As well as to be a tool for understanding and evaluating his final product, the present work was begun so as to apprehend the theological methodology Lonergan used in his own teaching and writing as a Roman Catholic dogmatic theologian prior to 1964. The

3

reason for the scope of this study extending only until 1964 will be explained at the end of this introduction.

The topic of this publication is Lonergan's use of the *via analytica* and the *via synthetica* as theological procedures during the period of his own theological productivity from 1940 till 1964. Our contention is that the emergence of historical consciousness into Catholic theology through the advances of exegetical and historical scholarship as well as through the focusing of the notion of the development of dogma caused a series of differentiations within Lonergan's use of the traditional procedures for doing theology according to analysis and synthesis. We will show that while Lonergan was remarkably careful and consistent in his development, nonetheless there was an intra-Lonergan dialectic as he wrestled with a shift from viewing theology's goal as almost exclusively speculative to the perspective that incorporated the exigencies of historical consciousness for dogmatic theology.

Theologians may be more interested in Lonergan's final work on theological specialization, *Method in Theology*, than in the efforts that led up to his definitive conclusions about the way of doing theology. Yet as Frederick Crowe indicated in *The Lonergan Enterprise*, Lonergan's final study of theological method "was indeed the end product of a lifetime of thought".[7] In order to grasp the meaning and import of the end product, we need a fuller appreciation of the steps taken to reach the conclusions of *Method in Theology*. Like Tracy, Crowe provided a broad outline of Lonergan's development of the twofold theological procedures according to analysis and synthesis, noting examples from natural science and ethics to show the difference between the starting point, goal, and process of each procedure.[8] Furthermore, he listed the fundamental places where data on the topic of the twofold way can be found.[9] In support of his contention that basic research is crucial for an understanding of Lonergan, Crowe specifically cited the topic of Lonergan's own early methodology and indicated that until the research is done to study the predecessor of the method of 1972, this lacuna about his use of analysis and synthesis will be an area of ignorance vulnerable to misinterpretation.[10]

4

In a thinker as nuanced and complex as Lonergan, this special kind of research is needed. Not only is his thought difficult because it is so dense, but as Crowe indicated, "his way has not been to turn out an article a month and a book a year, but has followed a pattern of quantum leaps at intervals of several years".[11] While these intervals encompassed striking developments, still this evolution of thought frequently was not exhibited in published works as much as in mimeographed lectures or classnotes taken by students. So the effort to recapitulate the development does not derive as much from published material as from the data available only to specialized research.

A number of scholars have pointed out the importance of studying Lonergan's use of analysis and synthesis, and have even indicated the texts, notes, lectures where germane references are contained. Still, there is remarkably little written about his use of the twofold procedures. For example, Lonergan directed theses by Robert Richard and John Connelly in Rome that adverted respectively to the systematic exposition of the *via doctrinae* and to the difference between the thought of Beumer and Lonergan on theological procedures.[12] Richard delineated the twofold way in an article that examined a theory of development to account for the evolution of dogma in Church history.[13] Peter Drilling alluded to Lonergan's use of the twofold theological procedures in his doctoral thesis on the development of Lonergan's thought on the material starting point of theology.[14] And Nicholas Fogliacco identified the *via dogmatica* with the *via inventionis* in his doctoral study of the first part of Lonergan's Roman period.[15] But all of these writers only alluded to the twofold procedures without treating Lonergan's development and use of them in any comprehensive way.

If there is little written about Lonergan's use of the twofold theological procedure, there is even less practical implementation of it. At the end of the period of Lonergan's work that we are investigating, Frederick Crowe structured his course at Regis College for 1965-1966 on the Trinity according to the *via analytica* and the *via synthetica*. After benefiting from an awareness of Lonergan's development of the twofold analytic/synthetic procedures that had been reached by 1964, Crowe explained the use of the procedures for his own course by giving an example of the two processes:

> A simple figure will illustrate the difference between the two orders: in the historical part, we are like men groping their way down a dark corridor, unable to turn on the light till they get to the end where the switch is; but in the systematic part, we are like men who have turned on the light and retrace their steps, seeing everything with a new clarity and understanding.[16]

As we shall see, the analytic/synthetic procedures promote learning in students that is both rapid and complete because the two processes complement each other. While the twofold processes cultivate good pedagogy, perhaps it is no wonder that the procedures have not received more widespread application. They require enormous breadth of scholarship and output of energy in the teacher to organize the material both historically and systematically. Even Lonergan only used these procedures in some of his theological writings, as in his trinitarian texts, for example. He did not follow a similar rigorous method of arranging the presentation of his thought in other works, not even in his major classnotes on the Incarnation.

The Method of this Study

If we apprehend theological method according to the model that Lonergan elaborated in *Method in Theology*, then we view it as a discipline composed of eight independent and yet related functional specialties. This publication exemplifies the use of the first, second as well as the third specializations: research, interpretation, and history. In his own dissertation on Aquinas, Lonergan implemented these three specializations. He had to use both interpretation and history since the various expressions about *gratia operans* by Aquinas could only be adequately interpreted in light of their historical contexts. So our initial goal will be to exercise the three exegetical operations that make up the aim of interpretation:

> (1) understanding the text; (2) judging how correct one's understanding of the text is; and (3) stating what one judges to be the correct understanding of the text.[17]

The initial step, then, will be to come to an understanding of Lonergan's writings on the twofold ordering of ideas. This first task will be to identify the various relevant classnotes, books and texts, locate the writings according to place and time, discover their audiences, ascertain their aims, procedures, and elements. In this work, the purpose will be to understand what Lonergan meant by the various new names he gave the ways of ordering ideas (e.g., the *via resolutionis, inventionis, certitudinis, analytica*; or the *via compositionis, doctrinae, probabilitatis, synthetica*). But we will not be content with an exegetical understanding of texts (we want an historical understanding as well). Moreover, we are not simply seeking an exegetical understanding of Lonergan's thought since his texts are already systematic in conception and execution. Unlike texts written in popular language that admit endless interpretation (such as the plays of Shakespeare or the gospels), systematic texts are composed of technical terms that yield a precise meaning and curtail the possibility of misinterpretation and misunderstanding. Still, our first task is to delineate the correct understanding of the various ways the twofold analytic/synthetic procedures evolve.

The subsequent goal of the present work is to gain an historical understanding of Lonergan's thought on the development of the analytic and synthetic procedures he used in doing theology. Our method is to examine his relevant theological texts in chronological order. The aim of reaching historical understanding will be met in the process of scrutinizing the germane materials because from this examination there will emerge both a general and a specific viewpoint.

As Tracy has shown, Lonergan's work to specify and to elaborate a comprehensive theological method has provided theology with a general and a moving viewpoint. Our study will show that the specific movement of Lonergan's viewpoint about the development of the analytic/synthetic procedures relates to the general movement as lower to higher differentiation. The development of the twofold procedures relates to the general movement as one organic stage of growth relates to the transposition to a subsequent stage. A movement from biology that mirrors this development is the evolution of the zygote to the embryo. For as we shall see, the twofold way is not abandoned in theological method any more than the insights of faculty psychology about human cognition are invalidated by the elaborations of intentionality analysis. Rather, Lonergan's use of analysis and synthesis is further differentiated and transposed to a new methodological context.

The aim of an historical understanding of Lonergan's development of the analytic/synthetic procedures is to make explicit the problems, questions, and difficulties that he was implicitly seeking to solve. The basic arrangement of the questions and problems arises from a study of the chronological succession of his works. The most significant shift in his thought can be traced to the 1962 *"De methodo theologiae"* where he responds to problems already identified in his developing methodological reflections, and where he establishes the terms that will eventually become the functional specialty, dogmatics, in *Method in Theology*.

We will see him spelling out the implications of this shift in his new reflections about the place of history in theological method as contained in the 1964 revision of his trinitarian texts. Our arrangement of the presentation of his work functions only to state his development of the analytic/synthetic ways of doing theology and does not pretend to be a normative compartmentalizing of his theological or methodological corpus.[18]

Division of the Development

A division of Lonergan's work on the analytic/synthetic processes according to chronology yields three periods of development. The first period of the 1940s till 1954 is characterized by his acceptance of theology's goal as the classical, Thomist aim of speculative theology, namely, to understand the truths of faith. Although he adverted to the *via inventionis* in the *Verbum* articles, his main interest was the *via doctrinae*, that is, speculative development. Our first two chapters will trace the primitive expression of his original methodological horizon. The first chapter is on the Introduction to his *Gratia Operans* dissertation followed by an exposition of some schematic supplements, especially *De ente supernaturali*. The second chapter shows him reaching up to the mind of Aquinas in the *Verbum* articles, in *De scientia atque voluntate Dei*, and in *Insight*.

A second period began from the 1954 article, "Theology and Understanding", where he thematized his own use of analysis and synthesis. Here he was still content with the classical formulation of theology's goal in terms of seeking an understanding of the truths of faith. But now he admitted four methodological issues that stretched the elegant simplicity of the analytic/synthetic procedures. These problematic issues culminated in the introduction in the 1957 *Divinarum personarum conceptio analogica* of a "third, historical process" to complement the analytic/synthetic pair. Later in this period in 1959, in the "*De intellectu et methodo*", there were three main problems that were the component parts of his struggle to relate speculative theology and emerging positive scholarship. The foundational problem occurs within a system when a new kind of problem arises whose solution does not seem available within that system. The problem of historicity arises because the ordering of theological data in a tract does not emerge automatically from logical deduction, but requires the act of understanding to discover what is the *causa essendi*. The problem of the chasm is the gulf that exists between systematic presentations of doctrine and the belief of simple people. Actually, these are three aspects of the single methodical problem that arises when the historical perspective (introduced by positive studies) forces a rethinking of the task of speculative and dogmatic theology.

We will cover the material of this second period in chapters three through five. The third chapter is on Lonergan's 1954 thematic statement of the twofold way as well as on his 1956 comments on method in *De constitutione Christi*. The fourth chapter is on the Introduction to his 1957 *Divinarum personarum conceptio analogica*. The fifth chapter covers the problems evolving from theological understanding as seen in his 1959 doctoral seminar on understanding and method. In fact, the bridge between the methodical problems raised by accounting for the develop- ment of doctrine -- hence, the bridge between this second period and the third period of Lonergan's amplification of the twofold procedures -- was the graduate course of 1959, *"De intellectu et methodo"*.

A third period was inaugurated in 1960 when Lonergan sought to account for theology's historical dimension, but now in a way that questioned whether to place the historical task more in the camp of the analytic procedure, or to posit the movement of history as the prior context for both the analytic and synthetic procedures. He wrote about these new perspectives in the 1960 lecture, "The Philosophy of History", and in the Introduction to the 1961 *De Deo Trino: Pars Analytica*, and most significant- ly, in the 1962 graduate course, *"De methodo theologiae"*, where his turn to the subject and attention to issues of historicity generated the terms for establishing what eventually becomes functional specialization (our chapter six); in the 1964 revisions of his twin trinitarian volumes which we treat as the term of his development of the analytic/synthetic procedures, on dogmatics (our chapter seven) and on systematics (our chapter eight).

One final note about the 1964 limit of our study. Originally, the plan of this investigation was to trace the beginnings of Lonergan's theological method as expressed in the analytic/synthetic procedures and to discover how they were related to functional specialization in *Method in Theology*. It soon became apparent, however, that there was a massive amount of data to be covered from his inchoate statements on method in 1940 until he last used analysis and synthesis explicitly as the organizational principles for his theological work in 1964. After 1962 and *De methodo theologiae*, Lonergan seemed to move beyond the hitherto engulfing and captivatingly magnetic influence of St. Thomas into the more historical viewpoint reflected for theology in functional specialization. It became apparent that answering the initial question about the origin and term of Lonergan's early methodical development was sufficiently broad a task without adding the second question about how the twofold procedures were transposed into functional specialization. This second question has the foundation for its answer in the present work, but it represents a superstructure that would carry us well beyond the blueprint of our already complex and extensive construction. So we have chosen Lonergan's explicit treatment and use of the twofold analytic/synthetic processes as the term of our study.

As will become evident, practically the rest of this entire book has been written in the *via inventionis*, the gradual accumulation of insights by a study of the history of a development. A large proportion of the work here has been to present a precis of Lonergan's views. While the amount of space given to summaries of Lonergan's work may seem great, it is not without worth since it contributes to the first functional specialty, research, especially when a work such as *"De intellectu et methodo"* is available only in Latin. Once the work of the "way of historical discovery" has been done, the *via doctrinae* can accomplish its task rapidly in the "way of logical simultaneity", and present its findings with brief deductions and a compendious statement of insights. So while the conclusions of the present work are narrow in terms of working out the aims of interpretation and history, our aim is also to contribute to the functional specialty, research, by seeking out, accumulating, arranging, and presenting a body of evidence on the topic of Lonergan's use of analysis and synthesis in theology.

NOTES

INTRODUCTION

[1]David Tracy, *The Achievement of Bernard Lonergan* (New York: Herder and Herder, 1970), p. 205.

[2]*Ibid.*, p. 199

[3]*Ibid.*, p. 183

[4]Bernard J. F. Lonergan, S.J., *Method in Theology* (London: Darton, Longman & Todd, 1972).

[5]Tracy, *The Achievement of Bernard Lonergan*, p. 193, footnote 24.

[6]Frederick E. Crowe, S.J., "Early Jottings on Bernard Lonergan's *Method in Theology*", *Science et Esprit*, 25 (1973), 126.

[7]Frederick E. Crowe, S.J., *The Lonergan Enterprise* (Cambridge, Massachusetts: Cowley, 1980), p. 23.

[8]*Ibid.*, pp. 19-20.

[9]*Ibid.*, p. 49. See Frederick E. Crowe, S.J. ed., "Introduction" in *Collection* (New York: Herder and Herder, 1967), p. xxv; Conn O'Donovan, "Translator's Introduction" in *The Way to Nicea* (London: Darton, Longman and Todd, 1976), pp. xviii-xx; David Tracy, *The Achievement of Bernard Lonergan* (New York: Herder and Herder, 1970), pp. 192-196.

[10]Crowe, *The Lonergan Enterprise*, p. 49.

[11]*Ibid.*, p. 48

[12]Robert L. Richard, *The Problem of an Apologetical Perspective in the Trinitarian Theology of St. Thomas Aquinas* (Rome: Gregorian University Press, 1963); John J. Connelly, *"Ordo Doctrinae* in the *Summa Contra Gentiles* of St. Thomas Aquinas" (S.T.D. dissertation, Pontifical Gregorian University, Rome, 1956).

[13]Robert L. Richard, "Contribution to a Theory of Doctrinal Development" in *Spirit as Inquiry: Studies in Honor of Bernard Lonergan, S.J.*, ed. Frederick Crowe, S.J., *Continuum,* 2 (1964) pp. 505-530, especially 506-507.

[14]Peter J. Drilling, "A Study of the Development of Bernard Lonergan's Thought on the Material Starting Point for Theology", (Ph.D. dissertation, University of St. Michael's College, Toronto, *Science et Esprit,* 31 (1979), 303-321.

[15]Nicholas Fogliacco, I.M.C., *"Lo sviluppo del dogma nel pensiero di Bernard Lonergan"*, *Dissertation Abstracts International,* 34 (1974), 2749-A to 2750-A.

[16]Frederick Crowe, S.J., *The Doctrine of the Most Holy Trinity* (Willowdale: Regis College, mimeographed classnotes for use of students, 1965-1966), p. 141. See Robert J. Egan, "New Direction in the Doctrine of Original Sin" (Ph.D. dissertation, Fordham University, New York, 1973). He explains his use of the twofold procedure in the Introduction, pp. 12-27.

[17]Lonergan, *Method in Theology*, p. 155.

[18]There are almost as many ways of dividing up the chronological sequence of Lonergan's writings as there are commentators on his corpus. My arrangement of his work has taken into consideration the various orderings made by different scholars. See Crowe: "The Exigent Mind: Bernard Lonergan's Intellectualism" in *Spirit as Inquiry: Studies in Honor of Bernard Lonergan, Continuum* 2 (1964), 316-333; "Bernard Lonergan" in *Modern Theologians, Christians and Jews*, ed. Thomas E. Bird (New York:

Association Press, 1967), 126-151; "Dogma Versus the Self-Correcting Process of Learning", *Theological Studies*, 31 (1970), 605-624; "Early Jottings on Bernard Lonergan's *Method in Theology*", *Science et Esprit*, 25 (1973), 121-138; "Lonergan's New Notion of Value", *Science et Esprit*, 29 (1977), 123-143; *The Lonergan Enterprise* (Cambridge, Massachusetts: Cowley, 1980), pp. 19-22, 49. See Drilling: "A Study of the Development of Bernard Lonergan's Thought on the Material Starting Point for Theology", (Ph.D. dissertation, University of St. Michael's College, Toronto, 1978), pp. 13-14. See Thomas A. Dunne, S.J., "Lonergan on Social Progress and Community: A Developmental Study" (Ph.D. dissertation, Institute of Christian Thought, Toronto, 1975), pp. 112-113, n. 4. See William F.J. Ryan, S.J. and Bernard Tyrrell, S.J., ed. in the Introduction to *A Second Collection* (London: Darton, Longman & Todd, 1974), pp. vii-xii. See Tracy: *The Achievement of Bernard Lonergan* (New York: Herder and Herder, 1970); "The Development of the Notion of Theological Methodology in the Works of Bernard J. Lonergan, S.J." (S.T.D. dissertation, Pontifical Gregorian University, Rome, 1969).

CHAPTER I

THE PRELIMINARY CONTEXT
FOR LONERGAN'S ORDERING OF IDEAS

A Biographical Note

With the rumblings of world conflict echoing throughout Europe in 1939, Lonergan hurried to finish his doctoral thesis in the spring of 1940. He began his first teaching assignment as a professional theologian in the summer of 1940 at the College of the Immaculate Conception, the Jesuit seminary in Montreal. He was responsible for teaching dogmatic theology to Jesuit students for the priesthood who were engaged in their last phase of ecclesiastical education before ordination. After joining the faculty of *L'Immaculee* (as it was called), he taught various courses in Montreal from the summer of 1940 until Christmas, 1946: sacramental and eucharistic theology, creation, eschatology, and the two most influential classes, Trinity and grace.[1] In 1943, he began collecting materials for an account of Aquinas' views on understanding. From 1946-1949 he published a series of articles in *Theological Studies* called "The Concept of *Verbum* in the Writings of St. Thomas Aquinas".[2] In 1947, he was assigned to the Jesuit seminary in Toronto where, until the spring of 1953, he continued teaching theology to men preparing for the priesthood. After he had finished the *Verbum* articles, he began writing *Insight* in 1949 while continuing to teach in Toronto. During the first three years of writing *Insight*, his intention was to explore methods generally in preparation for a study of the method of theology. But in 1952, he was told to begin readying himself to teach theology the following year at the Gregorian University in Rome, so he changed his plan and rounded off what he had done and submitted it for publication in 1953 under the title, *Insight, A Study of Human Understanding*. It was not published, however, until April of 1957.

Lonergan was transferred from Toronto to his alma mater, the Gregorian University in Rome in the summer of 1953. For the next ten years he lectured in alternate years on the incarnate Word and on the Trinity to classes of 650 second and third year theologians. In addition, he composed articles, book reviews, and supplements to the ordinary texts for use by students in his classes. Moreover, he taught doctoral seminars on method in theology to students in Italy, Canada, and the United States from 1954 to 1964.[3] In this setting, briefly sketched in simple categories of space and time, we have now to outline the series of his writings that deal with the twofold way.

A Schematic Outline of the Twofold Way's Development

Lonergan's interest in method can be traced back at least as far as the late 1930s, when he was writing in Rome his doctoral dissertation on Aquinas' thought on operative grace. The dissertation begins with a long theoretical discussion of speculative development that contains his first attempt at specifying a method for theology.[4]

The interest in method appears again in Lonergan's early Latin class notes. In a schematic supplement to the course on grace written in 1946 at Montreal with the title *De ente supernaturali*, he refers in the introduction to a twofold order of ideas. The first is the "way of resolution" that proceeds from revealed truths to their intelligible ordering, and the second is the "way of composition" that descends from the intelligible ordering to the ordered elements. He adopts the second order in the tract itself because he understands the "way of composition" to be the appropriate order for teaching advanced students. This is the first place in which Lonergan alludes to the exploration, lasting from 1946 to 1964, of what are eventually called the analytic and synthetic processes in theology.

In the 1946-1949 *Verbum* articles, Lonergan begins the discussion of method in the context of trinitarian theology. In the section on the "way of teaching" (*via doctrinae*), he reviews how our grasp of a twofold ordering of our trinitarian concepts is necessary for an appreciation of what St. Thomas did in his treatment of the Trinity in the *Summa theologiae*. By

1950, the way of resolution and the way of composition have become the "way of discovery" and the "way of teaching" as they are treated in another Latin schematic supplement called *De scientia atque voluntate Dei*.[5]

The first thematic statement of the twofold way of discovery and the way of teaching comes in the 1954 article titled "Theology and Understanding".[6] This article is a book review that is principally concerned with the nature and role of speculative theology. Lonergan cites the Thomist treatment of Trinity in the *Summa theologiae* as a concrete instance of the order of teaching. In addition, he indicates schematically how the order of discovery and the inverse order of teaching are related in trinitarian theory. The 1956 class notes, *De constitutione Christi*, contain a brief chapter on theological understanding that alludes to the twofold ordering of ideas. But from this time forward, it seems that Lonergan mainly worked out his method in theology in the texts he composed for teaching the course on the Trinity. For example, in 1957 he published the *Divinarum personarum conceptio analogica* in which he elaborated in an introductory chapter on theological understanding the twofold way of ordering theology according to analysis and synthesis. But here he introduced a third, historical process that reflected the influence of positive studies on speculative theology.[7] In the doctoral course of 1959 there was transcribed a student *reportatio* version of his course called "*De intellectu et methodo*". He investigated there the problems generated for theology by the historical study of the evolution of dogma.[8] In 1961, he wrote the *De Deo Trino: Pars Analytica*. In its Introduction, he faced the issue of how to arrange the elements of doctrinal history in the light of positive studies.[9] In the 1961 doctoral seminar, "*De methodo theologiae*", he transposed the twofold processes by shifting to methodical theology that included history in a new way. The shift to the subject in methodical theology transformed the twofold process of analysis and synthesis in order to prepare the way for the eventual breakthrough of doing theology according to functional specialization.[10] Finally, he returned to the ordering of ideas in the introductions to the twin volume *De Deo Trino I: Pars Dogmatica*; *II: Pars Systematica*.[11] The former focuses on the methods used by the positive and dogmatic theologian, and introduces further reflections about the development of dogma. The latter is a revision of the 1957 *Divinarum personarum* and adds a new section on the evolution of systems in speculative theology. He now called the twofold way of organizing theology the dogmatic process and the systematic process. Such is the series of writings which we shall investigate for details of Lonergan's ideas on the twofold way.

The Introduction to the *Gratia Operans* Dissertation

Lonergan does not write anything in his doctoral dissertation, *Gratia Operans*, about the twofold ordering of ideas. Yet in the Introduction to the dissertation, he writes what is his first approximation to a method for theology. While his dissertation was a work of historical interpretation, he did not focus on the role of positive theology with its contributions coming from specialized research in scripture, the Fathers, the councils, especially in medieval theology. If he were troubled with the problems arising from the contributions of positive theology, he did not address them in any comprehensive way. In the Introduction to his dissertation, he noted some difficulties in passing: that historians need to be attentive to their use of terms, that terms change their denotation and connotation when used by various authors, that correct interpretation requires a correct chronology of an author's collected works. The problems of positive theology will become central later. In the beginning of his theological career, he focused his thought on method on the difference between speculative and dogmatic development.

Speculation, according to Lonergan, is the system in systematic theology. It provides the unity, cohesion, and order of the theology manual. It develops theorems and terms, uses dialectic and the technique of philosophy to assimilate the truth. Yet speculation has a subordinate role to dogmatic theology. Dogmatic theology presents the objects that are to be defined, arranged, and put into order. It is primary because it embodies the Word of God upon which speculation reflects. Finally, speculation and dogmatic development are different because the former seeks to express deeper understanding of the truths of faith while the latter only wants to state the truths of faith in a way that is true.

The Early Latin Writings

In his early Latin writings, Lonergan focused his attention on the procedures and elements of speculative exposition. It was in the context of speculative development (not dogmatic or positive) that he initially used the ways of arranging ideas first called the "way of resolution" and the "way of composition". At first, he borrowed these terms from St. Thomas, but as his understanding of the requirements of speculation increased, he developed new terms that expressed new roles within each process. Our present interest, however, is simply to understand how he used the process of resolution and the process of composition in the process of a speculative exposition.

When Lonergan began teaching dogmatic theology to seminarians in Montreal and later in Toronto and Rome, the usual procedure was to present the dogmatic material contained in an approved manual, or to write one's own notes, or finally, to add a supplement to a standard text. The approved manuals used the thesis format to transmit to the students the dogmas and doctrine of the faith. We will look at two sets of early supplements that Lonergan wrote. They are examples of the usual organization of a manual and form a basis of comparison between the usual speculative supplement and the striking breakthrough Lonergan achieved in the structuring of his supplementary tract, *De ente supernaturali*.

The first set of notes was a speculative addition to the manual on the sacraments by Lennerz, *"De sacramentis in genere: supplementum"* and *"De materia confirmationis"*, probably written in 1940-41.[12] These supplements are interesting because they manifest the structure of the manual format and the procedure in the style then current for writing a thesis. Let us take the four-page *"De materia confirmationis"* as an

19

illustration of these points. The arrangement of the supplement follows the structure of the manual format: thesis, definition of terms, questions, solutions, proofs, and objections. As other theological treatments, it attempts to inculcate a modicum of understanding in the students. It begins by collecting the teachings accepted by faith and arranges them in the various expressions received from scripture, patristic studies, conciliar decrees, pontifical pronouncements, and theological opinions. It gathers elements from various sources that pertain to a single speculative question. It appeals to the authority of scripture or theologians rather than seeking to discover how or why the thesis reaches the conclusions it does. This characteristic of appealing to authorities is central to this style of proceeding. The other trademark of the contemporary theological manual of the middle 1940s is the refutation of error and the handing on to students of dogma the reliable facts gleaned from the history of doctrine.

The second set of notes was called "*De notione sacrificii*", a schematic supplement that Lonergan wrote for the 1943-1944 course on the eucharist for students at *L'Immaculee*.[13] These notes contain current teachings about the eucharist, its meaning, its causes, the difference between the sacrifice of the cross and of the Mass. Two points are significant for understanding why Lonergan used the thesis format here. First, he is aware that St. Thomas considered the role of wisdom to be the correct arrangement of data, and so he followed the procedures of St. Thomas. Second, at this point he seems to lump together under the category of "positive data" both what comes from revelation and from the teaching of the Church and of theologians. He is more interested in the speculative aim of his presenting the positive data according to a systematic, coherent analysis than he is in distinguishing the aims of positive or dogmatic theology.

In the school year 1945-1946, Lonergan first taught trinitarian theology, and the following year instructed students on divine grace, the subject investigated in his doctoral dissertation and reworked for publication four years earlier. It was for this course that he wrote his important *De ente supernaturali: supplementum schematicum* in the fall of 1946, in the last semester in which he taught regularly at Montreal before taking a new assignment at Regis College, the Jesuit seminary in Toronto.[14]

Written in the customary Latin of the ecclesiastical system prevalent in the 1940s, the *De ente...* was a work supplementary to the regular set of notes written by Pere Paulin Bleau. Lonergan used the manual, *Tractatus de Gratia*, by Pere Bleau, as the ordinary text for his course on grace, and presented the entire positive and dogmatic part of the treatise there. He would devote his own special attention to the theoretic side of an issue "...sometimes by way of lectures, sometimes by way of a written supplement (as in the present case), and sometimes by way of a full-scale book, as happened later in regard to both Christology and the Trinity".[15]

The content of *De ente...* is interesting in its own right as a further elaboration of ideas that first appeared in the *Gratia Operans* dissertation. This schematic supplement investigated the structure of the supernatural order, the basis for distinguishing between the natural and the supernatural, and the initial stages of relating the two orders. Yet *De ente...* is significant as well because it contains inchoate insights about the structure of the theological treatise itself. As Frederick Crowe wrote in the *De ente...* Introduction

> ...this is the first work Lonergan wrote in what he would later call the order of the *via synthetica* and, though he does not seem at this time to have given the same thought to the contrasting *via analytica*, this initial effort at methodical theology is of immense importance to the historian of his thought.[16]

To that importance we now turn.

THE ROAD TO LONERGAN'S *METHOD IN THEOLOGY*

The *De Ente Supernaturali* and the *Via Compositionis*

In his Introduction to the *De ente supernaturali*, Lonergan asked two preliminary questions. First, why consider supernatural being at all? And second, why begin a theological treatise with a term as abstract as supernatural being? He answered his first question by stating that he wants to explain the gratuity of grace.

> If the gift of God were not gratuitous, it would not be grace. Of course, a partial explanation of this gratuity is that we have sinned in Adam, and therefore we are justly deprived of qualities which Adam enjoyed before the fall. But this explanation is partial -- indeed, an easier and less important part of the entire answer. Grace is gratuitous chiefly because it has no proportion with our nature, that is, because it is supernatural.[17]

The response to the first preliminary question is significant because it reveals that Lonergan wants to *explain* the gratuity of grace. He responds to anyone who might hold that one gains enough light from the sayings of scripture and the Fathers and does not need the explanations of theologians:

> ...Aquinas pointed out that a disputation could be directed to either of two ends. If directed to removing a doubt about what was so, then in theology one appealed principally to the authorities that the listener recognized. But if directed to the instruction of the student so that he be brought to an understanding of the truth in question, then one must take one's stand on the reasons that bring to light the ground of the truth and enable one to know how what is said is true. Otherwise, if the master settles the question only by an appeal to authorities, he will make his pupil certain of what is so; but so far from giving him any understanding or science, he will send him away empty. *Quodlibet* IV,q. 9, a. 3 (18). [18]

In order to discover what Lonergan meant by this text, it is well to review the context in which St. Thomas composed it. Aquinas wrote in response to the question, *"Utrum determinationes theologicae debent fieri auctoritate, vel ratione?"*[19] In the first part of the argument, St. Thomas stated the view that teachers should use authorities more than reasons in instructing students because

> in any science, questions are best determined with reference to the first principles of that science. But the first principles of the science of theology are the articles of faith, which we know from authorities. So we should make a determination about theological questions especially by referring to authorities. [20]

In the *sed contra* part of the argument, however, St. Thomas quotes the Letter to Titus 1:9 that says that the role of the bishop is to hold firm to the sure word as taught "so that we may be able to give instruction in sound doctrine and also confute those who contradict it". This line of thought says that opponents of doctrine can be better overcome by reasons than by authorities. The context of the first part of the argument, then, is the context of instructing students. The *sed contra* context, on the other hand, is for answering the opponents of doctrine.

St. Thomas wrote as well that there is a second goal in disputations, and that aim is to understand the facts. Instead of giving students some citations from authority to establish this or that fact, St. Thomas proposed giving to learners "reasons that bring to light the ground of the truth".[22] As we have already witnessed in the *Gratia Operans* Introduction, Lonergan wanted to identify the nature of speculative theology. As he said in the Introduction of his dissertation, "Anyone who reflects on religious doctrine enters the field of theological speculation; the question of the child, the difficulties of the adult, the flood of books and articles on the 'religious problem', -- all are essentially speculative".[23] Because his aim here is speculative, he concentrated his energy in these class notes on this second kind of disputation that seeks understanding.

Now we come to the second preliminary question that pertains directly to meeting speculation's aim of arranging ideas according to the "way of composition". The second preliminary question asked in the *De ente supernaturali* Introduction is why we begin our treatment with an issue as abstract as supernatural being. This is the question about the proper order or organization of the material of the tract. Lonergan writes that it is evident that there are two possible ways of organizing the material in a speculative study. The first is the "way of resolution" that advances from revealed truths to their intelligible organization. This ordering is appropriate for teaching young students who learn best from a large number of examples, each example repeated numerous times. The second way of ordering ideas is the "way of composition" that descends from an intelligible principle of organization to the matter that is organized. This is a pedagogy for mature students who have the power of achieving insight into an entire issue from a few examples. This second way has the obvious superiority over the "way of resolution" because it does not burden the memory and it allows the thrill of insight to reduce the toil of learning theology.[24]

Lonergan's aim in the tract on the supernatural order is to explain the reason that grace is gratuitous. He accomplishes his task both by giving a structure to the supernatural order and by stating the fundamental ground for the distinction between the natural and the supernatural order. But our concern here is with yet another significant contribution he made in writing the *De ente supernaturali*. What he does here is to create a methodological breakthrough for theology. His breakthrough is to pinpoint and use the structure for the theological treatise that St. Thomas was first to discover in his own speculative development that culminated in his arrangement of ideas in the *Summa theologiae*.

Lonergan's methodological innovation was to write the tract on the supernatural order entirely in the "way of composition". The aim of the "way of composition" is to descend from an intelligible principle of organization to the matter that is organized. At this early stage in his development, he does not explain that the role of the intelligible principle of organization is to unify and to contain in itself the rest of the development. And he does

24

not explain how he arrived in this treatise at the intelligible principle of organization from which he descends back to the material that is organized. He is content to work out the "way of composition" in practice and to leave reflection about it for later. If we examine the elements that make up the "way of composition" process, we can discern how Lonergan accomplished the structuring of his treatise. The organization principle here is the scholastic metaphysical notion of being. The explanation of the tract's structuring according to the "way of composition" is that there is a correspondence between the scholastic metaphysical notion of potency, form, and act and the organization of the five theses. Just as in the natural composition of a being, potencies derive from essence or form, acts derive from potencies. The first and second theses, then, are on supernatural habits; the third and fourth theses are on the virtues as the habitual formation of potencies; and the fifth thesis is on the acts of the intellect and will. This structure is implicit, however, and Lonergan does not explicitly declare his own organizing principle other than to say that it is the "way of composition".[25]

The aim of the "way of composition" is speculative in that it seeks increased understanding -- not simply deriving from citations of authorities but generated by reasons why matters are so. And these reasons are not given in any order, but they are arranged to a principle of unity, clarity, simplicity. The "way of composition" is the descent through the intelligible arrangement of truths organized according to a seminal principle. This process sheds new light on the truths we have already seen in other tracts on such topics as habitual grace or the infused virtues. The materials treated in the "way of composition" become increasingly concrete as we move from the theoretical starting point and advance to the concrete details that have been organized. It is important to recall that this strategy aims at a fuller explanation of the data than was originally possible when each of the tracts dealt with its own material separately. The "way of composition" begins with the basic point that presupposes nothing else, and like the blossoming of a bud into a flower, gradually unfolds the meaning hidden in the most basic terms of the matter under consideration.

NOTES

CHAPTER I

[1]Frederick E. Crowe, S.J., in the editor's Introduction to *Early Latin Works of Bernard J.F. Lonergan*, Vol. II: *De ente supernaturali: supplementum schematicum* (Toronto: Regis College, 1973), pp. x-xi. He did not defend his thesis until June 8, 1943 in Montreal, a year after the dissertation was rewritten for publication in a series of articles for *Theological Studies* with the title, "St. Thomas' Thought on *Gratia Operans*," 2 (1941) 289-324; 3 (1942) 69-88, 375-402, 533-578.

[2]Bernard J.F. Lonergan, S.J., "The Concept of *Verbum* in the Writings of St. Thomas Aquinas," *Theological Studies*, 7 (1946) 349-392; 8 (1947) 35-79; 404-444; 10 (1949) 3-40; 359-393. The articles appeared in book form under the editorship of David Burrell, C.S.C. with the title, *Verbum: Word and Idea in Aquinas* (South Bend, Indiana: University of Notre Dame Press, 1967).

[3]The titles of these courses were (1) "A Theoretic Inquiry into Methods in General" (1954-55); (2) "Intellect and Method" (1958-59); (3) System and History" (1959-60); (4) "Method in Theology" (1961-62, and 1963-64).

[4]Bernard J.F. Lonergan, S.J., *Gratia Operans: A Study of the Speculative Development in the Writings of St. Thomas of Aquinas*, (Rome: *Dissertatio ad lauream in facultate theologica Pontificiae Universitatis Gregorianae*, 1940). The dissertation was published as four articles in *Theological Studies* with the title,"St. Thomas' Thought on *Gratia Operans*," 2 (1941) 289-324; 3 (1942) 69-88, 375-402, 533-578. These articles were published as *Grace and Freedom*, edited by J. Patout Burns, S.J. (London: Darton, Longman & Todd, Ltd., 1971). Lonergan did not publish the forty-seven page introduction probably because his later theorizing superseded his inchoate statements.

[5]*De scientia atque voluntate Dei*, Vol. III of *The Early Latin Works of Bernard J.F. Lonergan, S.J.*, ed. Frederick E. Crowe, S.J. (Toronto: Regis College, 1973). Written in 1950, this supplement is almost contemporary with the *Verbum* articles, which treat the two *viae*. See *Verbum: Word and Idea in Aquinas*, pp. 212-215.

[6]Bernard J.F. Lonergan, S.J., "Theology and Understanding", *Gregorianum* 35 (1954) 630-638. Reprinted in *Collection: Papers by Bernard Lonergan, S.J.*, edited by F.E Crowe, S.J. (New York: Herder and Herder, 1967), pp. 121-141.

[7]Bernard J.F. Lonergan, S.J., *Divinarum personarum conceptio analogica* (Rome: Gregorian University, 1957).

[8]Bernard J.F. Lonergan, S.J., "*De intellectu et methodo*" (mimeographed student notes, Rome: St. Francis Xavier College, 1959).

[9]Bernard J.F. Lonergan, S.J., *De Deo Trino: Pars Analytica* (Rome: Gregorian University, 1961).

[10]Bernard J.F. Lonergan, S.J., *De Deo Trino I: Pars Dogmatica; II Pars Systematica* (Rome: Gregorian University, 1964)

[11]Bernard J.F. Lonergan, S.J., "*De methodo theologiae*" (mimeographed student notes, Rome: North American College, 1962). This course was repeated in English at Regis College, Toronto, in the summer of 1962. A transcript by John Brezovec of the Regis tapes, along with some additions made by Lonergan for the summer course, are available at the Lonergan Research Institute of Regis College, Toronto.

[12]Bernard J.F. Lonergan, S.J., "*De sacramentis in genere: supplementum*" (Montreal: *L'Immaculee-Conception*, 1940-1941), pp. 1-12 and 1-14. "*De materia confirmationis: supplementum*" (Montreal: *L'Immaculee Conception*, 1940-1941), pp. 1-4.

[13]Bernard J.F. Lonergan, S.J., *"De notione sacrificii: supplementum"* (Toronto: Regis College, 1959-1960), pp. 1-18. The reason for the later date is that the notes were not gathered for editing until then.

[14]Bernard J.F. Lonergan, S.J., *De ente supernaturali: supplementum schematicum* in *The Early Latin Works of Bernard J.F. Lonergan, Vol. II*, edited by F.E Crowe, S.J. (Toronto: Regis College, 1973). Hereafter citations will be abbreviated to *De ente...*

[15]Lonergan, *De ente...*, editorial Introduction, p. x.

[16]*Ibid.*, p. xii.

[17]*Ibid.*, p. 2. This section is quoted from an unpublished English translation, *On the Supernatural*, done at Weston College, Weston, Massachusetts in 1966, p. 2. It is available at the Lonergan Research Institute of Regis College, Toronto.

[18]*Ibid., p.* 4. This paraphrase of the Latin citation to St. Thomas is taken from Lonergan's later use of it in *Method in Theology* (London: Darton, Longman & Todd, 1972), p. 337.

[19]S. Thomas Aquinas, *Quaestiones Quodlibetales* (Paris: P. Lethielleux, 1926), p. 154.

[20]*Ibid.*

[21]*Ibid.*, pp. 154-155.

[22]Lonergan, *De ente...*, p. 2.

[23]Lonergan, *Gratia Operans*, P. 16.

[24]Lonergan, *De ente...*, p. 2. Since there are frequent citations to *De ente supernaturali* in the following section, they will be made directly in the text.

[25]Lonergan   did not declare his own organizing principle, and perhaps because his typist got the pages of the text mixed up, there was some confusion about the proper order of the *scholia* in the tract. In the original Latin mimeographed edition of the *De ente supernaturali*, produced at *L'Immaculee-Conception* in Montreal in 1946, and in all the editions copied from that, the fourth scholion appears after the *fifth* thesis. It is clear from Lonergan's own typescript, now available in the Lonergan Research Institute of Regis College, that it belongs after the *fourth* scholion of thesis four. The inner logic of the sequence gives the same conclusion, because it deals with the efficacy of the divine concursus, and because thesis five contains elements that are presupposed as already treated in this scholion. For example, this scholion deals with the property of an efficient cause that is efficacious, that is, indefectible and irresistible. Through the distinction between absolute necessity and hypothetical necessity, St. Thomas solves every difficulty arising either from God's knowledge, will, or activity against the contingency of creatures. This scholion settles the issue of physical premotion that needs to be handled before we can understand how to solve the difficulties raised by the disciples of Molina and those of Banez in thesis five.

CHAPTER II

RECOVERING THE MIND OF AQUINAS

The first place where Lonergan alluded to the twofold way of organizing ideas according to the "way of resolution" and the "way of composition" was in the classnotes, *De ente supernaturali*, written for the course on grace in the fall of 1946. The second context in which he attended directly to the twofold ordering of ideas was the *Verbum* articles, originally published in *Theological Studies* from 1946-1949, then in book form in 1967, *Verbum, Word and Idea in Aquinas*.[1]

The twofold ordering of ideas according to the *via compositionis* and the *via resolutionis*, as they are now called, appears in two contexts in the *Verbum* articles. The first place is the discussion of the term, resolution to principles (*resolutio in principia*). The second place is the section on the "way of teaching" (*via doctrinae*) used by Aquinas in setting forth his speculative treatment of trinitarian doctrine.

The central question of the *Verbum* articles asks what is the nature of human intelligence as discovered by Aristotle and more fully understood by Aquinas. Given the unlimited capacity of intellect as dynamism, Lonergan works out the process of human cognition from insight into phantasm to its term in the *verbum*. The goal, however, is an understanding of the trinitarian processions, first, that of the inner Word, and ultimately, that of the Holy Spirit.

Resolution to Principles

The first context in which our twofold order is discussed occurs in the second chapter. After developing in his first chapter the notion of the word as definition, Lonergan examined the Thomist reflections about the word as judgment. In the discussion about the way we reach this second

31

type of inner word, Lonergan refers to the term, "resolution to principles". The trouble with the term "resolution to principles" is that it is ambiguous. At times it has to do with the reflective activity of the mind when it examines its knowledge, the "way of judgment" (*via judicii*). But this usage is not relevant to our topic, so we mention it only to set it aside.

In contrast to the reflective activity of the mind that reaches a judgment by a reduction of issues to naturally known first principles, there is the process by which we study a science according to its historical unfolding in the "way of discovery" (*via inventionis*). The "way of discovery" uses a "resolution to principles" by following a process that examines the historical development of a science. This resolution to principles is accomplished by the "way of resolution" that duplicates in the classroom the discovery over the years that takes place in the accumulation of insights that now constitutes a science. We can find an example of this procedure from natural science. It is possible to study chemistry only in the laboratory in a series of experiments that follow the history of the development of the science. The place to begin, then, would be from common material objects. After learning the arts of qualitative and quantitative analysis, we would slowly and gradually move on to the discovery of the periodic table and the sub-atomic structures. The "way of resolution" duplicates the historical discoveries of a given science and examines these discovered elements in such a way as to reduce them to their first principles. The analysis of conclusions that leads to a reduction of them to their first principles is the meaning of the term, "resolution to principles" (*Verbum*, pp. 61-62).

Although Lonergan's main purpose in the second chapter of the *Verbum* articles is to explain the "resolution to principles" by which the mind reaches its word of judgment, he explains as well that there are two different orders by which a science might be studied, the "way of resolution" and the "way of composition". In contrast to the study of a science that reproduces the historical discoveries that accumulated over the years and reduces these discoveries to first principles (the "way of resolution"), there is the study of a science that begins where the "way of resolution" leaves off. This is the "way of composition". It begins with the theoretic principles that are the product of the analysis effected by the resolution to principles. So this ordering of ideas can begin "with pure mathematics, then posit hypotheses regarding electrons and protons and neutrons, work out possible atomic and then molecular structures, develop a method of analysis, and finally turn for the first time to real material things" (*Verbum*, p.62). This way of arranging the data of a science starts not with material things but with hypotheses. And this explanation of the "way of composition" coincides with the brief account of it that Lonergan used in putting together his supplementary theological class notes for *De ente supernaturali*.

Both the "way of resolution" and the "way of composition" are merely abstractions because actual thinking oscillates dialectically between the two lines of approach. The mind uses the one and the other of these procedures in seeking and finding understanding. Lonergan borrowed the terms "resolution" and "composition" from Aquinas, who used them in his commentary on Aristotle's metaphysics.[2] In the "way of resolution", the mind uses analysis and moves from the whole to its parts. In the "way of composition", the mind uses synthesis and proceeds from parts and returns to the whole. These procedures indicate the lines along which the mind moves in coming to its knowledge of the truth. As we shall see, the mind can use its powers of analysis or synthesis in a variety of settings in the setting of an historical study of a science, or in the setting of a systematic study of a science. At this early stage of his development, when Lonergan is intent on recapturing the mind of Aquinas, he quotes St. Thomas who says that the historical study of a science (the "way of discovery") can use both resolution (*S.T.*, I, q. 79, a. 8 c) and composition (*S.T.*, I, q. 79, a. 9 c). Lonergan merely adverts to the opinion of St. Thomas without reflecting whether resolution and composition are both processes that belong in the "way of discovery". Actually, by 1956 in the *De constitutione Christi*, Lonergan has firmly distinguished the roles of the historical "way of discovery" and the speculative "way of teaching" and has aligned the process of resolution with discovery and the process of composition with speculative teaching. Here in the *Verbum* articles, he does not see the need to make a careful distinction between the mind's processes of resolution and of composition and the contexts in which these processes might be exercised -- the historical reduction of a science to its first principles in the "way of discovery", or the speculative synthesis of a science's theoretical elements leading to deeper understanding in the "way of teaching".

In fact, although Lonergan adverts to the "way of resolution", it is the second order, the "way of composition", that claims his special attention in these articles. And discussion of this process by which the mind composes new understanding by starting from principles occurs in the second context that was mentioned at the beginning of this chapter, the context of the speculative treatment of Aquinas' notion of trinitarian theology. The term that St. Thomas used here for the speculative presentation of doctrine is the "way of teaching" (*via doctrinae*) that uses the mind's procedure identified as the "way of composition". Lonergan borrowed the term, *via doctrinae vel disciplinae*, from the Prologue of the *Summa theologiae* where St. Thomas explained his method for the rest of the work. It is this *via doctrinae* that Lonergan sought to emulate in his speculative presentation of trinitarian doctrine.

The *Via Doctrinae*

The second context in the *Verbum* articles that refers to the twofold ordering of ideas occurs at the end of the last article, *Imago Dei*, in the section called *Via Doctrinae*. In this section, Lonergan reported that at the time of his writing, there were two systematic divisions of work in medieval trinitarian thought. One division of thought is the "Trinity *in fieri*", and the other is the "Trinity *in facto esse*" (*Verbum*, p. 206). Confusion arises if it appears that these two divisions of thought correspond to the "way of resolution" and the "way of composition" that we have examined thus far. The twofold resolutory/compository processes are different ways a science may be studied. Within the second process, the "way of composition", there is a systematic division of concepts *in fieri* and *in facto esse* -- a

34

separation of concepts "in their unfolding" and "as they exist as an established fact". So thought on the Trinity *in fieri* corresponds to the systematic arrangement of the concepts about God in which the processions precede the relations and the relations precede the persons. And thought on the Trinity *in facto esse* corresponds to the systematic ordering of concepts about God in which there are the persons as persons, the persons considered individually, the persons compared to the divine essence, to the relations, and to the notional acts.

The early speculative writings of Aquinas on the Trinity imply a becoming in God since they start from God the Father and next state the generation of the Son and then the procession of the Holy Spirit. Aquinas' later trinitarian work in the *Summa theologiae* eliminates even the appearance of a logical fiction of a becoming in God (*Verbum*, p. 206). The way St. Thomas accomplished this in the *Summa theologiae* was by using the "way of teaching" -- first, to treat of God as one, then to turn to God as triune.

If the *via doctrinae* does not simply repeat the earlier ordering of ideas used by Aquinas that starts with the Trinity given in revelation, how does it work? In the "way of teaching", the starting point is not God the Father but God. The first question in the "way of teaching" is not whether there is a procession from God the Father to the Son. Instead, it asks whether there is a procession in God. Next, it establishes that there are two processions in God. Then it treats the existence of real relations in God. Only after both the processions and the relations have been treated is the question of persons raised (*Verbum*, p. 206).

The significance of this procedure, as far as Lonergan is concerned, is that it puts "Thomist trinitarian theory in a class by itself" (*Verbum*, p. 206). Recall that the entire *Summa theologiae* was structured by St. Thomas according to the "way of teaching". There are three results from this use of the *via doctrinae*. First, it eliminates what is called the *crux trinitatis*; second, it reveals the significance of the *imago Dei* in trinitarian thought;

and third, it provides an excellent example of theology as science (*Verbum*, pp. 206-215).

A. The *Crux Trinitatis*

The benefits derived from the use of the *via doctrinae* reveal what it is and how it works. Let us examine these three benefits that arise from the "way of teaching". First, what is the *crux trinitatis*? This problem has to do with some apparent contradictions surrounding the fatherhood of God. If the Father is a Father by a relation to the Son, then that relation supposes a procession -- so the Father must generate before being constituted as Father. On the other hand, if the Father is Father not by a relation, "then he must be Father either by something absolute or by negation" (*Verbum*, p. 206). Neither possibility (an absolute factor or a negative) is acceptable. We are faced, then, with the *crux trinitatis*.

In order to appreciate the Thomist solution to this problem, we must grasp the structure of the *Summa theologiae*. The structure embodies two inverse orderings of our trinitarian concepts. The first ordering of our trinitarian concepts as they develop systematically has the processions coming before the relations and the relations coming before the persons. The other way of ordering our trinitarian concepts at their term studies the persons as persons, the persons considered individually, the persons compared to the divine essence, to the relations, to the notional acts.

The key to understanding how these two systematic orders solve the *crux trinitatis* is the realization that the two orders are inverse. The *via doctrinae*, then, uses both the ordering of trinitarian concepts in their systematic development and in their term to bring about a fuller understanding of the Trinity than either ordering of ideas could accomplish by itself.

Let us note briefly how the inverse structure of these two orderings of trinitarian concepts functions in the "way of teaching". The pivotal insight

seems to be that what are called "processions" in the developing arrangement of ideas and what are termed "notional acts" in the final ordering of
ideas are the same reality. "But the processions are in God prior, in the first
order of our concepts, to the constitution of the persons. On the other
hand, the notional acts are acts of the persons and consequent to the
persons conceived as constituted" (*Verbum*, p. 207). Thus St. Thomas
distinguished between the property of the Father as relation and the same
property as constitutive of the Father. As relation, the property of
fatherhood is subsequent to generation. As constitutive, the same property
of fatherhood is prior to generation. This is a perfect solution to the *crux
trinitatis*. How can the property of fatherhood be both prior and subsequent? The question is not about the property "fatherhood" itself, but about
the systematic order of our concepts. When there are two systematic
orders that are inverse, necessarily what is prior in one order will be
subsequent in the other order (*Verbum*, p. 207)

B. The *Imago Dei*

The second benefit deriving from the change in the ordering of
trinitarian concepts is the application of the psychological *imago Dei*. First,
what is the application of the psychological analogy? To answer this
question it is necessary only to reflect that our desire to know *quid sit Deus*
in this life can only proceed through analogy. Philosophy composes
analogies from pure perfections by the ways of affirmation, negation, and
eminence. So by natural reason we can know that God is absolute being,
absolute understanding, absolute truth, absolute love. But natural reason
by itself cannot establish that there are intelligible processions in God. This
additional understanding through the analogy of what God is does not
come from reason alone, but from what the First Vatican Council calls the
limited but most fertile understanding that can be attained when reason
operates in the light of faith. So through the data of faith, theology uses the
Augustinian psychological analogy just as philosophy uses the naturally
known pure perfections. Moreover, the structure of the *Summa theologiae*
according to the way of teaching reveals the significance of the *imago Dei*.

As long as our concepts are developing in systematic order, our minds use the psychological analogy as the vehicle for carrying our understanding along. But once the concepts of the psychological analogy reach their limit, our minds transcend the analogy and we are confronted with the mystery. Thus the "way of teaching" embodies two orders that stand on different levels of thought. The developing order of ideas achieves insight through analogy, but that insight does not penetrate to the very essence of God where alone can trinitarian doctrine be contemplated in its full intelligibility. Lonergan's example of the two orders of thought here is helpful:

> Just as an experimental physicist may not grasp most of quantum mathematics, but under the direction of a mathematician may very intelligently devise and perform experiments that advance the quantum theory, so also the theologian with no proper grasp of *quid sit Deus* but under the direction of divine revelation really operates in virtue of and towards an understanding that he personally in this life cannot possess.[3]

C. Theology as Science

The third benefit stemming from the method of proceeding according to the "way of teaching" in the *Summa theologiae* reveals how the trinitarian speculation of St. Thomas is a masterpiece of theology as science. Lonergan argues here against what he calls a conceptualist theory of human intellect and of science. Conceptualists think that concepts simply emerge in a machine-like fashion from the mind like sausages from the sausage roller. So for them, the operations of human understanding are not an apt foundation for an analogy by which to penetrate the depths of trinitarian speculation (*Verbum*, p. 211).

In contrast to the conceptualist position on theology as science, there is what Lonergan calls the intellectualist concept of theology. It is within the intellectualist framework of theology that the development of the *via doctrinae* occurs. First, the intellectualist knows what the human mind can attain, then he neither settles for less than what is possible nor reaches beyond its grasp. Second, the intellectualist knows that for theology the synthetic principle from which all trinitarian speculation flows is the divine essence which we cannot understand directly. But instead of despairing of any synthetic understanding, the intellectualist sets as his systematic goal the imperfect understanding which begins where natural theology leaves off. Entering what St. Thomas characterizes as a "way of teaching", the intellectualist uses the Augustinian psychological analogy as the natural theologian uses his pure perfections. He elaborates the key concepts of procession, relation, person. Then shifting to a higher level, he consciously confronts mystery as mystery, and in so doing, transposes relations to properties and processions to notional acts. What guarantees the perfection of the method is an accurate grasp of the goal and scope of theological understanding (*Verbum*, p. 213).

In the earlier context of his discussion of the "way of resolution" and the "way of composition", Lonergan gave an example of the two ways in which a natural science might be studied. He illustrated the difference between studying a science according to a recapitulation of its historical discoveries and studying a science according to its speculative treatment of its material by a synthetic principle of unity. So it is clear from what he wrote about the two ways of studying a science that in theory, at least, he understands what they are. His application to trinitarian theology in this second context of the *via doctrinae* can be seen, with present hindsight anyway, to correspond accurately enough to the theoretic exposition given earlier about the "way of composition". But two factors contribute to a kind of confusion in this second context (*Verbum*, pp. 206-215).

First, there is little evidence that Lonergan at this point in his theological career is much interested in the *via inventionis*, in the historical study of a science according to the unfolding of its development. True, he mentions it earlier in *Verbum*, pp. 61-62, and again here briefly in *Verbum*, pp. 213-214. But the mention here is only one paragraph in an entire section devoted to his real interest, the *via doctrinae*. In that paragraph, he distinguishes between dogmatic development and speculative development, but only the second has the name *via inventionis* attached to it. Perhaps he intends for it to be understood as a dogmatic development as well, but the likelihood is that the question hardly occurred to him, since his primary, almost his entire concern is for the *via doctrinae*. In order to understand Lonergan's later wrestling with the way of including the concerns of historical scholarship in doing systematic theology, it is well to note that in his early career, when he concentrated on recovering the mind of Aquinas, his chief interest was in the speculative procedures for doing theology according to a "way of teaching" exemplified by St. Thomas.

Because there is not much attention given to the role of the *via inventionis*, there is confusion here in this section when Lonergan alludes to development. Does he mean the kind of historical development that unfolds over time with new findings in a science, or does he mean the kind of systematic development that occurs when there is a systematic arrangement of ideas in a speculative treatment? He is not troubled by the distinction -- he simply puts historical elements and speculative elements together at this point. In the *Verbum* articles, the way of arranging ideas in the *via doctrinae* presupposes the accumulation of dogmatic and speculative elements. So there are the dogmatic elements that evolved from the apostolic Church through the early Fathers and councils. Then he says that there are speculative elements of the "way of discovery" present in the deduction of St. Athanasius that immaterial generation must reach its term in a consubstantial being. Similarly, the Cappodocians and St. Augustine worked out the doctrine that what makes possible the distinction between persons is their relations. He says that "speculative thought ... was clearly present as *via inventionis*" in the elaboration of the notions of person and nature summarized for the East by St. John Damascene and for the West by Boethius (*Verbum*, p. 213). But the role of the *via inventionis* is to move to a reduction of a complex whole to its most basic elements. And here it is clear that this reduction takes place in both an historical context and in a speculative context. So at this point, Lonergan is not much interested in distinguishing types of development. Only later, when the aims and procedures of historical scholarship will challenge the legitimacy of dogmatics to account for its own development will the question of differentiating kinds of development become important.

There is a second factor that contributes to a kind of confusion in the *via doctrinae* context. In the *crux trinitatis* section, Lonergan introduced two orders of development in the systematic context of the *via doctrinae*: the order of thought as it develops (*in fieri*) and the order of thought at its term (*in facto esse*). Since we are studying another pair of ways of arranging ideas (the historical "way of discovery" that uses a "way of resolution"; a systematic "way of teaching" that uses a "way of composition"), it is possible to confuse our terms. What we must do is to remember that the order *in fieri* and an inverse order *in facto esse* occur in the systematic context, that is, in the "way of composition". But when one of the systematic orders is called "the order of thought as it develops" (*in fieri*), there is bound to be confusion about what kind of development is meant -- historical or speculative. Apparently Lonergan did not advert to this possible confusion because he was not much interested in the aims and procedures of the *via inventionis*. This interest will become clear in more lucid fashion in 1954 with his review article, "Theology and Understanding", and in 1957 with the introductory chapter of *Divinarum personarum conceptio analogica*.

The *De Scientia Atque Voluntate Dei*

The last of the *Verbum* articles appeared in the September, 1949 issue of *Theological Studies*. At the time, Lonergan was already at work composing *Insight: A Study of Human Understanding*. But his primary commitment was to his assignment as a teacher to instruct Jesuit theological students at the College of Christ the King (now Regis College) in Toronto.

At Regis College, the sequence of the dogmatic courses on God for the academic year 1949-1950 was: Trinity in the first semester, and the one God (*De Deo uno*) in the second. Lonergan taught the course on the Trinity and shared teaching duties during the second semester with Father

THE ROAD TO LONERGAN'S *METHOD IN THEOLOGY*

Peter Mueller. Lonergan took the second half of the second semester to address the questions dealing with predestination, divine dominion over humankind, human effort and freedom. The basic text he used was the manual of H. Lennerz, *De Deo uno*, issued in 1948 at Rome in its fourth edition. He began to lecture some time in March, 1950 on the third and fourth parts of the text: *De scientia Dei and De providentia et praedestinatione*. His own organization of key ideas appeared in a typescript he provided as an aid to students for following his lectures and for promoting study. As with the *De ente supernaturali*, the original manuscript was subtitled *supplementum schematicum*.[4] We will now examine the relevance of these supplementary classnotes to the twofold way of organizing ideas in theology.

The *De scientia...* is about the relation of divine will and dominion with human effort and freedom. At the beginning of the first chapter, "on the end of this work", Lonergan mentions that "sacred theology is so divided that through the way of discovery what must be believed is determined from sacred scripture, from the fathers, councils and theologians. Next through the way of teaching, what is sought is that most fertile understanding illustriously exemplified by St. Thomas which although limited, is what the Vatican Council praises" (*De scientia...*, p. 1, paragraph 1). As Conn O'Donovan points out in his translator's Introduction to *The Way to Nicea*, the way of discovery and the way of teaching by 1950 have become in Lonergan's writing "two different parts of theology, the first concerned with faith, the second with understanding".[5] As with the other supplementary schemes written to accompany texts, the basic theological concern is still speculative. Within the speculative context, however, Lonergan adverts to the division of theology between what is determined by the way of discovery (what must be believed), and what is understood by the way of teaching (the understanding itself that is sought through the way of teaching).

Granted that the schematic supplement seeks understanding, there is in the De scientia...a noticeable difference in procedure from that used in the *De ente supernaturali*. In the *De ente...*, Lonergan organized his work in a deliberately systematic fashion and presented his ideas in the "way of composition". Here in the *De scientia...*, he does not have a similar method in mind. "The order of exposition is not so much logical as pedagogical. First we set forth the simpler elements separately. After we accumulate and digest them, we can understand the more complex ideas" (*De scientia...*, p. 2, paragraph 3). Instead of organizing the whole set of ideas according to the *via compositionis* in which a unifying overview weaves disparate elements into a new synthesis, he is content to develop individually various points of understanding. The stated reason for this choice of procedure is pedagogical. The organizing principle used by Lonergan is "not one that allows positive insight and consequent deductive reasoning" (*De scientia...*, p. xi). When he reviews in his Epilogue what he has accomplished in the little work, he writes that his method

> has been to run through a large number of questions always meeting new difficulties with new solutions, trying to exclude errors rather than to gain positive insight into the truth, piling up principles instead of organizing them synthetically. In this way we have produced a set of statements in which we can affirm coherently that God is Lord with dominion over all things, that man has dominion over himself, and that the sinner is guilty of his sin.[6]

As he discovered later in St. Thomas' *Summa Contra Gentiles*, it is a good pedagogical procedure to let the same arguments recur over and over in ever slightly different forms.[7] What guides his ordering of the *De scientia...* classnotes, then, are his concerns for wise pedagogy, for finding solutions to difficulties, for excluding errors, and for accumulating principles in a piecemeal arrangement.

The question arises, of course, why Lonergan did not organize the material of the *De scientia...* according to the "way of composition". It may seem that since the object of the classnotes is the mind and will of God, which is mystery, that the topic is too difficult to admit its synthetic treatment according to a principle of unity in the "way of composition". Yet Lonergan later treated the speculative part of the course on the Trinity according to the *via compositionis*. So it is not because the material of the *De scientia*... was too abstruse that prevented its presentation according to the "way of composition". A conjectured response to this question is that Lonergan had already taught the first semester in the 1949-1950 academic year and was only helping Father Mueller with the last half of the second semester course. Any possible fatigue aside, Lonergan was busy at work on *Insight*, and it may be that he did not want to spend the extra time and labor required to mold the *De scientia*...elements into a unified whole.

Insight: The Appropriation of One's Own Mind

In a paper recounting the composition of his first book, Lonergan affirmed that as soon as he finished the *Verbum* articles, he began writing *Insight*.[8] In the Epilogue to *Insight*, Lonergan says that the detailed investigations of the thought of Aquinas on *Gratia Operans* and on *Verbum* have been followed "by the present essay in aid of a personal appropriation of one's own rational self-consciousness".[9] As with the first two works on the mind of Aquinas, *Insight*'s aim is to contribute to Pope Leo XIII's program, *vetera novis augere et perficere*, only this time his focus is on the *nova*.

It is clear that *Insight* was written as a general exploration of methods in order to provide the foundation for a method in theology. Yet there is no mention in the entire volume about the twofold ordering of ideas according to the way of resolution or to the way of composition -- whether in science generally or in theology specifically. This is striking in light of Lonergan's subsequent development of the two procedures in his trinitarian thought. It is a vexing question why he did not allude explicitly to these two procedures if he found them important enough to use in his own later theological writing. One possible explanation is that he did not thematize the twofold way until 1954 when he explicitly treated them in his review article, "Theology and Understanding", by which time *Insight* had been completed. Another possible reason is that he focused on the importance of the historical dimension for theology only later when he wrestled with the part shed on cognitional theory, epistemology, and metaphysics, there is little concern in *Insight* for the dimension of history.[10] We will note several passages from *Insight* that reveal what Lonergan does think as of 1953 about points that eventually become germane to the "way of resolution".

In the first sentence of Chapter XVII on "Metaphysics as Dialectic", Lonergan writes

> If Descartes has imposed upon subsequent philosophers a requirement of rigorous method, Hegel has obliged them not only to account for their own views but also to explain the existence of contrary convictions and opinions.[11]

Insight's method enables its practitioner to measure any possible philosophy against the dynamic structure of cognitional activity and thus to discover whether the philosophy is correctly conceived or distorted by oversights and by incorrect orientations. After Hegel, moreover, philosophers need to account for positions and counterpositions. So there is a clear advertence to the element of dialectic in method, but there is no explicit explanation about how the dialectic will work in theology. A possible reason is that the question of the development of dogma with its various positive, historical studies has not yet created for Lonergan a state of the question in which dialectic could operate. The example that does come to Lonergan's mind, however, is the question of the Mystical Body of Christ and its historical unfolding.

Another passage from *Insight* that prepares the ground for the eventual thematizing of the twofold way of organizing ideas occurs in the Epilogue. Here it is said that the method of theology embodies a dialectical technique that analyzes the opposition between positions and counterpositions. Dialectical technique has a threefold theological significance:

> It lays bare the roots of the revolt of pietists and modernists against dogma, for as the philosophic counterpositions appeal to experience generally against the 'Yes' of rational

It lays bare the roots of the revolt of pietists and modernists against dogma, for as the philosophic counterpositions appeal to experience generally against the 'Yes' of rational consciousness, so they appeal to religious experience against the 'Yes' of articulate faith. Secondly, the same dialectical technique that cuts short the disputed questions of metaphysicians will contribute at least indirectly to the systematic demise of not a few disputed questions of theologians. Finally, the clarification we have effected of the role of understanding in knowledge recalls to mind the impressive statements of the Vatican Council on the role of understanding in faith; and a firm grasp of what it is to understand can hardly fail to promote the limited but most fruitful understanding of the Christian mysteries that results both from the analogy of nature and from the inner coherence of the mysteries themselves.[12]

This threefold relevance of dialectical technique for theology has a bearing on the ordering of ideas. The ordering of ideas requires prior thought about theology as science, about the role of positions and counterpositions in theological speculation, about the role of understanding as an aim of theology. Furthermore, the crisis for the ordering of ideas according to the way of resolution and the way of composition comes when positive theology raises the issue of cultural relativism and thereby places in jeopardy the possibility of continuity in dogmatic development and theological understanding.

A final passage from the Epilogue relevant to our topic is on understanding history. After examining the elements that compose the development of an individual under the action of divine grace, there is a consideration of the cumulative, historical development of the chosen people and of the Catholic Church. In what department of theology might the historical aspect of development be treated? The historical aspect belongs to a treatise on the Mystical Body of Christ. As we have seen, any theological treatise has a material and a formal element. The material element comes from scripture, patristic texts and dogmatic pronounce-ments. The formal element consists in the terms and relations through which the materials are gathered in a single, coherent view. What are illustrations of the formal element from the tracts on grace and on the Trinity that reveal a pattern of terms and relations issuing in a coherent, unified view? The theorem on the supernatural is an example of a formal element in the treatise on grace, just as the theorems on the notions of procession, relation and person illustrate the formal elements in the treatise on the Trinity. But the issue here is the historical aspect of development. The treatise on the Mystical Body requires not only the scriptural, patristic, and dogmatic materials, but also a correct theory of history. This theory of history must consider "the concrete universal that is mankind in the concrete and cumulative consequences of the acceptance or rejection of the message of the Gospel".[13] This statement is significant because it reveals Lonergan's desire to include considerations derived from concrete historical development in the theological ordering of ideas. And while *Insight* has already elaborated in chapters seven and twenty what a theory of history should entail, at this point he simply states that a correct theory of history is necessary for theology, but he does not say what impact history might have on the ordering of ideas.

The Epilogue concludes by explaining how *Insight* has contributed to Pope Leo XIII's aim *vetera novis augere et perficere*. What results from the historical investigation of medieval thought are texts, information about sources and chronology, a steady flow of monographs upon doctrinal issues. Such historical research creates a climate of critical thinking that does not tolerate the substitution of rhetoric for history or fancy for fact. An even more important contribution coming from historical research is its aim to penetrate the mind of the thinker under investigation. After years spent at reaching up to the mind of Aquinas, Lonergan realized that he himself had been profoundly changed, and that the change made him capable of grasping what the *vetera* really were as well as opening challenging vistas on what the *nova* could be.[14] Still, the advances in cognitional theory, epistemology, and metaphysics are one thing, the practical implications for theology from these advances are another. It will take considerable work with theological issues before the method of theology equals the development of *Insight*'s philosophic foundations.

Concluding Overview

In the *Verbum* articles, Lonergan wanted to vindicate and to retrieve the genius of St. Thomas both in the substance of his trinitarian thought as well as in the method of his theological procedure. Lonergan wrote in response to the manualist tradition, which lumped together dogmatic and speculative elements to meet its aim of establishing proofs of faith. In contrast to the manualist aim, Lonergan took as his goal the Thomist theological ideal of understanding the truths of faith. Since understanding was his aim, he focused on the speculative procedure used by St. Thomas in the *Summa theologiae* to reach theological understanding, the *via doctrinae* that is an example of the way a science may be studied according to the "way of composition". In contrast to the manualist tradition that did not distinguish between proving truths and understanding them, Lonergan separated the two processes by which a science may be studied and concentrated on the "way of composition". He was not much interested yet in the historical way of studying a science, and because he was interested primarily in the goal of seeking understanding, he did not distinguish at this early point in his development between the dogmatic and the speculative elements of a development.

In the manualist horizon, the task of history was to provide an array of opinions that apologetics could use to oppose or defend a position. So history was seen as an ancillary discipline to theology, only a preparation for the real work of speculation. It seems that Lonergan was mostly interested in history only as a support to the part of theology he saw as central, namely, speculation. So while he opposed the manualist aims and procedures, it seems that he shared the contemporary opinion of the 1940s that history was only needed to dig up and to present grist for the speculative mill. Since the work of the "way of composition" in theology was to set out from theological hypotheses and to return to the truths of faith with deeper understanding than was possible to achieve in a "way of historical discovery", it is no wonder that Lonergan -- who strove to recover the mind of Aquinas, for whom theology was equivalent to deeper understanding -- concentrated on the procedure that sought precisely a fullness of understanding. Although Lonergan also showed an interest in the functions of auxiliary disciplines such as dialectic, interpretation, and history, it does not seem at this early period of his development that he was thinking about the relationships between branches of theology as he will think about them later. By 1950, he was intent on exonerating the theological procedure used by St. Thomas and developing the "way of composition" that aimed at deeper understanding of the truths of faith.

NOTES

CHAPTER II

[1]Bernard J.F. Lonergan, S.J., *Verbum, Word and Idea in Aquinas*, ed. David B. Burrell, C.S.C. (South Bend, Indiana: University of Notre Dame Press, 1967). The chapters of this book originally appeared as articles in *Theological Studies*: chapter I: VII (1946), 349-392; chapter II: VIII (1947), 35-79; chapter III: VIII (1947), 404-444; chapter IV: X (1949), 3-40; chapter V: X (1949) 359-393. Since there are frequent citations to this work in the following section, the references will be to Burrell and will be made directly in the text with the abbreviation, *Verbum*, and the page number.

[2]*S. Thomae Aquinatis, In Duodecim Libros Metaphysicorum Aristotelis Expositio* (Rome: Marietti, 1950), II, I., paragraph 278, p. 81. *Est autem duplex via procedendi ad cognitionem veritatis. Una quidem per modum resolutionis, secundum quam procedimus a compositis ad simplicia, et a toto ad partem, sicut dicitur in primo Physicorum, quod confusa sunt prius nobis nota. Et in hac via perficitur cognitio veritatis, quando pervenitur ad singulas partes distincte cognoscendas. Alia est via compositionis, per quam procedimus a simplicibus ad composita, qua perficitur cognitio veritatis cum pervenitur ad totum. Sic igitur hoc ipsum, quod homo non potest in rebus perfecte totum et partem cognoscere, ostendit difficultatem considerandae veritatis secundum utramque viam.* See *S. Thomae Aquinatis, Summa theologiae* (Rome: Marietti, 1950), I-II, q. 14, a. 5, editor's footnote 3, p. 74.

[3]Lonergan, *Verbum*, p. 208. A slight misprint in the text corrected.

[4]Frederick E. Crowe, S.J., in the editor's *Introduction to The Early Latin Works of Bernard J.F. Lonergan, Vol. III: De scientia atque voluntate Dei: Supplementum Schematicum* (Toronto: Regis College, 1973), p. ix. Citations to this text will be abbreviated to *De scientia...*.

[5]Bernard J.F. Lonergan, S.J., *The Way to Nicea*, trans. Conn O'Donovan (London: Darton, Longman & Todd, 1976), p. xix. See F.E. Crowe, S.J., "Early Jottings on Bernard Lonergan's *Method in Theology*", *Science et Esprit*, 25 (1973), 124.

[6]Lonergan, *De scientia. . .*, p. 66, paragraph 228. This translation is from the editorial Introduction, p. x.

[7]*Ibid.*, p. xi. See Bernard J. F. Lonergan, S.J., *Method in Theology* (London: Darton, Longman & Todd, 1972), p. 30.

[8]Bernard J.F. Lonergan, S.J., "*Insight* Revisited", *A Second Collection*, ed. William Ryan, S.J. and Bernard Tyrrell, S.J. (London: Darton, Longman & Todd, 1974), p. 267.

[9]Bernard J.F. Lonergan, S.J., *Insight: A Study of Human Understanding* (New York: Philosophical Library, third edition, 1970), p. 748.

[10]That is, for history as what he later calls a functional specialty. Lonergan does distinguish the exegete and the historian on p. xxix of the Introduction to *Insight*, and he notes the role of history in the treatise on the Mystical Body cited in the Epilogue, p. 743. There are as well recurring passages on, and analysis of, the objective course of history, for example, in the chapters on common sense.

[11]Lonergan, *Insight*, p. 530.

[12]*Ibid.*, pp. 733-734.

[13]*Ibid.*, p. 743.

[14]*Ibid.*, p. 747.

CHAPTER III

A THEMATIC STATEMENT OF
THE *VIA INVENTIONIS* AND THE *VIA DOCTRINAE*

Lonergan's earliest concern for developing a theological method began with the writing of his unpublished Introduction to his doctoral dissertation. As the Introduction to the *Gratia Operans* thesis focused on speculative thought and its developing character, so the supplementary class notes *De ente supernaturali* organized the treatise according to the way of composition, called in the language of St. Thomas, the *via doctrinae.*

Next, the Thomist teaching on the Trinity became a model instance of theological ordering of ideas in the *Verbum* articles. In the *De scientia atque voluntate Dei*, however, we see Lonergan distinguishing a second theological task that complements the task of theological speculation in the "way of teaching". This ordering of ideas organizes the elements of a science according to their historical development; it is called the "way of discovery" (*via inventionis*). It studies the scriptures, the Fathers, the councils, and the theologians to set down what the Church ought to believe.[1] Then we saw that *Insight* suggests a theological task that runs parallel to speculative theology. This task that is complementary to speculation is the procedure used by the historical theologian. The historical theologian does not focus on what is to be believed. He seeks to formulate identity in the various historical moments of a doctrine.[2]

"Theology and Understanding"

The next place where Lonergan adverts to the twofold way of arranging ideas in theology is in his article, "Theology and Understanding".[3] This article is a thematic statement not only about the way of discovery and the way of teaching, but also about the manner in which these two orders relate to one another. At first it was conceived as a review of the book by

THE ROAD TO LONERGAN'S *METHOD IN THEOLOGY*

Johannes Beumer, *Theologie als Glaubensverstandnis*. The article can be seen now, at least from the perspective of historical interpretation, to be pivotal for Lonergan because it is a thematic exposition of the method that will guide his theological work for the next ten years. In his editorial Introduction, Crowe explains how important the *via inventionis* and the *via doctrinae* are for Lonergan's theological method.

> In so far as they result from something like a transcendental
> deduction, they are not likely to be changed. That is, just as
> cognitional structure is a transcendental settling the way men
> have to know if they are going to know anything at all, so
> there are natural inevitabilities in the two orders of the his-
> torical growth of knowledge and of its systematic communica-
> tion, and such a transcendental order seems to lie behind the
> sketch of theological method proposed here.[4]

Of course, these remarks need to be placed in the ongoing context of Lonergan's further development of theological method. It will be revealing to discover just how apt this assessment is after we have reviewed the struggles that Lonergan overcame to harmonize the historical growth of knowledge with its systematic communication.

Originally published in *Gregorianum* in 1954, this review article was composed during Lonergan's first year in Rome when he taught at the Gregorian University. He had already substantially completed *Insight* in which the empirical human sciences "were allowed to work out their basic terms and relations apart from any consideration of metaphysics".[5] His new challenge came from the problems of hermeneutics and critical history, "from the need of integrating nineteenth-century achievement in this field with the teachings of Catholic religion and Catholic theology".[6] He had already begun lecturing to second and third year theologians on the Incarnation and the Trinity in alternating years. He gave these classes to 650 students at a time who among themselves distributively "seemed to read everything ".[7] Since he came to prize intellectual honesty during his own philosophical studies in Heythrop College, he worked to meet the challenges his students brought him through their reading. One such challenge was crystallized by Beumer's remarks about the aim of theology. It is in the context of explaining how St. Thomas ordered his theological ideas that Lonergan defends his own more elaborated exposition of Aquinas' thought against Beumer's critical remarks. Before we turn to Lonergan's presentation of Aquinas' thought on the *via inventionis* and the *via doctrinae*, it is necessary to set the context for this exposition by summarizing briefly his review of Beumer's thought.

A. Lonergan's Review of Beumer

Lonergan begins with a concise summary of the book. In his *Theologie als Glaubensverstandnis*, Johannes Beumer tried to make a case for basing a definition of theology's task on the declarations of the First Vatican Council. The first part of the book unearths the groundwork of the foundation for what the Council said. Lonergan is entirely in sympathy with Beumer's goal -- his later exposition of the aim, proper object, and the process for achieving the goal of speculative theology is based on the First Vatican Council's declarations. But as we shall see, Lonergan thinks that Beumer neglected to take the meaning of the declarations far enough.

The main section of Beumer's work elaborates the *intellectus fidei* as derived from the exposition of the *Constitutio de fide catholica* on the meaning of the very fruitful but imperfect understanding of the mysteries of the faith. The author narrates the positions of fideists and traditionalists which oppose one another and traces the history of the text from the original schema through its multiple variations to the ultimate content accepted by the Vatican Council in the third session. Also included in this section is a complete account of the meaning of *intellectus fidei*. The section concludes with an appraisal of the impact of the decree both in its nineteenth-century context and in its pertinence to a general theory of knowledge and method in theology.[8]

Lonergan agreed with Beumer's interpretation of the Council's decree, but he felt that Beumer's understanding of St. Thomas and of the relations between Thomist thought and *Glaubensverstandnis* needed critical attention. Our procedure will be to summarize his critical reflections on Beumer's work, and then turn to his own ideas which oppose and supersede those of Beumer.

Glaubensverstandnis means "an understanding of the truths of faith". Beumer separates this term from *Glaubenswissenschaft*, "a science of the truths of faith" (T & U, p. 123). According to him, theology's goal and purpose is the understanding of faith. The science of faith, on the other hand, specifies the method for reaching the purpose and goal. For him, the understanding of faith and the science of faith should be interacting components of the same reality. Because the purpose and goal of theology is an understanding of faith, the conclusions deal fundamentally "with a positively intelligent understanding of the truths of faith themselves" (T & U, p. 123). Because the method is the science of faith, then as science it uses syllogisms and theological conclusions.

By understanding of mysteries (*intelligentia mysteriorum*), Beumer meant an obscure and imperfect yet positive and most fruitful understanding of the truths of faith -- but not an understanding of the mysteries in their internal content or substance. The element of positive illumination consists in a grasp of the relations that stand in an analogy of proportion with naturally known truths and link the mysteries to one another and to our ultimate end (T & U, pp. 123-124).

Beumer wants to argue in two directions. First, he maintains that a science of faith will develop in the direction of an understanding of faith. Second, he opposes a notion of theology that conceives the science of faith to move away from the truths of faith into other areas. According to the view that Beumer opposes, revealed truths provide the initial premises of theology. So the job of theology is to defend these foundational truths, to show that they are free from inner contradiction. Beumer opposes the viewpoint that maintains that revealed truths do not constitute the object or objective of theology as science. Although he believes that the theologian's job is to proceed from revealed truths which he accepts on faith, he is against moving to other truths which the theologian as a scientist elaborates, proves, and demonstrates (T & U, p. 124).

Beumer does not deny the central task of deduction in theology, nor does he deny that theologians validly draw inferences that have not been revealed. He maintains that the pivotal importance of deduction in theology is not for reaching new certitudes, but for gaining a fuller understanding of what is already believed with the certitude of faith. He accepts that Aquinas was correct in drawing upon Aristotle to provide the term *intelligentia fidei* with a precise scientific context. He maintains, however, that Aristotle's scientific framework was not adequate and that it led Aquinas and his students away from a correct scientific emphasis and a fully satisfactory specification of objectives in theological understanding (T & U, p. 124).

Actually, Beumer did not object to the early works of St. Thomas that stood well within the Augustinian and medieval tradition of *intelligentia fidei*. It is only in the *Summa theologiae*, according to Beumer, that the Thomist method has used Aristotelian notions of science to reduce the understanding of faith to the negative content of an absence of inner contradiction. His opinion is that the later writings of St. Thomas do not express "a pure gain in the forward march of Catholic thought on the nature of theology..." (T & U, p. 124).

B. Lonergan's Objections to Beumer

After presenting five objections to Beumer's conclusions, Lonergan's sixth objection becomes the locus for his exposition of an analysis of the elements in the way of discovery and the way of teaching. His sixth objection concedes that St. Thomas writes about theology "as a science that deduces conclusions from the articles of faith" (T & U, p. 127). What he maintains in opposition to Beumer, however, is that Aristotle's theory of science and Aquinas' theological practice are the context in which to understand this statement about deduction.

Lonergan observes that Aristotle distinguished between explanatory and merely factual syllogisms. Aristotle also contrasted explanatory middle terms that assigned the *causa cognoscendi* and others that assigned the *causa essendi*. The example that Lonergan uses repeatedly to explain the syllogism is stated here to distinguish these two kinds of causes. The phases of the moon are the *causa cognoscendi* that the moon is a sphere, but the sphericity of the moon is the *causa essendi* for the phases being what they are. He goes on to state that the cause of our knowing is also *prior quoad nos* and so it is first in the way of discovery. But the cause of the moon being what it is *prior quoad se* and so it is first in the way of teaching or learning (T & U, p. 127).

These distinctions are not some moldy artifact from the history of thought. To see their relevance to the presentation of scientific knowledge, all one need do is to compare a history of chemistry with a textbook on chemistry. The history book discloses that the course of actual discovery (the *via inventionis*) proceeds from sensible data to ever more abstruse theoretical elements until finally these elements "may be constructed into explanations of all known phenomena" (T & U, p. 128). So the history of a science discloses that we first discover the causes of our knowing, and only after further work can we construct the cause of an object's being what it is.

After distinguishing between the *causa cognoscendi* and the *causa essendi* in Aristotle's theory of science, Lonergan advances to Aquinas' theological practice. The theologian's *causa cognoscendi* are the articles of faith, and these articles of faith provide the *prior quoad nos* and are first in the way of discovery. A problem arises when one tries to carry into theology the other complementary terms from science -- the *causa essendi* which is *prior quoad se* and the first in the way of teaching. While it is clear that God is always the *causa essendi*, it is also patent that in this life we do not attain a positive understanding of God. It is not possible, moreover, to use the expression *priora quoad se* with regard to God because "in the Blessed Trinity there is *nihil prius aut posterius*" (T & U, p. 128). Keeping these limits in mind, the question that requires attention is whether Aquinas attached any importance to the "way of teaching".

C. The Importance for St. Thomas of the *Via Doctrinae*

Lonergan enumerates three reasons that demonstrate the importance for St. Thomas of the way of teaching as a technique for ordering ideas. These reasons set the stage for Lonergan's thematic exposition of the elements and function of the *via doctrinae* (here also called the *via disciplinae*).

Evidence from the writings of Aquinas shows that he not only attached importance to the way of teaching but also used it extensively. One good example of his deployment of the way of teaching is within the *Summa Contra Gentiles*. Lonergan contends that it was intended as a theological work even if it was not composed in the way of discovery, which moves from revelation to conclusions that have not been revealed, but instead in the "way of teaching" that moves from the conclusions of the way of discovery to a systematic presentation of the revealed truths. In a footnote, he cites Book IV, chapter 11 as starting from a conceptual construction and terminating with a passage from scripture (T & U, footnote 20, p. 128). So one way of ordering ideas in the *Summa Contra Gentiles* which Aquinas adopted proceeds from theoretical premises to conclusions that are confirmed by texts of scripture. Aquinas does not argue from revelation to theological conclusions that are apart from revelation. Rather, he argues from nonscriptural premises to conclusions that run parallel to scriptural statements. It appears in these instances that he was writing as a theologian rather than as a philosopher. The general indications are that Aquinas never considered himself to be a philosopher since he regarded mere philosophers as pagans. He explicitly enunciated his purpose, moreover, in writing the *Summa Contra Gentiles*. He wanted to manifest the truth professed by the Catholic faith and to refute contrary errors. So

St. Thomas used scripture, not to supply premises but to confirm his conclusions even when issues in the *Summa Contra Gentiles* fell entirely outside the scope of philosophy.[9]

A second reason for concluding that St. Thomas valued the *ordo doctrinae* is a justification he gave for the procedure he used in writing the *Summa theologiae*. St. Thomas said that ordinary theology books contained useless questions and articles; they did not use an orderly method in selecting and in treating issues, but chose topics according to the opportunities presented by the subjects for commentary and debate. What is worse, these theology books kept dealing with the same issues until students grew bored and muddled. What these books did not use is the way of teaching. It is clear, then, that to follow the way of teaching means "to eliminate the irrelevant, to prevent mere repetitions, and to provide an alternative to the commentary and to the free debate" (T & U, p. 129).

A third reason for concluding that St. Thomas valued the *ordo doctrinae* is the tangible instance of this order provided by the questions in the *Summa theologiae* on the Trinity. It is clear in the early and later writings of Aquinas that he conducted an extensive experiment in theological method. The arrangement of material on the Trinity in the way of teaching, for example, begins from the processions, goes on to the relations, and then deals with the divine persons. This arrangement in the *Summa theologiae* differs sharply not only from the haphazard arrangement of the *Scriptum super sententias* but also from the careful orchestration of the *Summa Contra Gentiles* and from the yet different order of the *De potentia* (T & U, p. 129).

Now that it is clear that St. Thomas knew and used the way of teaching, it will be instructive to move to an investigation of the relationship between the way of discovery and the way of teaching. The place where Lonergan treats how the two orders relate to one another is in the realm of trinitarian theory.

A THEMATIC STATEMENT

The way of discovery (*ordo inventionis*) is the order which one uses to find rigorous proofs for trinitarian theses. This order begins from the dogmatic affirmation of three consubstantial persons given in the truths of faith. Because the persons are consubstantial, it follows that their real distinctions cannot be based on anything absolute but on something relative. For example, all three persons are omniscient, omnipotent, all wise. So we cannot distinguish the Father from the Son on the basis of power or wisdom. What distinguishes them, then, are relations. Because our purpose is to distinguish the persons, then the relevant relations must not be prior to the distinction if we are to ground distinctions. The only relations that are not presupposed, moreover, are relations of origin. Now these relations of origin presuppose processions, and the only processions we can conceive in God are analogous to the processions of human rational consciousness (T & U, p. 130).

Notice how the way of discovery works. It poses dilemmas and eliminates the more ostensibly unacceptable alternatives. After concluding to the existence of relations (*quia sunt*), we obtain a first hint about their nature (*quid sint*) when we argue further to the existence of processions. In a familiar fashion, we get a hint about the nature of the processions only when we advance to an elaboration of the argument on the existence of an analogy. In summary, then, the aim of the way of discovery is to find rigorous proofs. Its procedure is to pose dilemmas and to eliminate the clearly wrong choices of the dilemma. It turns the mind's attention to demonstrations of existence.

The aim of the way of teaching (*ordo doctrinae*) is to generate in students what understanding is possible. So in trinitarian study, the aim of the way of teaching is to bring about in students the limited understanding of the mystery that it is possible to gain in this life. It directs the pupil's thought "to the synthetic or constructive procedure in which human intelligence forms and develops concepts" (T & U, p. 130). In its trinitarian development, the way of teaching parallels, in effect, the procedure which the mind spontaneously expresses in its forming and elaborating concepts. To see how the way of teaching works in trinitarian theory, all we must do is to examine how Aquinas fabricated his understanding of the Trinity. He began by elaborating point by point the notion of God without inquiring about trinitarian understanding. Then he asked whether there are processions in God. This question presupposes that he has already figured out what processions are in human cognition. The trouble with the question is that it seems to ask *utrum sit* rather than *quid sit*. While it is a question of existence of processions, still the question makes us face the necessity of determining in what sense we can speak of processions in God. It is clear that as we do not understand God himself, so we do not understand the processions identical with God. So a clarification about the sense in which we can understand processions in God is all we can hope to attain this side of the grave. What follows in Aquinas after the clarification of the divine processions is an illumination of the subsistent relations in God. Last, St. Thomas advances from three mutually opposed subsistent relations to some penetration of the truth that there are three really distinct yet consubstantial persons (T & U, p. 130).

We may now summarize what we have discovered so far about the way of teaching. St. Thomas used it in the *Summa theologiae* in a constructive fashion to form and develop concepts. Paralleling the procedure of the human mind, the way of teaching does not base its trinitarian conclusions on any *priora quoad se* because in the Trinity there is nothing prior or posterior. Rather, it aims at generating understanding instead of proof. Its method is to work out in detail what one already knows, for example, about human cognition, and then to determine in what sense we can clarify what we understand. This clarification leads to a new understanding.

Lonergan agrees with Beumer that understanding of mysteries (*intelligentia mysteriorum*) is a fundamental concern of speculative theology. He disagrees with Beumer, however, who says that we must drop the anti-quated Aristotelian and scholastic views on the nature of science. Beumer writes that the notion of a *Glaubensverstandnis* (understanding of the truths of faith) is lacking in clarity and precision, and so runs the risk of fostering fuzzy, uncritical thinking. And while he believes that Aquinas instilled in the study of theology a spirit of scientific precision, he has to insist that this benefit does not reach *Glaubensverstandnis*. Lonergan, however, asserts that St. Thomas not only grasped fully the notion of understanding mysteries, but he also placed it in a rich theoretical context that enables one to relate speculative theology to (A) the truths of revelation, (B) the illumination of reason by faith, and (C) the teaching authority of the Church. Let us examine each of these relationships in turn (T & U, p. 131).

"Theology and Understanding": Old Problems

A. Speculative Theology and the Truths of Revelation

The premises of the "way of discovery" come from revelation. The truth of these premises forms the basis not only for the conclusions of the "way of discovery", but also of the subsequent development of the "way of teaching". It follows that the theologian's work does not create new motives for the assent of faith. In fact, the assent of faith forms the basis for his labors. What makes the deductions of the way of discovery all the more sure is not only that the initial premises are revealed, but also that the conclusions are confirmed by revelation. Inversely, the more extensively revelation confirms the conclusions of the way of discovery, the greater the section of revealed truth the way of teaching unifies. Finally, it is instructive to see how the distinction between the way of discovery and the way of teaching is drawn. Clearly, the distinction does not derive from finding out which truths come from revelation. Revelation figures in both because the truths admit different arrangements. Nor is the distinction between the two orders derived from inquiring into the chronology of discovery. The basis of the distinction is a discrimination between types of arguments. One type of argument settles matters of fact and is in the realm of judgment (*utrum sit* -- the way of discovery). Another type of argument throws some light on the nature of things and seeks understanding (*quid sit* -- the way of teaching). Recall that we have already seen this distinction in the Introduction to the *De ente supernaturali* where Lonergan cites the Thomist fourth *Quodlibet*, question 9, article 3 (18) that distinguishes between disputations that settle matters of fact by appealing to authorities, and disputations that aim at understanding reasons why things are the way they are. As Crowe wrote in the editorial Introduction to the "Theology and Understanding" article, this passage from Thomas has been paradigmatic for Lonergan during his entire career. The correct ordering of details in a theological issue according to a unifying idea contributes both to the understanding of the historical evolution of theological thought (the way of discovery) and of its systematic exposition (the way of teaching). Now we see that the basis of these distinct procedures is a discrimination between the aims of the two different arguments.[10]

B. Speculative Theology and the Illumination of Reason by Faith

How does the rich Thomist context help the theologian relate speculative theology to the illumination of reason by faith? Lonergan answers this question by stating that, although there is a twofold aspect in the illumination, there are not two illuminations, one coming from the truths of revelation and the other coming from the truths of reason. There is one illumination of reason by faith coming from the deductions of the way of discovery. But the illumination has a twofold aspect. First, theology helps the efforts of human reason in reason's pursuit of its own proper philosophical goals. It is well known that natural reason can attain a correct philosophy, yet it is equally apparent that it frequently fails to do so. The way of discovery used in theology helps reason because it elaborates a series of alternative philosophical conclusions. Second, the illumination of reason by faith comes about because revelation is supernatural. The implication here is that revelation presents reason with truths that it could not know otherwise. The analysis of these truths in the way of discovery "leads to the discovery of the theoretical elements that 1) stand beyond the confines of man's natural knowledge, 2) possess something like an immanent systematic structure of their own (*nexus mysteriorum inter se*), and 3) may be approximated through the analogies offered by scientific knowledge in the natural and human fields" (T & U, p. 132).

A THEMATIC STATEMENT

This one illumination of reason by faith has a twofold aspect that implies both the unity of the subject and the unity of the goal. An individual thinker does not have many intelligences but only one. And it is the dynamism of the one mind to grasp everything in a comprehensive view. Now we assume that the truths of revelation are congruent with the truths of reason. And so the illumination of reason produces the necessary dispositions for the illumination of faith. Lonergan uses the helpful comparison that just as grace is beyond nature yet perfects nature, so faith is beyond reason yet perfects reason. What about the Thomist synthesis created by the way of teaching? It communicates an understanding of mysteries which does not always easily show just where the philosophic analysis ends and theological understanding begins. Lonergan holds that Beumer's concept of theology as *Glaubensverstandnis* seems to regard the philosophical component in speculative theology as a perhaps required but unfortunate intruder. Yet Beumer's viewpoint is at odds with the Thomist position that the primary subject of theology is God, but the secondary subject includes all things in their relation to God (T & U, pp. 132-133).

C. Speculative Theology and the Teaching of the Church

In Lonergan's view, the point of the way of teaching is to provide a limited understanding of the truths of faith, not to expect its syllogisms to create evidence by which to make indisputably certain conclusions. The way of discovery is the procedure for expounding the certitude that comes from faith. The way of teaching, moreover, does not generate additional certitude by understanding the truths of faith -- our apprehension of the mysteries in this life remains imperfect. The only aim of the way of teaching is to express our imperfect understanding of the mysteries. It would betray this aim if a theologian were to pretend to find evidence for certitude where such evidence is lacking, or if he were to dismiss *argumenta convenientiae* (the so-called "proofs from reason") as proofs that do not prove (T & U, p. 133).

You might wonder what use the way of teaching is if it neither provides certitude nor generates perfect understanding. One important contribution is that it approximates a viewpoint on God and on all things in relation to God that is unified. This single viewpoint then gives rise to a grasp of the precise content and implications of the various mysteries in their varied aspects. This single viewpoint has a threefold benefit. It simplifies and deepens a person's spiritual life. It grounds teaching in sureness of doctrine with versatility of communication. It tends to remain in the mind because it is an intellectual memory (T & U, p. 133)

The speculative theologian uses the conclusions of the way of discovery as the starting point in his use of the way of teaching. These conclusions of the way of discovery are theoretical elements. In the way of teaching, the understanding will combine these theoretical elements into principles and science will expand them into deductions. It is clear that the work of the way of discovery is crucial for the way of teaching, much the same as a solid foundation is crucial for the stability of the rest of the house. What happens when the formulation of the theoretical elements is inaccurate or incomplete is that the entire structure of the way of teaching shudders. And this defect is as common as heresies in the history of religion. Heresy, after all, is the use of some but not all of the relevant components from the fonts of revelation. The obvious question that comes to mind has to do with the selection and use of the way of teaching's theoretical elements. How are these elements to be controlled? St. Thomas taught that wisdom superintends both understanding and science. Lonergan realized that the principles of understanding depend upon the terms that they unite. Following Aquinas, he held that wisdom controls the selection of terms and so the validation of both understanding and science (T & U, p. 134).

The relationship of speculative theology to the teaching authority of the Church depends on the practice of the speculative theologian. If he has some knowledge of philosophy and some measure of the gift of wisdom given everyone with sanctifying grace, then he is not completely unwise. Yet no matter how wise he is, his wisdom will be inadequate because the beatific vision alone is proportionate to the reality that speculative theology would understand. So the speculative theologian stands between wisdom and folly. He endeavors to know the basic theoretical elements that then he elaborates as fully and as accurately as possible. The more he knows his subject, the more grateful he will be for both God's revelation of supernatural truth as well as for the divinely assisted teaching authority (T & U, p. 134).

The basic relation of speculative theology to the teaching authority of the Church is wisdom's direction of both understanding and science. Understanding and science are subordinate to wisdom, a supernatural subordination parallel to the natural subordination of speculation to judgment, of *quid sit* to *an sit*. This subordinate relationship matches a subordination that has already come to light. The truth of the conclusions of the way of discovery and thereby the truth of the components that enter into the way of teaching rests upon the truth of the assent of faith. So the truth with which the way of teaching begins is certain.[11] Observe that the way of teaching adds a further synthetic element by its selection of related basic terms. Because this selection of terms and its consequences are not obvious or explained, then the mysteries remain hidden behind the curtain of faith. The theologian knows that he cannot account for all of his hidden assumptions and unexplicated ideas. So he acknowledges that his best theorems are merely probable -- that is, uncertain. "Because his clearest theorems are only probable, he is ever ready to leave an ultimate judgment upon them to the further exercise of faith that discerns in the church's dogmatic decisions the assistance of divine wisdom" (T & U, p. 135).

There are two further relations between speculative theology and the teaching authority of the Church. As is clear from glancing through the history of conciliar developments, the Church's dogmatic pronouncements borrow from the previous writings of theologians. The basis of the way of discovery, on the other hand, is each new dogmatic pronouncement of the Church. These dogmatic teachings receive an increase in clarity and precision that the way of discovery passes on to its conclusions. These more luminous conclusions form a corresponding increase in the precision of the way of teaching and in the understanding of revelation (T & U, p. 135).

"Theology and Understanding": New Problems

In the final section of his book review, Lonergan declares that, while the Aristotelian and scholastic notions of science are adequate for the formulation of *speculative* theology, still there are methodological problems that derive from *positive* theology. This recognition that there is more to theology than speculative concerns shows up in the large section he devotes to the methodological issues. Since these four problems influence the development of the twofold way, we will examine each of the issues briefly.

A. Methodological Issues: The Problem of Patterns of Human Experience

The *Imitation of Christ* expresses a contrast between feeling compunction and defining it, between pleasing the Trinity and teaching brilliantly about it. This raises the perennial philosophical issue between doing and merely knowing, between practice and theory. But Lonergan distinguishes between practice and theory as between two types of knowing. There are two types of knowledge involved in defining compunction and in experiencing it. But these two types of knowledge are distinct from one another. Methodology's problem is to define the exact nature of each kind of knowledge, the uses and perils of each, and above all to express the principles that regulate the transpositions from one to the other. As we shall see later, this issue becomes the foundation for his exposition of the antithesis between the worlds of common sense and of theory in his 1962 *De methodo theologiae*.

A THEMATIC STATEMENT

B. Methodological Issues: The Problem of the Relation Between Speculative and Positive Theology

The second methodological issue which needs attention is the problem of the relations between speculative and positive theology. The First Vatican Council urged an understanding of mysteries. It fostered as well an individual and collective progress "in the understanding, science, and wisdom with which the same revealed truths in the same sense are apprehended down the ages" (T & U, p. 137). The difficulty is to find the methodological principles for doing the Council's bidding. This brings us to the realm of positive theology. Positive theology provides a sea of monographs on the Fathers, the scholastics, the heretics, the councils, the Bible, and the decrees of the Holy See. Methodology's task is to reduce such multiplicity to unity. First, the special methods of different branches of scholarly research cannot plot the chart of a synthesis that unifies the results of different kinds of research. Second, specialists in one area will not permit a nonspecialist from another field to settle either what the conclusions really signify or how the result should be arranged into a unity. Third, who can perform a synthesis if we exclude specialists and nonspe-cialists? Even if such a synthesis could be effected after the research were completed, the value of the synthesis would be fleeting. For it is a com-monplace that contemporary scholarly conclusions are endlessly likely to be overruled by the conclusions of tomorrow's researchers. These difficulties regarding synthesis elicit from Lonergan five observations toward a method of synthesis.

Five Observations on the Method of Synthesis

The first observation relates to historical questions. There seem to be two types of historical question. The first type of historical question per-tains to the more positive and material details of time and place regarding documents, artifacts. As the raw material of the historical process, this type of question is not relevant to theology. The second type of historical question is extraordinarily relevant to theology. Historical questions of the

69

second type are not so much influenced by the cumulative labor of researchers as by the philosophical assumptions that scholars implicitly or explicitly invoke in their interpretations of the nature of the scientific method.

A second observation about the method of synthesis has to do with the illumination of method by faith. For if we can distinguish clearly and precisely these two types of historical question, we can be illumined by faith. Since method is "simply reason's explicit consciousness of the norms of its own procedures, the illumination of reason by faith implies an illumination of method by faith" (T & U, p. 138).

A third observation pertains to the study of scientific methods. Just as historical questions of the second type are influenced by philosophical assumptions -- be they empiricist, naturalist, existentialist, idealist, relativist or realist -- so the presuppositions and assumptions of the scientist influences his method. A scientist is never certain of his conclusions. What he is sure of is the validity of his method. So a study of scientific methods is most valuable when it examines the scientist's presuppositions and assumptions. The study of these assumptions also generates the principles for a systematic critique of the results of the scientific investigation.

A fourth observation is simply that just as there is a correspondence in the scientific method of the physical sciences between pedestrian techniques and the relatively *a priori* differential equations, so there is a relationship in the scientific method of the historical sciences between mundane monographs and higher level hermeneutic controls.

A fifth and final observation regards this "higher level control" of the historical method. If this element of the historical method can be discovered, defined, and put to work, then the probability is that the distinction between the two types of historical question referred to above could be established within the context of methodology not by whim, therefore, but "in the light of clear and distinct ideas intrinsic" to that field and context (T & U, P. 139).

A THEMATIC STATEMENT

C. Methodological Issues: The Relation Between Speculative Theology and the Empirical Human Sciences

Lonergan now returns to his original four problems for an elaboration of speculative theology in its relations to other things. This third problem is the relation between speculative theology and the empirical human sciences. The science that treats all things in their relation to God is the queen of the sciences. And that is the aim of speculative theology, so it is the queen of the sciences. Now speculative theology down the ages has delegated to philosophy as to a handmaid the exercise of certain functions. With the advent of empirical human sciences, however, there is a new situation. For the human sciences are empirical inasmuch as they treat of men and women as in fact they are. That is, men and women in the present order labor under the effects of original sin and of personal sin. Only through supernatural grace can human beings escape the darkening of the mind and the weakening of the will flowing from original and personal sin. It follows that the human questions of this earth cannot receive satisfactory superintendence from philosophy if it conceives its task in terms of what prescinds from the concrete intelligibility of the developing human scene. If the human sciences studied human experience in the abstract, then they would be automatically subordinate to philosophy and thereby subordinate to theology. But the human sciences are empirical, that is, they aim to understand all the data on men and women as they are -- in the concrete and specific. Yet the only correct general form of that understanding is theological; only the theological correctly assumes the source and direction of human weakness (T & U, p. 139).

D. Methodological Issues: The Critical Problem and Historical Interpretation

The entire problem of knowing what one's knowing is can be exemplified in Beumer's approach to theological method. Instead of turning to St. Thomas as the theologian who best illustrates the teaching of the First Vatican Council on the nature of theology, he turns to M.J. Scheeben. He does so because he judges that the *Summa theologiae* and increasingly the Thomist tradition became over the years inattentive to the Augustinian notion of theology as the understanding of faith. Lonergan disagrees with Beumer's interpretation of *Summa theologiae*, and he believes that no teacher can fail to communicate some understanding of the faith to students who examine it with the requisite literary, philosophical, and historical knowledge (T & U, p. 140).

Lonergan contends that Beumer fails to give the facts of human understanding sufficient merit or attention in his scrutiny of the works of Aquinas. What results from this inattention to the facts of human understanding is confusion about the procedures of historical interpretation. The issues of historical interpretation become complicated "by the self-knowledge of the interpreter, by his difficulty in grasping clearly and distinctly just what he is doing when he understands and conceives, reflects and judges" (T & U, p. 141). The critical problem, however, is not the relatively easy question whether we know. It is the far more difficult and important issue of what exactly happens when we are knowing. "Until that issue is settled in the luminous fashion that will make philosophy as methodical as science, there are bound to remain basic and unsolved problems of theological method" (T & U, p. 141). Of course, Lonergan had already composed *Insight* as his attempt to solve the critical problem for philosophy, so he alerts his article's readers in a footnote to *Insight*'s imminent publication.

De Constitutione Christi

During the two years following the publication of the "Theology and Understanding" article, Lonergan continued to teach large classes at the Gregorian University. It is evident that he still pursued an interest in the ordering of ideas because he returned to the topic explicitly. In a Christological textbook published in 1956 for his students, Lonergan set forth his ideas on the constitution of Christ.[12] The *De constitutione Christi* elaborates his position that the doctrine of one person with two natures transposes into the modern psychological terms of a single subject of both a divine and a human consciousness.[13] In the third part of the six part text, he sets down his ideas "On Theological Understanding". Since this is the next locus for his discussion of the ordering of ideas, we will turn our attention to his statements in this part.

On Theological Understanding

In section 42, Lonergan makes a division of the tasks of theology. In this life, we know God only mediately by the divine essence, and this knowledge is mediated in two ways. One way is through the natural revelation of creation. The likeness to God expressed by each creature and by the order of the entire universe is the origin both of metaphysics and of natural theology.

The other way we come to know God is through a formal, supernatural revelation. It is through supernatural revelation that there emerges dogmatic theology, a subalternated science. And dogmatic theology is usually divided into positive theology and speculative theology. Here Lonergan says that the task of positive theology is to discover the same truth, dogma, and opinion that appears in many different cultural guises throughout our continuously emerging understanding of the same truth. Why has the need for positive theology arisen at all? It has come about because different languages within various cultures, eras, and locations have expressed the very same truth in different ways, but always under the magisterium of the Church. And as the First Vatican Council reiterates, it is the same revealed truth which we owe to the economy of divine grace that can be apprehended with ever more understanding, knowledge, and wisdom.[14]

Positive theology discerns the *quoad nos* which varies according to historical differences. What makes positive theology possible, however, is speculative theology. The proper goal of speculative theology is the *quoad se* which remains true despite past cultural and historical changes. So positive theology could not discern the same truth if speculative theology had not first discovered and then expressed accurately the *quoad se* which always stays the same. The goal of theological speculation, then, is to understand the revealed word of God and to express precisely and clearly that understanding.

Section 46 states that every ordering of truths is twofold. As Lonergan stated earlier in the *Verbum* articles (pp. 61-62), the two ways we have for arranging what we know in the natural sciences are the "way of resolution" and the "way of composition". Here he explicitly aligns the "way of resolution" with the "way of historical discovery"; and the "way of composition" with the "way of teaching". This connecting of resolution with historical discovery and of composition with teaching is a new synthesis in his way of proceeding. He seems bothered by the faith/reason dispute and wants to show that faith and reason connect with one another in the same way as the two ways of ordering ideas correspond with one another. These connections between resolution/discovery and composition/teaching are important because they give him new ways of arranging what we naturally and supernaturally know about God. In arranging what we natural-ly know about God, we might begin by an ascent from created things to God. And then we posit some first truth about God (such as divine power or wisdom), and then we demonstrate the divine attributes and explain created realities under the influence of a kind of divine guidance.[15]

What we know supernaturally about God we can likewise arrange in two ways. First, faith illumines reason. Second, once reason is illumined by faith, it achieves some understanding of mysteries. We call faith's illumination of reason the "way of theological discovery" (*via inventionis theologicae*). And we term the understanding of faith by illumined reason the "way of theological teaching or discipline" (*via doctrinae vel disciplinae theologicae*).[16]

Let us look more closely at the two ways in which Lonergan arranges what we can know about God supernaturally. In the way of discovery, when faith illumines reason, we begin with what is better known to us (*notiora quoad nos*), namely, what is revealed by God and contained in the written word which tradition gives us. In the way of teaching, when reason enlightened by faith achieves some understanding of mysteries, we begin from theological grounds which are better known in themselves (*notiora quoad se*) and we conclude to what has been revealed and understood through those theological grounds. The movement is circular. Faith illumines reason inasmuch as we conclude theological reasons from what has been revealed (*via inventionis*); and reason has some understanding of the mysteries inasmuch as we conclude from these theological grounds to the same revealed mysteries (*ordo doctrinae*). He concludes that since it is similar to reduce a thing to causes and truth to grounds, the method of scientific resolution (*via resolutionis*) and the method of theological discovery (*via inventionis*) are similar. And since it is similar to compose a thing out of causes and deduce a truth from grounds, so the method of scientific composition (*via compositionis*) is like the method of theological doctrine or teaching (*via doctrinae vel disciplinae theologicae*).[17]

Section 47 deals as well with the issue whether theology is analogically called science. Lonergan notes the Aristotelian distinction between a cause of being (*causa essendi*) and a cause of knowledge (*causa cognoscendi*). A *causa essendi* is some being which gives existence to another being. A *causa cognoscendi* is not being but some truth which is the ground of another truth. In the natural sciences, we begin in the way of resolution with the cause of our knowledge and end up with the cause of something being what it is. In the way of composition, natural science uses the causes of things being what they are as causes of our knowledge.

Theology admits a different ordering. God does not exhibit either intrinsic or extrinsic causes of being. Since God is in every way simple and necessary, then in theology only causes of knowledge are posited. Our knowledge of God, however, is composed of many truths related to one another as ground. A truth which is the ground of another is also the cause of the knowledge of that other. Since the ordering of all truths is twofold, namely, from what is better known to us (*notiora quoad nos*) to what is better known in itself (*notiora quoad se*), and from what is better known in itself to what is better known to us, this arrangement has an implication for theology.

In theology, there are some causes of knowledge better known to us (*causae cognoscendi notiores quoad nos*) from which we begin inasmuch as faith illumines reason in the way of theological discovery. And there are other causes of knowledge better known in themselves (*causae cognoscendi notiores quoad se*) from which we begin inasmuch as reason illumined by faith understands to some degree the mysteries of faith in the way of theological teaching.[18] We can conclude, then, that the scientific causes of being and the theological causes of knowledge are really different from one another. Yet as far as our knowledge is concerned, we can also conclude that the scientific causes of being are similar to our theological causes of knowledge.

Just as a scientist concludes from the understood essence of a thing to the attributes of the thing, so also the theologian proceeds from the essence of God analogically conceived to the attributes of God analogically conceived. This difference in the reality and similarity in the knowledge of something is the analogy between other sciences and theology. For just as science is certain knowledge of things through their causes, so theology is certain knowledge of God through the causes of our knowing that are better known in themselves.[19]

These explanations correspond to the ones given to the trinitarian procedures of the *via doctrinae* written in the *Verbum* articles and reiterated in the "Theology and Understanding" article. So for Lonergan at this point in his thought, theology properly speaking is the realm of the understanding achieved in the way of teaching, the realm of the causes of our knowing that are better known in themselves.

A summary of the *De constitutione Christi* section on theological understanding discloses that supernatural revelation is the source of dogmatic theology. Dogmatic theology in turn has two tasks. One task is positive. Positive theology discovers the same truth expressed *quoad nos* which varies according to historical differences. So there is attention to the issue of maintaining continuity of revealed truth from one age to the next. But the emphasis is on dogmatic theology's other task which is speculative. Speculative theology aims at understanding the revealed Word of God and the *quoad se* which remain true despite past cultural and historical changes. Furthermore, there are two ways we can arrange what we know about God. First, faith illumines reason in the way of discovery that begins from the *notiora quoad nos* (revelation and tradition). Second, reason enlightened by faith achieves some understanding of mysteries in the way of teaching that begins from the *notiora quoad se*. Just as natural science is certain knowledge of things through their causes, so theology is certain knowledge of God through *causa cognoscendi notiores in se*. So while philosophy and theology are similar, they have different objects, aims, and procedures. Finally, theology is only analogously a science because it seeks an imperfect understanding based on analogy.

Concluding Overview

We can now summarize what we have seen about the "way of discovery" and the "way of teaching" in "Theology and Understanding". In theology, the way of discovery (*via inventionis*) is the course of actual discovery over the ages. The cause of our knowing in the way of discovery is the articles of faith given in revealed truth. The cause of our knowing is *prior quoad nos* and first in the way of discovery. It is the order one uses to find rigorous proofs for theological truths. It poses dilemmas and eliminates the more obviously unacceptable alternatives. Its realm is the argument that settles matters of fact. Through the way of discovery, faith illumines reason. So the way of discovery is the procedure for expounding the certitude that comes from faith. It provides the theoretical elements that are the starting point of the way of teaching. Recall that in the *Verbum* articles, Lonergan seemed to say that the two ways proceed simultaneously and dialectically. Yet here, one picks up after the other.

As of 1954, the *via inventionis* is not an end in itself but is a preparatory stage that provides the elements for the *via doctrinae*. It is subordinate to the system that the way of teaching elaborates to achieve the true goal of speculative theology, the understanding of the mysteries of faith. Although Lonergan does not advert to this problem yet, the real difficulty he will encounter in the arrangement of theological ideas pertains to the place of history. Because he is so concerned with the understanding of mysteries, he does not at this time pay sufficient attention to the problems that can arise if theologians conceive the way of discovery as proceeding atemporally, as containing truths without minds thinking them.

The aim of the *ordo doctrinae* is to provide a limited understanding of the truths of faith. It moves from the conclusions of the way of discovery to a systematic presentation of the truths that have been revealed. Its realm is the argument that throws some light on the nature of things and seeks understanding. It argues from nonscriptural premises to conclusions that run parallel to scriptural statements. Instead of aiming at proof, the way of teaching works out in detail what we already know, and then determines in what sense we can clarify what we only vaguely understand. This clarification leads to a new understanding. And the new understanding gives some approximation to a single view and so is synthetic.

In the final section of the book review, Lonergan states that the Aristotelian and scholastic notions of science are adequate for an elaboration of the nature of speculative theology. Why does Lonergan still defend the scholastic notion of science in 1954 when he has already substantially written *Insight*, a study that reveals a sophisticated understanding both of modern science and of the limits of the Aristotelian scientific ideal? Perhaps he was cautious about wanting to adhere to the Church's directive to defend and to follow the procedures of Aquinas who used the Aristotelian framework of science. Perhaps he was aware how massive the task would be to transform theology's entire way of proceeding. Perhaps he needed the further wrestling with his own trinitarian work and with answering the question of the development of dogma to require him to work out new procedures. But the most likely explanation for his loyalty to the Thomistic

scientific model at this time was his awareness of its widespread acceptance in the schools and its limited although still adequate value as a
system within which to accomplish speculative theological goals.

Although Lonergan was still primarily interested in the theoretical
underpinnings of *speculative* theology as embodied in the "way of
discovery" and the "way of teaching", he recognized some methodological
issues stemming from positive theology and its relation to speculative
theology. The four issues he mentions are: (A) the problem of patterns of
human experience; (B) the problem of the relations between speculative
and positive theology; (C) the problem of the relations between speculative
theology and the empirical human sciences; and (D) the problem of the
relations between speculative theology and epistemology as illustrated in
historical interpretation. These methodological issues seem to strain and
to bulge out of the neat procedures outlined thus far as the "way of
discovery" and the "way of teaching".

It may seem that these methodological considerations are superfluous to an account of the ordering of ideals according to the "way of
discovery" and the "way of teaching". But the relationship of speculative
theology to positive theology and to the empirical human sciences raised
questions about the aim and scope of speculative theology that had only
recently been asked. The speculative goal of scientific theological
understanding -- to reach necessary and immutable truths about God and
all things in their relation to God -- was no longer the only aim of theology.
The new goal of positive theological studies seeks to understand human life
in its particular, unique circumstances and events. The fresh difference in
goals between speculative theology and the positive human sciences
becomes the context for Lonergan's wrestling with the ordering of ideas.

NOTES

CHAPTER III

[1]Lonergan, *De scientia. . .*, p. 4: *Verbum*, pp. 213-214.

[2]Lonergan, *Insight*, p. 740.

[3]Bernard J.F. Lonergan, S.J., "Theology and Understanding", in F.E. Crowe, S.J. ed., *Collection* (New York: Herder and Herder, 1967), pp. 121-141.

[4]F.E. Crowe, S.J., Introduction, Collection, pp. xxv-xxvi.

[5]Lonergan, *"Insight* Revisited", *A Second Collection*, p. 277.

[6]*Ibid.*

[7]*Ibid.*, p. 276.

[8]Lonergan, "Theology and Understanding", p. 122. Since there are numerous references to this article in this section, the citations will be made directly in the text with the abbreviation, T & U, and the page number.

[9]As Lonergan himself points out in the 1957 trinitarian textbook, *Divinarum personarum conceptio analogica*, there are in Book IV of the *Summa Contra Gentiles* elements from the "way of teaching" (chapters 10-14, 19-26, 40-49) and elements from the "way of discovery" (chapters 2-9, 15-18, 27-39). See Bernard J. F. Lonergan, S. J., *Divinarum personarum conceptio analogica* (Rome: Gregorian University Press, 1957), p. 9.

[10]F.E. Crowe, S.J., Introduction to *Collection*, p. xxv.

[11]The important distinction between revealed truth (with which the "way of discovery" begins) and theological truth consequent to revelation (with which the "way of teaching" deals) needs to be more carefully examined. But Lonergan does not advert to this issue until his 1957 first

A THEMATIC STATEMENT

chapter in *Divinarum personarum conceptio analogica* on the aim and proper object of speculative theology.

[12]Bernard J.F. Lonergan, S.J., *De constitutione Christi ontologica et psychologica* (Rome: Gregorian University Press, 1956). An English translation by Timothy P. Fallon is available at the Lonergan Research Institute of Regis College, Toronto. *On the Ontological and Psychological Constitution of Christ: A Supplement* prepared by Bernard Lonergan, S.J. for the use of his students (University of Santa Clara, Santa Clara, 1979).

[13]Bernard J.F. Lonergan, S.J., "The Dehellenization of Dogma", a review in *Theological Studies*, 28 (1967), 336-351 of *The Future of Belief: Theism in a World Come of Age* by Leslie Dewart (New York, 1966), reprinted in William Ryan, S.J. and Bernard Tyrrell, S.J. editors, *A Second Collection* (London: Darton, Longman & Todd, 1974), p. 25.

[14]Lonergan, *De constitutione Christi*, pp. 42-43. These points pick up the theme about the relationship between positive and speculative theology first enunciated as the second methodological issue in the 1954 review article, "Theology and Understanding", p. 137.

[15]*Ibid.*, p. 46.

[16]*Ibid.*, p. 47.

[17]*Ibid.*

[18]*Ibid.*, pp. 48-49

[19]*Ibid.*, p. 49.

CHAPTER IV

THREE PROCESSES IN SPECULATIVE THEOLOGY:
ANALYSIS, SYNTHESIS, AND THE HISTORICAL EVOLUTION
OF UNDERSTANDING

When Lonergan moved to Rome in 1953 as professor of theology at the Gregorian University, he taught courses in Latin on the Trinity and the Incarnation in alternate years till 1963 when he began to concentrate on the Incarnation. He offered the course on the Trinity five times in all, the first during the year 1954-1955, the last during the year 1962-1963. He composed a set of Latin class notes called *De sanctissima Trinitate* which he used as a supplement to the standard text for the course when he first taught it in 1954-1955.[1]

Although Lonergan contributed to the understanding of Trinitarian and Christological theologies, his main work remains his thought on the nature of theology itself. As we shall see in the development of the two volumes of his trinitarian theology, the key methodological problem he faced is the need to differentiate and relate the three emerging contemporary theological specializations: positive, dogmatic and systematic theology.

Lonergan's first textbook on the Trinity appeared in 1957 with the title *Divinarum personarum conceptio analogica*.[2] He published a second edition in 1959 in which he corrected misprints and made two minor additions (pp. 91, 297). And he produced a third, final edition in 1964 called *De Deo Trino II: Pars Systematica*. This volume contains extensive revision, particularly in the opening chapters where he treated further reflections on the nature of systematic theology. Before we focus on *Divinarum personarum's* first chapter on theological understanding and upon how it develops, it is worth noting in passing that Lonergan deals with the dogmatic and positive elements of theology in another volume, the *De Deo Trino: Pars Analytica*, first published in Rome in 1961. In its revised form in 1964, it becomes *De Deo Trino I: Pars Dogmatica*. The change of name indicates a significant development to which we shall return.

Our procedure in this chapter will be to outline Lonergan's thought on the twofold ordering of ideas, now called the *via analytica* and the *via synthetica*. While his main concern is still to explain the goal of speculative theology, which is the understanding of the truths of faith, there are new issues that impel him to consider more fully the *via inventionis* (now called the *via analytica*). Recall that the four contemporary methodological issues of the 1954 article, "Theology and Understanding", had already begun to stretch the structure of the twofold ordering of ideas. Here there are questions about how to explain the continuity of truth in the development of dogma. Lonergan still thematizes the elements of the twofold ordering of ideas in the scholastic terminology of object as end (God), object as immanently produced (intelligible truth), and moving object (revealed truth). But instead of maintaining that speculative theology's goal of understanding is reached merely by a twofold process of analysis and synthesis, he introduces a third, historical consideration. The question that prompts this historical consideration is how the same truth can be understood now more, now less. In order to explain that there is variation not in the object understood but in the manner of understanding, he introduces the historical dimension. While we will focus on his thematization of the ways of analysis and synthesis, we must also cite the issues that the introduction of the historical dimension raises for the twofold way of ordering ideas in theology.

The First Chapter of *Divinarum Personarum*: Theological Understanding

In the preface to the *Divinarum personarum*, Lonergan mentioned that his effort to distinguish and relate the several parts of theology had taught him to note how different from dogmatic and positive theology were the aim, proper object, and the method of speculative theology (DP, p. 5). The first chapter, "Theological Understanding", treats speculative theology's goal both in itself and in its relation to the rest of theology. In order to promote a positive understanding of speculation rather than to catalog and refute opposed errors, he proposes to organize his material according to the following three headings: (1) the goal that is intended; (2) the act by which we attain the goal; (3) the way by which we advance to the act of attaining the goal (DP, p. 7).

The goal intended in speculative theology (1) is that imperfect and yet most fruitful understanding which the First Vatican Council promotes (DB 1796, DS 3016).[3] The act by which we attain the goal pertains to the first act of understanding. It is imperfect, analogous, obscure, slowly evolving, synthetic, and yet highly fruitful (DP, pp. 9-13). In some further reflections about theological understanding's relation to truth, the tenth point is that there is continuity in the development of theological understanding (DB 1800, DS 3020). This tenth point contains a thorny problem. How can there be "growth...and all possible progress in understanding, knowledge, and wisdom...but only within proper limits, that is, in the same doctrine, in the same meaning, and in the same purport (DB 1800, DS 3020)"?

This question raises the issue of the way in which theology is similar to or different from natural science. It is possible that the same truth can be understood theologically now more, now less. This variation in theological understanding is possible not because there is a change in the object that is understood but in the manner of understanding.

There are four examples given of a variation in the manner of understanding. First, a person can read scripture and understand correctly each of the truths written by the sacred authors. Yet since a person understands each element of truth separately, such a one simply lacks comprehensive understanding. Second, a person can read scripture, understand individual truths correctly, and go one step further. This person compares various texts of scripture, passes over accidental elements and discovers what are the substantial truths that occur in many passages. This second reader then conceives and expresses in accurate technical terms this substantial identity. This one arrives at the expression of the same truth, understood in the same sense, and yet composed in new technical terms (DP, p. 18).

Third, there is the person who advances beyond these previous two and enters the theological way. This person not only peruses all of scripture, understands individual passages, and expresses the essential matters of scripture in technical terms. He has investigated even more deeply. Revealed truths even when reduced to their essential parts are not easily grasped in their inner coherence. What are some examples of these difficult revealed truths? God is one in such a way that there are three Persons; Christ is God and nonetheless is man; everything depends on the gracious will of God in such a way that without our merits we will not gain the reward of heaven. One who has entered the "theological way" is one who not only makes a systematic exegesis of scriptural statements and discovers theological problems. Such a one also seeks an understanding of what scripture teaches to be the truth. Although the theologian introduces another kind of understanding, still it is the same revealed truth that one seeks to understand. The meaning of revealed truth does not change through theological understanding. But the revealed truth itself understood in the same sense is what the theologian grasps more fully, clearly, and systematically (DP, p. 18).

Fourth, a theologian can understand the same revealed truth in such a way as to reach a new step in comprehension. According to Aristotle, science is twofold: one kind of science is science in potency, when it is only knowledge of universals. The other science is science in act, when it is applied to particulars. Beyond systematic exegesis, therefore, there exists historical exegesis which no longer omits the accidentals but includes them synthetically. Besides systematic theology, there is more concrete and comprehensive theology which reflects upon the economy of salvation in its historical evolution and seeks to understand it (DP, p. 19).

What makes this new advance in theological comprehension possible? Lonergan attributes this possible advance to the groundwork provided by positive research in biblical, conciliar, patristic, medieval, liturgical and ascetical fields. Yet the synthetic character of a systematic theology that includes the historical development of understanding has not yet emerged because, as Lonergan put it, scholars of his day resemble twelfth century compilers rather than thirteenth century theologians (DP, p. 19).

The Threefold Process by Which We Attain the End of Theological Understanding

The fourth section of the 1957 edition of *Divinarum personarum conceptio analogica* is about the triple way by which we proceed to the goal of theological understanding. Here Lonergan adopts new terminology for what we have seen was the "way of resolution" and the "way of composition". The processes now are called analysis, synthesis, and the historical evolution of understanding.

A. Analysis

In natural science, we arrive at some knowledge of causes through inquiry and investigation. There necessarily exists a certain common and prescientific knowledge of things whereby we grasp things without as yet knowing their causes. Therefore, the first process by which we progress toward the acquisition of scientific knowledge begins from a common and pre-scientific knowledge of things and terminates in a knowledge of their causes. This initial process is called (1) *analysis*, because it advances from a confused grasp of things to causes or reasons that are clearly defined; (2) *via resolutionis*, because it reduces those very things to their causes; (3) *via inventionis*, because by it causes are discovered which until now were unknown; (4) *via certitudinis*, because from this common and prescientific knowledge, which for us is the most obvious and certain, we draw up arguments to demonstrate more remote and obscure conclusions (DP, p. 20).

B. Synthesis

Science is more than knowledge of causes (understanding). It is also the understanding of the things themselves through their causes. So we complete this initial scientific process by a second which begins from the causes already discovered, and terminates in an understanding of things themselves in their causes. This process we call (1) *synthesis*, because we supply fundamental reasons to define things and to deduce their properties; (2) *via compositionis*, because we use the causes already discovered to produce or constitute things; (3) *via doctrinae seu disciplinae*, because we begin from concepts that are the most simple and fundamental, and by gradually adding others, we advance to an ordered understanding of the entire science (DP, p. 21).

An illustration of the distinction between these processes emerges from Lonergan's familiar comparison between the historical chronicle of physics or chemistry, on the one hand, and textbooks by which physics or chemistry are taught. The reason for the different starting points is that the explorer, pioneer, or apologist begins from what is most manifest and easy to grasp with common sense. Yet a good teacher begins from those concepts whose understanding does not presuppose the understanding of anything else (DP, p. 21). The teacher starts with the unifying idea of a subject. The unifying idea is not the same as the ones that common sense easily grasps. The point here is that the "simple" concept from which the synthetic process begins is simple in the sense of being fundamental, of presupposing nothing else. It does not mean "simple" as in "easily understood" or effortlessly discovered.

C. The Historical Evolution of Understanding

As these two processes evolve over generations, there emerges a third process we can call the evolution of understanding that completes the twofold process of analysis and synthesis. The movements of analysis and synthesis as described above are not perfected once and for all, but continuously repeat their operations. The process is never identical in the repeated performances, because later investigators discover truer and more remote causes by which the earlier analysis is corrected, and the earlier synthesis sometimes becomes totally reformed. So this third scientific process is the evolution of understanding in the history of the sciences which in its concrete unity comprehends the entire succession of those truths which down the ages have been discovered in the *via resolutionis* and systematically taught in the *via compositionis* (DP, p. 21).

D. A Comparison Between Natural Science and Theology

Lonergan next compares in four points how these processes of analysis, synthesis and the evolution of understanding occur in natural science and in theology. First, just as in naturally known truths there is a kind of prior and common grasp of things (where things themselves are manifestly known although their causes remain obscure), so also in supernaturally known truths there is a kind of prior knowledge common to all the faithful whereby we believe with complete certitude all divinely revealed truths, although as yet we have not achieved theological under-standing of them.

Second, there is an analytical process in both natural science and theology. Just as science begins with a manifest knowledge of things and proceeds to the discovery of their causes, definitions, and proofs, so also human reason illumined by faith begins from the truths of faith and by earnest, devout, and sober inquiry arrives at some understanding of mysteries (DB 1796, DS 3016). This analytic process was the chief occupation of the Fathers. They sought both to understand revealed truths and to refute heretics.

Third, there is a synthetic process in both natural science and theology. In science, one who proposes a scientific theory must system-atically define all the causes which were previously discovered. To do so, the theoretical scientist proceeds from an orderly arrangement of the more fundamental causes to the intermediate and complex ones, until he knows clearly and distinctly the objects according to all their reasons and accumulated causes and controls them effectively. In a similar fashion, the theologian who unites to the understanding of particular revealed truths a synthetic understanding of all of them, systematically defines all their reasons and causes. As in the natural sciences, the theologian's task is to proceed in an orderly fashion from the more basic fundamental questions through the intermediate ones until at last one can expound systematically all data which pertains to God and his creatures, as it were, according to their intimate reasons and ultimate causes. We have an example of this synthetic process in theology through its development in the Middle Ages when scholars systematically collected testimonies of scripture and the opinions of the Fathers, and when the scholastics constructed with the help of philosophy the summas of theology to promote synthetic understanding according to the *ordo doctrinae seu disciplinae* (DP, p. 22).

Fourth, there is an evolution of understanding both in the natural sciences and in theology. Lonergan notes that the condition for the possibility of the evolution of a synthetic process is that in the order of intelligent beings, humans exist only as a potency. So the integral science possible to mankind cannot reach such a peak of perfection in any given age that the rest of the human race throughout the centuries can be only humble disciples of their predecessors. Hence, in the natural sciences we see new theories and hypotheses succeeding the old, while in the supernatural order it is clear that there has been a kind of evolution not only of theology but even of dogmas. If an evolution of theological understanding and of dogma were not possible, then the Vatican Council's hopes would be vain that "there be growth...and all possible progress in understanding, knowledge, and wisdom whether in single individuals or in the whole body, in each person as well as in the entire Church, according to the state of their development..." (DB 1800, DS 3020). The current theology manuals provided examples of this mixed procedure that used both analysis and synthesis. In the theology manuals of the middle 1950s, what illustrate the analytic process are the arguments from scripture, the councils, the Fathers, and the agreement of theologians, while what exemplify the synthetic process are the series of theses, and the solutions of difficult problems (DP, p. 23).

E. A Comparison Between the Analytic and Synthetic Processes

Now that we have outlined the three processes that lead to theological understanding, we can reach even greater comprehension by comparing the analytic process with the synthetic process. Lonergan uses the schematic outlines of trinitarian theology as a concrete example of this comparison.

In the analytic process (which is also the *via resolutionis, via inventionis*, and *via certitudinis*) we start from the missions of the Son and Holy Spirit as narrated in the New Testament. Next, we proceed to the trinitarian dogma which affirms that there are Three who are really distinct (in opposition to the Sabellian teaching), and that God is only one (in opposition to the Subordinationists) (DB 48, 51, DS 112, 115). Next we affirm the consubtantiality of the Three (DB 54, 86, DS 125, 150); then there are distinguished real personal properties (Cappadocians). Then we learn that these properties are relative and that the relations are of origin. Last, we seek an understanding of these origins and we invoke the psychological analogy (DP, pp. 23-24).

In the synthetic process (which is also the *via compositionis, doctrinae, disciplinae*) there is an orderly approach to the doctrine of the Trinity which differs markedly from the analytic way. First, we consider the one God (S.T., I, qq. 2-26). Second, we posit intelligible relations in the one, intelligent, knowing and loving God (q. 27). Third, we ground the relations in these emanations (q. 28). Fourth, once we know emanations and relations (q. 29, introduction), we consider the Persons in general (qq. 29-32). Fifth, we consider the Persons one at a time (qq. 33-38). Sixth, we compare Persons with those realities which we considered before we examined the Persons, namely, the Divine Essence (q. 39), the relations or properties (q. 40), and the notional acts or emanations (q. 41, cf. q. 27).

Seventh, we compare Persons among themselves (q. 42) and with us (q. 43).[4]

With the outline of these two different approaches, we can proceed to a further explication of the two methods. Lonergan proposes to compare the analytic and synthetic processes under eight headings.

1. The two processes, the *via analytica* and the *via synthetica*, consider the same reality. The missions of the Son and of the Holy Spirit which the New Testament narrates are the same ones that Aquinas expounds in *S.T.*, I. q. 43. So the synthetic process is nothing but the ordered exposition of those truths that were discovered in the analytic process (DP, p. 24).

2. Although the two processes treat of the same realities, nevertheless the order is different. As we saw in the *via doctrinae* section of the last *Verbum* article, what occurs first in the systematic order is treated last in the order that traces development throughout history. For example, St. Thomas terminates his systematic treatment with the divine missions of the Trinity whereas the New Testament begins its narrative with the divine missions (DP, pp. 24-25).

3. Although the analytic process and the synthetic process deal with the same realities, they do not conceive those realities in the same way. For example, the creed, *Quicumque*, does not speak of three subsistent relations when it teaches that there are three Persons. The universally applicable reason to explain these differences is that the synthetic process includes the entire explication of the elements that have accumulated step by step in the analytic process. It is for this reason that the manuals customarily distinguish between the fact itself, which is demonstrated from authorities, and the understanding of the fact, concerning which theologians frequently argue and dispute (DP, p. 25).

4. The formal difference of concepts increases the more we compare the earlier elements of the *via analytica* with later elements in the *via synthetica*. The later an element occurs in the synthetic process, the more it presupposes and includes all of the previously accumulated understanding achieved up until then. On the other hand, the earlier an element occurs in the analytic process, the more it resembles a bare narration of fact which excludes all controversial questions for understanding (DP, p. 25).

5. The same formal difference of concepts diminishes the more we compare the later elements of the analytic process and the earlier elements of the synthetic process. It is the job of the *via analytica* to strive after understanding, to retain what is understood, and to accumulate this understanding. And the *via synthetica* in its initial stages does not expound immediately all of this understanding. Therefore, there is no great distinction between the psychological analogy which terminates the *via analytica* and the same analogy which is the point of departure for the *via synthetica* (DP, p. 25).

6. The two processes use different proofs because they have different formal concepts and because they intend different ends. So the analytic process demonstrates that relations certainly exist in God, arguing from the names "Father" and "Son", and from the necessity of a distinction only by means of relatives. But the *via analytica* ignores the relations insofar as they are somehow known before the Persons. And not until it is an established fact that there are relations does the *via analytica* begin to think about their basis. On the contrary, the *via synthetica* proceeds from the basis of the processions to posit relations. And since the synthetic process has not yet conceived Persons systematically, it cannot (except by some entirely unconventional anticipation) summon up arguments from the names of Persons, from their properties, and from notional acts. This difference again has a completely universal explanation. For every argument proceeds from earlier elements and prepares for what is later. But what is prior in the synthetic process is later in the analytic process, and vice-versa. Since this is so, it is easy to understand the peril of a

mixed procedure. Anyone who tries to use the analytic and synthetic processes simultaneously will have to cover nearly the entire tract in each thesis. This explains why Lonergan decided to treat the doctrine of the Trinity in one volume, the speculation about the Trinity in another (DP, pp. 25-26).

7. Theological notes or censures properly speaking belong to the *via analytica*. The analytic process is the same as the *via certitudinis*, which begins with manifestly known elements and proceeds to more recondite and subtle elements by demonstrations that can be made. But theological notes or censures say nothing more than the degree of certitude or probability which is coincident with individual assertions. It is for this reason that theological notes as in their own domain belong to the *via analytica* (DP, p. 26).

The proper goal of the synthetic process is not certitude but the understanding of truths that are already known to be certain. So it is unsuitable to have an exaggerated interest in theological notes or censures while working in the synthetic process. Actually, the value of the synthetic process is such that it cannot be grasped at the beginning or fully appreciated at the end except by using concrete comparisons that exemplify the great gulf there is between the mind of one who is certain but devoid of scientific knowledge, and the mind of one whose synthetic grasp of all things informs, orders, and directs his certitudes. Finally, there are no ordinary criteria by which to measure the security and solidarity of the synthetic process. Someone who seeks certitude customarily cites as many witnesses as possible of the common faith and doctrine. Yet someone who seeks understanding can safely pass by the opinion of the crowd and listen instead to those who are wise. For this reason, the Church proposes as a guide for our studies not all theologians equally, nor the more common opinions, but only St. Thomas and his thought (DP, p. 27).

8. Both the analytic and synthetic processes confront opponents, but each in its own way. The analytic process aims at removing doubts

and acquiring complete certitude. So the *via analytica* exposes the opinions of opponents with attention to historical detail. The synthetic process, on the other hand, aims at understanding the reason of things. So when the aim is to root up errors in such a way that others are not ensnared, then we must seek the root from which the error derives its semblance of truth and cut at the root. It does not matter whether opponents ever explicitly noticed the root of their error. So in the synthetic process, we should not spend much energy on opponents but should apply ourselves to the roots of their errors (DP, p. 27).

F. A Summary of the Analytic and Synthetic Processes in Comparison with One Another

Although the analytic and synthetic processes treat of the same divinely revealed truths, nevertheless they follow different and inverse orders, use formally distinct concepts, employ different kinds of proofs, approach in different ways their opponents and errors. Lonergan's reason for distinguishing the two processes derives from his reading of Aquinas who says that "every act is to be carried on in a manner consonant with its end. Theological disputation, however, can be ordered to a twofold end".[5] There is a real distinction between the operation of the intellect by which we reach intelligible truth *qua* true (the second act of understanding), and the operation by which we reach intelligible truth qua intelligible (first act of understanding). Since there are two distinct operations, then there are as well two distinct methods by which we advance to the operations. If you seek certitude, then begin from what is most manifest and gradually move toward a demonstration of what is obscure. If it is understanding that you seek, then begin from those notions whose understanding does not presuppose the understanding of anything else. Confusion results from a demand for understanding when there is a question of certitude, and a demand for certitude when you are looking for understanding. Yet a failure to distinguish adequately between the analytic and synthetic processes causes equal confusion. When there are in theological works different ends, different formal objects, different operations by which the ends are reached, different orders of questions, different formal concepts, different proofs and ways of considering errors, it is unreasonable to judge these theological works as if there were only one way of ordering ideas. While this confusion obfuscates the analytic and synthetic processes, there is even more possibility for confusion when the historical dimension comes into play (DP, p. 28).

The Historical Dimension of Theological Understanding

After thematizing the *via analytica* and the *via synthetica*, Lonergan in the next section of the *Divinarum personarum* deals with the historical dimension of theological understanding. In order to grasp the nature of the historical process as he conceives it, he proposes two tasks. First, we must deal with the significance of historical development (A) in general, and (B) in those particular areas which pertain more closely to the Catholic faith. Second, it is necessary to seek an understanding of the theological development which is so closely connected with what has been called the development of dogma (DP, p. 28).

A. General Outlines of the Historical Dimension of Theological Under-standing

To grasp the nature of the general outlines of the historical dimension of theological understanding, Lonergan distinguishes between nature and spirit, between the natural sciences and the properly human sciences. The *quoad nos* elements in nature seem almost to remain fixed whereas the *quoad nos* elements in the human sciences seem to undergo a slight but continual change. In the natural sciences, where things such as colors and sounds and textures are known through the senses, where these things participate in some way in the unchanging form of our bodies, we can find univocal categories to express the *priora quoad nos*. But there is one law of nature, another law of spirit. From the human sciences we receive a variety of languages and customs, mechanical and liberal arts, religions and politics. For each individual, what is prior, better known and more obvious is what each saw, heard, and did as an infant, a child, an adolescent, or a youngster. Hence, from a variety and inconstancy of human realities, the categories that express the *priora quoad nos* are rendered very equivocal. For the *nos* in question is not a single, fixed, and immutable reality, but rather changes with every age, nation, social class, and indeed for almost every individual. From these cultural differences there arises a fundamental problem, namely, to discover a transcultural principle by which we can pass systematically from what is prior in this individual's experience to what is prior for another person (DP, p. 29).

A solution to the problem of discovering a transcultural principle has three sources: depth psychology, scholarship, and comparative scientific inquiry. Depth psychology shows that people are alike not only in their sense impressions but also in the spontaneous symbols by which the sense faculty discloses its own finality to the spirit and in turn manifests and somehow interprets for itself the utterances of the spirit. Scholars can acquire the culture and mentality of another place and time if they are willing to undergo the slow and arduous learning process required. Finally, we can reach an understanding of the total life of another age if we not only read, compare, and arrange past events in one coherent account, but also if we use all the information we can generate from questions arising from our awareness in the categories of contemporary sciences.

These three elements of a solution to the transcultural problem may suffice to solve the issue from the side of the object, but the problem remains unsolved from the side of the subject. Even after the three solutions mentioned are employed, there remains the serious difficulty that there are usually as many accounts of past events and as many interpretations of documents as there are scholars, schools, and trends. We usually end up thinking that issues concerned with the material side of things can be scientifically determined. But issues which touch on the principles, judgments and counsels of men and women are abandoned to an apparently inevitable relativism. Because there is usually complete univocity in the physical order in what is considered prior, better known, and more obvious, then in those areas which are more material, certitude is admitted. But skepticism prevails in cultural and spiritual matters because in those issues that are properly human, there is extensive equivocity among different thinkers as to what is considered prior, better known, and more obvious.[6]

Historians, in Lonergan's view, are content to remain on the level of the relative, to labor in moving from what is relative to others to what is relative to themselves, and to avoid seeking what is prior, better known, and more obvious in itself. This is the same point as the one Lonergan made in the 1954 "Theology and Understanding" when he distinguished two types of historical question and stressed the need for moving beyond mere positive studies. [7] Some fall into this historicism because they consider it a safer course to avoid all the opinions of philosophers, while others maintain that a certain relativistic philosophy is the only true one. This kind of historicism with its philosophical presuppositions and theological consequences is what Pope Pius XII repeatedly condemned in his encyclical, *Humani Generis*.[8]

From these general considerations of the historical question it is possible to make several broad conclusions. First, there is a transcultural problem that becomes more acute to the degree that we move from the material aspects of an historical issue and attend to cultural differences. Second, it is not possible to solve this problem adequately by passing from one set of *priora quoad nos* to what another set of people considers *priora quoad nos*. Third, there is no adequate solution to the transcultural problem except by having recourse to those truths which in the interior life of humankind are found to be absolute. Fourth, there is prevalent outside the Church an historical and *a priori* relativism either because proponents of such relativism exclude methodically all philosophical positions or because they accept as valid a kind of philosophical relativism (DP, p. 31).

B. The Historical Development of Theological Understanding and the Transcultural Problem

We have seen how the transcultural problem is manifest outside the Church, and how the broad outlines of the historical question of understanding have emerged. Let us now turn to the historical development of theological understanding. It is obvious that the transcultural problem arises for Christians because divine revelation was given to a particular people at a particular time and under specific circumstances. On the other hand, the Church of God is for all people of all places and all cultures. From the very fact that the Catholic Church was founded under particular circumstances, there is set up the transcultural problem. Yet even the primitive experience of the Church witnesses to a solution to the transcultural problem. The problem arose when Judaizers opposed the preaching of the Good News to the Gentiles. And the early Church responded not only by preaching to the Gentiles, but also by allowing them to forego the Mosaic ritual (DP, pp. 31-32).

C. A Systematic Treatment of the *Via Analytica* and the *Via Synthetica* in Light of the Transcultural Problem

With a view toward solving the transcultural problem as it shows up in the Church, Lonergan next proposes to elaborate the distinctions he has already made between the *priora quoad nos* and the *priora quoad se*. This is his development of a systematic presentation of the elements he has already compared in the analytic and synthetic processes. What he intends to do here is to introduce into the analytic and synthetic movements the historical process.

What has come to be known as the *priora quoad se* is now amplified and identified by three new names: the *prius systematicum, prius theologicum,* and *prius dogmaticum*. What has come to be known as the *prius quoad nos* is now subdivided into three eras, *a prius scripturisticum, a prius patristicum,* and *a prius contemporaneum*. These terms relate to what was the *prius quoad nos* of the ancient Semitic or Palestinian mentality, of the faithful of the patristic era, or of the faithful of any given place, time, or culture (DP, p. 32).

Beyond the transcultural process, moreover, there are also elaborated the theological process and the dogmatic process. The transcultural process moves from what is the *priora quoad nos* of the scriptures to what is prior in the Fathers, or from what is prior in either of these to what is prior today. The theological process moves from what is the *priora quoad nos* of scripture or the Fathers to what is the *prius systematicum* (what is systematically prior). The dogmatic process advances from what is the *prius systematicum* to what the magisterium of the Church confirms, teaches, and defines. What are some examples of the transcultural, theological, and dogmatic processes? A function of the transcultural process was to bring the Gentiles into the Church, or for compilers to produce the medieval *catenae* and collections of patristic sentences. A function of the theological process was to conceive the Divine Persons as consubstantial, to conceive grace as absolutely supernatural habits. A function of the dogmatic process is seen in the Council of Nicea that defined that the Son is consubstantial with the Father; in the council of Chalcedon that defined Christ as one Person in two natures; in the Councils of Trent and First Vatican which used many theological elements to declare and even to define the faith (DP, p. 32).

From what has gone before we can see that there is not one understanding posited in scripture and another more correct kind posited by theology. The two say the same thing but according to different priorities. Finally, there is no difference between the primitive Palestinian faith and the Hellenistic or medieval or contemporary faith. Since all share the same faith, their belief is not different even though it is expounded according to different priorities (DP, p. 33).

If we compare these three processes with one another, it is apparent that the transcultural process concludes in a Hellenistic stage or in a medieval stage or in a contemporary stage. Since, however, the properly theological process terminates in what is *priora quoad se*, in no way can we say that it ends up at a Hellenistic or medieval or contemporary stage. The properly dogmatic process as well deals with the *priora quoad se*, so if *homoousion* is considered merely medieval, then there is a distortion of the dogmatic process. Finally, although theological and dogmatic processes may coincide in their concepts, still there is a huge difference between them. The theological process offers a judgment based on the private authority of a theologian. The dogmatic process infallibly declares under the guidance of the Holy Spirit the substance of the faith itself. So although there is a great difference between the general transcultural problem and the same problem as it manifests itself in the Church, still the Church perfects the transcultural process. The Church can speak with one and the same voice to all cultures and to all times because through the dogmatic process the Church not only ascends to what is *prius quoad se* (what is absolutely prior), but also judges infallibly that ascent (DP, p. 33).

It is clear that there is an intimate connection between this analysis of history and what has already been said about the end of theology, the act by which we obtain that end, and the process by which the act is realized. What has been added in the preceding section is a consideration of how ambiguous and equivocal is the category that expresses what is prior, better known, and more manifest *quoad nos*. Yet once this consideration is added, there immediately becomes obvious: (1) the outlines of a historical series of cultural differences; (2) the transcultural problem in the Catholic context; (3) the importance of the analytic process, the movement that goes from what is prior to this or that group of people to what is prior in itself; (4) the significance of the synthetic process, the movement that explores the *prius quoad se* in a systematic way; (5) the large differences among the transcultural, theological, and dogmatic movements. Once the ambiguity of the *quoad nos* category is grasped, not only are the analytic and synthetic processes viewed in their proper historical movement, but they appear as well to have a special function within the historical process itself (DP, pp. 33-34).

D. The Historical Process Considered in Its Own Right: The Evolution of Dogma and the Development of Theological Understanding

The historical unfolding and evolving of dogma and theological understanding is an intellectual process, and as such, cannot be understood until it reaches its term. It is not surprising, then, that those who effected this evolution -- the popes, the Fathers, the greatest theologians -- did not speak much about the evolution itself. Since every activity is understood by its end, then if one does not understand the end toward which one is heading, one cannot understand progress toward that end (DP, p. 34).

E. Examples of the Historical Process of the Evolution of Dogma Theological Understanding

We have seen that the terms of the historical process move from the *prius quoad nos* (whether scriptural, patristic, or contemporary) to the *prius quoad se* (whether dogmatic or theological). Lonergan now illustrates the historical process through four examples: (1) the *homoousion* of Nicea that abandons the scriptural *prius quoad nos*; (2) the two natures of Chalcedon that abandons the patristic *prius quoad nos*; (3) the medieval conflict between the Augustinians and the Aristotelians which brought about the advancement to the systematic *prius quoad se*; (4) the subsequent methodological uncertainty that impelled theologians to find a balance between different and opposed conflicts.

1. The Use of *Homoousion*

The primary question of the Arian controversy throughout the fourth century was whether the Son of God was a creature. A question secondary to this first one was whether the positive and required confession of faith could use words other than those written down in scripture. As a matter of record, the Council of Nicea did use the word *homoousion*. And after Nicea, there was never any hesitation about using non-scriptural words in the symbols of faith. It was *de facto* established, then, that it was lawful to pass from a scriptural *prius quoad nos* to something *prius quoad se.* In this affair, we can see how much the divine intention exceeds human intentions. St. Athanasius did not affirm the kind of development described above as a general principle. He considered that it was preferable to express every confession of the faith in scriptural words. But he wanted to root out the Arian heresy, so he argued for the necessity of using the term, *homoousion* (DP, p. 35).

2. The Two Natures of Chalcedon That Abandons the *Prius Patristicum*

The Council of Chalcedon not only went beyond the scriptural *prius quoad nos* but also beyond the patristic *prius quoad nos* in composing its understanding of *natura.* And a failure to notice this development was the basis of the error of Severus of Antioch. He saw that among the Fathers of the Church the word *natura* meant nothing other than a concrete and complete being, so that every being is a *suppositum.* So Severus acknowledged only one nature in Christ the God-man and attacked as Nestorian the proponents of the two natures at Chalcedon. We can conclude, then, that Severus and other monophysites defected from the faith not because of a Christological error but because of a methodological error that led them to ignore the conclusions of the ecumenical Council of Chalcedon (DP, p. 36). Of course it is one thing to point out that the Council of Chalcedon went beyond the scriptural and patristic *quoad nos,* and still another thing to explain how this was possible. Lonergan alludes here to a methodological error, but it is not until the 1959 "*De intellectu et methodo*" that he explains how these historical issues receive methodological attention.

103

3. The Discovery of the Systematic *Prius Quoad Se*

The medieval conflict between the Augustinians and the Aristotelians sets the stage for the next development. Lonergan quotes John Peckham, O.F.M., Archbishop of Canterbury, who described the controversy this way:

> ...and may the Holy Roman Church deign to consider that on all doubtful questions, the teaching of one Order is today almost completely opposed to that of the other; that the teaching of one of them, rejecting and sometimes ridiculing the opinions of the saints, relies almost exclusively on philosophical dogmas, so that the house of God is full of idols and the vanity of opposed questions, as the Apostle predicted. What a great danger as a result threatens the Church for the future. What is more certain than that the building will fall once the columns are broken? That if Augustine and other authentic teachers are held cheap, the devil will enter and truth will succumb to falsehood? (DP, p. 36).

Archbishop Peckham seems to mix together in his analysis the two operations of the intellect. One act of understanding asks *quid sit,* and another asks *an sit.* If in this second operation (which is the realm of judgment) one were to throw out the opinions of the saints and rely "almost exclusively on philosophical dogmas", then without doubt such a person would defect from the faith. But if there is no question of faith, if the entire argument is confined to debatable issues, then how can Archbishop Peckham make allegations such as "the house of God is full of idols" or that "Augustine and other authentic teachers are held cheap" or that the teaching of another Order relies "almost exclusively on philosophical dogmas"? The only explanation is that there really is no question of truth here -- but instead a question of understanding, and not philosophical but theological understanding. Just as we would fall into the trap of rationalism or historical relativism were we to conclude that *homoousion* is merely philosophical or dyphysism merely Hellenistic, so too it is clear how the whole medieval problematic that culminates in the systematic *prius quoad se* is a properly theological development (DP, p. 37).

While medieval theologians made a huge contribution to scientific theology by reducing the scriptural and patristic *prius quoad nos* to the theological *prius quoad se*, still the subsequent conflict between disciples of Augustine and those of Aristotle shows that they did not have an accurate grasp of the relationship between these two types of what is prior. It is not surprising that later theologians were unable to handle the methodological problems arising from the reduction of what is prior to us and what is prior in itself.

4. Methodological Uncertainty

The methodological problem resulting from the reduction of the *prius quoad nos* to the *prius quoad se* is the fourth and last example of the unfolding of the historical process. As we have seen, there is an intimate relationship between these two types of what is prior. Whatever the *via analytica* discovers and proves, that same truth the *via synthetica* intelligently and systematically brings to light. What happens when we neglect to pay enough attention to this conjunction or perhaps fail to understand the interdependence between the two processes? Then our speculations can gravitate toward systems that neglect the positive sources (DP, p. 37).

There are three ways to tend toward a theological system and yet to fail to attain a synthesis. First, philosophy can so dominate theologians that they give themselves mostly to questions with philosophical roots. An example of this first tendency is the decadence of the fourteenth and fifteenth century scholastics. Second, even if positive and speculative procedures receive equal attention, there can be a juxtaposition or mixture of the two instead of a conjunction and synthesis. The second tendency comes to the fore whenever in addition to philosophy's domination there arises an exaggerated emphasis on apologetics. Third, a system can receive more attention than it deserves, and then the positive elements in the theological process can seem superfluous because they are demon-strable. This third tendency made an appearance in the semi-rationalism of the nineteenth century, but the First Vatican Council quickly counteracted it (DP, pp. 37-38).

In addition to the three problems listed above that jeopardize the system in speculative theology, there are three possible aberrations in positive theology when synthesis is absent. First, archaism bids us reject the more recent synthesis in order to return to the ancient form of Christianity. Second, there is a kind of futurism that encourages us to ignore both the primitive and the more recent synthesis in order to subscribe to some novel theological vision. A third error is an exaggerated search for certitude. This happens when theologians become so exhausted by many different theories that they search for certitude in such a way as to exclude any attempt at understanding. The mania for certitude and the almost positivistic exclusion of speculation comes from placing a high value on the necessity of the positive approach. What can remedy this imbalance is a correct understanding of the relationship between analysis and synthesis in speculative theology (DP, p. 38).

The Object of Theology

The eighth section of the 1957 *Divinarum personarum* is titled, "The Object of Theology", and seeks a unified grasp of the elements we have already covered in earlier sections. There are six parts in this section. The fifth part covers the process from revealed truth to intelligible truth. Here we see that there are two different kinds of problems that impede the development of theological understanding. Some problems can be solved by increasing and developing the old understanding by the new. In other words, this type of issue can be solved by use of the analytic and synthetic ways. But there is a far graver problem, namely, when there is a difference of opinion about the true nature of the problem itself. Then what we must investigate are the opposed principles that lead to opposed conclusions (DP, pp. 45-46).

THREE PROCESSES IN THEOLOGY

Lonergan notes that the examination of theology's procedures has an important implication for the exposition of theological understanding. The same truth is expressed in both the scriptural *prius* and in the systematic *prius*. But there is a danger in imagining that the systematic *prius quoad se* is the same as the contemporary *prius quoad nos*. If this were true, then we would teach children, blue collar workers, professionals and teen-agers all with the same pedagogy as used for theology students. On the other hand, if we imagine that the systematic *prius quoad se* belongs only to medieval thought, then we open ourselves to the conclusion that scholastic theology is something relative and antiquated.[9]

Concluding Overview

Although Lonergan in the 1954 "Theology and Understanding" article thematizing the processes of speculative theology had noted the problems that positive historical scholarship raised for speculative theology, he did not focus his primary attention on these methodological problems in the 1957 *Divinarum personarum*. He decided to work out the speculative part of trinitarian theology before elaborating the dogmatic or positive parts. He could have focused his attention on the aim, proper object, and method of dogmatic or positive theology. Instead, he used the introductory chapter of his first trinitarian text to elaborate the method of speculative theology. Perhaps he judged that dogmatic and positive theology had already received sufficient attention in recent years, especially with the positive investigations in so many fields. Perhaps he thought that the dogmatic treatment of trinitarian teaching was less in need of revision than was the manual tradition's treatment of the speculative part. In any case, the fact remains that he chose to draw up the speculative part of his trinitarian theology before working out the dogmatic part. And it is clear that his main interest was in accounting for speculative theology's aim that stressed understanding of revealed truth. It is likewise clear that while the elements of the analytic process emerge historically before those of the synthetic process, he stresses the need to distinguish the two and treat them separately -- and the reason he emphasizes the distinction is so as to avoid confusing the aims and methods of each.

When Lonergan composed the *Divinarum personarum,* he was somewhat critical of theologians who would not advance beyond the requirements of positive historical scholarship. At this point in his career it was bold of him to assert the possibility of reaching beyond the goal of speculative understanding to reach an even higher goal, namely, the comprehensive theological understanding that includes particular, historical elements synthetically. While it does not seem likely that anyone had attempted such a theological understanding before, and while others might agree that such a blending of systematic and historical elements would be desirable, it was not at all clear in 1957 what the requirements of such a theological understanding that included historical elements might be.

The treatment of the two processes in the *Divinarum personarum* first chapter adds new terms to the ones already given in the original themati-zing of the *via inventionis* and the *via doctrinae* in the "Theology and Understanding" article. Now connected to the *via inventionis* are two new terms, "analysis" and "the way of certitude". Note that in addition to moving from confusion to clarity in this process, one also advances from what is obvious to the observer to what are demonstrations of conclusions that are not so obvious. Note as well that this process derives from its application in natural science and has a special adaptation for use in theology. Now connected to the *via doctrinae* is the new term, "synthesis". Synthesis not only means a joining of disparate elements -- it is also the movement in which reasons are given so that things can be defined and their properties be deduced. And insofar as deduction is used, the difference between the analytic and synthetic processes is that the latter derives its principles not simply from logic but from the act of understanding.

Lonergan stresses that the proper goal of the synthetic process is not certitude but the understanding of truths that are already known to be certain. But there are no ordinary criteria by which to measure the security and solidity of the synthetic process. So we should listen to those who are wise, especially to St. Thomas. While this assessment may be accurate enough, it leaves questions unanswered. What is the foundation of theological understanding? If it is the wisdom of St. Thomas, in what does that wisdom consist? Although *Insight* provides the background through its cognitional theory for figuring out adequate criteria for the synthetic process, it is not until his 1959 graduate course, *"De intellectu et methodo"*, that he explicitly returns to the issue of wisdom and how it provides the foundation for theological understanding. It is necessary to wait until we see how he deals with wisdom before we can judge whether he gives sufficient criteria by which to measure the synthetic process.[10]

In the section that relates how the analytic and synthetic processes confront opponents, each in its own way, there is an emphasis in Lonergan's thought worth noting. Although he adverts to the role of historical detail in the analytic process, he is far more interested at this time in the synthetic process, with its goal of increasing understanding. It is almost as if historical analysis only provided an instance of a problem which he would rather reduce to its theoretic elements and deal with in a systematic way. At least he prefers the synthetic process that aims at understanding the reasons of things to the bare apologetic task of confronting opponents.

The key question in *Divinarum personarum's* introductory chapter regarding understanding is whether the same truth, understood in the same sense, can be understood now more, now less. We have seen that understanding the same truth admits a steady advance from the comprehension of individual parts to systematic exegesis, from exegesis to the systematic questions of the theological way, and from systematic understanding to the fuller comprehension that encompasses the historical evolution of understanding. Can the same truth, understood in the same sense, be understood now more, now less? The answer given is that it can increase or decrease not because of an alteration in the object understood but because of a change in the manner of understanding. With a brilliance that seems so simple in hindsight, Lonergan identified the ambiguous category, the *prius quoad nos*, as the core of the transcultural problem. Recall that in the 1956 *De constitutione Christi*, he had explained the connections between what is "prior to us" and the *causa cognoscendi*; and between what is "prior in itself" and the *causa essendi*.[11] As we shall see in the section on historicity in *"De intellectu et methodo"*, there must be a fuller explanation of the transition from one way of ordering ideas to another than is given here. At this point, Lonergan only adverts to the transition from the *prius quoad nos* to the *prius quoad se* without explaining how this transition is accomplished.

We have already seen that there is not one understanding that is posited in scripture, and another more correct kind posited by theology. The two say the same thing but according to different priorities. But Lonergan does not say what the different priorities are according to which scripture and Church definitions say the same thing. Implicit here are some difficult questions. Do scripture and Church definitions use the same mode of expression? If not, how do we move from one way of communicating the revealed truth to another way? These questions only receive explicit treatment later in the 1959 doctoral seminar, *"De intellectu et methodo"*.

Although earlier Lonergan had raised four methodological issues in the 1954 article, "Theology and Understanding", issues that stretched the structure of the analytic/synthetic process almost to the breaking point, he returned to that twofold structure in order to elaborate his systematic solution to the problem of whether the understanding of the same truth can increase. After an exposition of analysis and synthesis, he introduced the consideration of a third movement, the historical unfolding of understanding throughout the ages as theologians use the analytic and synthetic processes to reach fuller understanding. He exhibited a breadth of historical awareness as he traced the evolution of theological understanding from the *homoousion* of Nicea, from the abandoning of the *prius scrip-turisticum* of Chalcedon, from the medieval conflict that ended in the discovery of the *prius quoad se*. By introducing the historical process, he demonstrated from the facts of theological history that the manner of understanding the same truth can change. The trouble is, he did not explain yet *how* this change in the manner of understanding is possible.

THREE PROCESSES IN THEOLOGY

Lonergan introduced the third, historical consideration of the unfolding of the analytic/synthetic theological procedures in order to identify the fact of an evolution in understanding. The question remains whether viewing the evolution of theological understanding in its successive moments according to a third, historical process that complements the analytic/synthetic processes is a perspective that is helpful in forming a theological methodology. Can this way of considering the historical process prove to be an adequate vehicle by which to carry the explanation for how this evolution of understanding takes place? This problem is methodological -- it asks about the foundation of theological understanding itself.

What about the four new methodological problems raised in 1954? Although this first chapter of *Divinarum personarum* attempts to explain the aim, proper object, and method of speculative theology, it does not answer the questions raised by these new methodological problems. Recall that these four problems touch on the relationship between speculative theology and the patterns of human experience, positive theology, empirical human science, and correct cognitional theory in historical interpretation.

This introductory chapter on theological understanding has established the fact of an increase in understanding the same truth by considering the historical evolution of the twofold way of ordering ideas. While this historical consideration helps to establish the fact of a development of understanding, it has an awkward drawback. It seems to be like the unicorn's horn on an otherwise normal horse. The twofold processes of analysis and synthesis seem to be a self-contained unit, and yet there is added a consideration of a third, historical process in order to explain the development of understanding. It remains to be seen whether this historical consideration will have any part to play as Lonergan faces the methodological issues that were raised earlier in 1954 as well as the new ones that emerge here: How do we make the transition from the prescientific stage of theology to the scientific phase that uses technical terms and procedures? What is the systematic explanation that establishes how it is possible for there to be an increase of understanding the same truth? What is the foundation for systematic understanding itself? These are questions that we see Lonergan addressing explicitly in the next work we will study, his 1959 graduate course, "*De intellectu et methodo*".

NOTES

CHAPTER IV

[1]Bernard J.F. Lonergan, S.J., *De sanctissima Trinitate: supplementum quoddam* (Rome: Gregorian University, 1955). These fifty pages of notes contain three articles: (1) Certain general notions; (2) The image of God in man; (3) From the image to the eternal exemplar. The first two articles appear with slight alterations as appendices I and II in *Divinarum personarum conceptio analogica*. This set of notes is an early step in the preparation of Lonergan's first textbook on the Trinity.

[2]Bernard J. F. Lonergan, S.J., *Divinarum personarum conceptio analogica* (Rome: Gregorian University, 1957). This text was published *ad usum auditorum*. There is an English translation of the first chapter titled, "Theological Understanding". Bernard Lonergan, S.J., "Theological Understanding", English translation by Francis P. Greaney of *Divinarum personarum conceptio analogica, caput primum* in *The Modern Humanist* (Student Journal at Weston College, Weston, Massachusetts, 1961). This translation was edited by Edmund Morton, S.J. and mimeographed in 1966. References to the *Divinarum personarum* text in this chapter rely upon the Morton edition of the Greaney Translation, both of which are available at the Lonergan Research Institute, Toronto. Since there are frequent references in this chapter to the *Divinarum personarum* text, the citations will appear directly in the chapter with the abbreviated notation, (DP,) followed by the page number.

[3]*Ibid.*, p. 13. Lonergan's reference is to Denzinger's *Enchiridion Symbolorum*, edited by Cl. Bannwart, S.J., hence the letters "DB", followed by numbers which indicate the sections and paragraphs of the book. Today's standard reference to Church teachings is contained in the Denzinger volume edited by A. Schonmetzer, S.J., hence the letters "DS". Our references to DB will also give the corresponding references to DS. *Enchiridion Symbolorum, Definitionum et Declarationum De Rebus Fidei et*

Denzinger volume edited by A. Schonmetzer, S.J., hence the letters "DS". Our references to DB will also give the corresponding references to DS. *Enchiridion Symbolorum, Definitionum et Declarationum De Rebus Fidei et Morum.* Henricus Denzinger, editor, and Adolfus Schonmetzer, S.J., editor. Editio XXXII. (Rome: Herder, 1963). The translation we use for DB is *The Church Teaches. Documents of the Church in English Translation*, Gerald Van Ackeren, S.J., editor (St. Louis: B Herder Book Company, 1955).

[4]*Ibid.*, p. 24. This outline of the analytic and synthetic approaches makes the same references to St. Thomas as contained in the earlier *Verbum* articles, pp. 206-207.

[5]S. Thomae Aquinatis, *Quaestiones Quodlibetales* (Paris: P. Lethielleux, 1926). *Quodlibet* IV, q. 9, a. 3 (18), p. 154.

[6]Lonergan, *Divinarum personarum*, p. 30. This is a re-statement of the second methodological problem cited in the 1954 article, "Theology and Understanding", pp. 137-139.

[7]Lonergan, "Theology and Understanding", pp. 138- 139.

[8]Lonergan, *Divinarum personarum*, p. 31. The root of historicism is exposed in *Insight*, pp. 342-347, 493 ff., 662-694.

[9]*Ibid.*, pp. 48-49. This brief passage relating to missiology and effective preaching only hints at Chapter Fourteen of *Method in Theology's* functional specialty, "Communications". The word "communication" does not so much as appear in this present, 1957 *Divinarum personarum* context, but the concern for effective communication is already clear.

[10]Bernard J.F. Lonergan, S.J., *"De intellectu et methodo"* (mimeographed edition, Rome: St. Francis Xavier College, 1959). The section on wisdom covers pages 17-22.

CHAPTER V

PROBLEMS DERIVING FROM THE EVOLUTION
OF THEOLOGICAL UNDERSTANDING

Lonergan's earliest theological productivity was characterized by theology done in the classical scholastic style. Theological method was envisioned as including two procedures, the *via inventionis* and the *via doctrinae*. We saw that he struggled to determine how theology could study the multiple expressions of faith in the scriptures and the Fathers, and at the same time maintain some sense of identity of faith in its various historically differing expressions.

In the 1954 article, "Theology and Understanding", he examined and affirmed the validity of Aristotelian and scholastic notions of science for speculative theology, yet he adverted to other, more contemporary methodological issues. First, theologians need to be concerned not only about the rational and universal, but also about "the more spontaneous intersubjective categories of ordinary human experience and ordinary religious experience".[1] Second, there is the problem of the relations between speculative and positive theology.[2] Third, there is the problem of the relations between speculative theology and the empirical human sciences. Theology will exercise its superintending role "primarily through the illumination of method by faith...."[3] Fourth, there is the critical problem that arises because the issues of historical interpretation are complicated by the self-knowledge of the interpreter.[4]

Lonergan continued to wrestle with these problems in the 1957 work on the Trinity, *Divinarum personarum conceptio analogica*. In the introductory chapter, theology was conceived as being a discipline analogous to the natural sciences. The natural sciences contain an analytic and synthetic movement. Theology also embodies the two movements. Natural sciences in the analytic movement start from the *priora quoad nos* and advance to the *priora quoad se*, which are made the basis for the systematic order in the synthetic process. Theology proceeds in a similar fashion. Believers come to know divinely revealed truths in two ways. The first way of knowing is through the *priora quoad nos*, the particular and concrete conditions of various cultures. The other way of knowing is through the *priora quoad se*, and here the same truth as that of the first way is distinguished and affirmed in universally accessible, theoretic language. In a way analogous to the sensible data in the natural sciences, then, the divinely revealed truths are the starting point for the analytic movement. And the concluding point for the synthetic movement (the speculative theology that seeks understanding) is the same truths, but now formulated and defined with fuller understanding.

The "*De Intellectu et Methodo*"

Two years after the publication of *Divinarum personarum conceptio analogica*, Lonergan was no longer writing of theology as simply analogous to the natural sciences. In some Latin class notes collected and transcribed by students from a course he gave at the Gregorian University in 1959 titled "*De intellectu et methodo*", he presented a further illumination of the problem of theological ordering of ideas.[5]

The "*De intellectu et methodo*", contains five main headings: (I) on the notion of the question; (II) on the notion of science; (III) on the twofold way of human thinking; (IV) on method and its precepts; (V) conclusion. It is clear from the *Divinarum personarum* introductory chapter that Lonergan was concerned about understanding. In this doctoral seminar, he pays attention not only to understanding, but also to method. In light of the extensive treatment he gave to analysis/synthesis in the 1954 "Theology and Understanding" and in the 1957 *Divinarum personarum*, it is significant that he writes so little here on the twofold procedures in these pages specifically devoted to theological method. We see here that other issues generated by the rise of positive theology's historical consciousness now compete for his attention -- an attention that formerly was almost entirely given to the concerns of speculative theology. We will examine each of the sections of

PROBLEMS OF THEOLOGICAL UNDERSTANDING

"De intellectu et methodo" with particular detail given to the issues that shape Lonergan's emerging thought on theological method. It will become apparent that these new issues form an intra-Lonergan dialectic that cause him to modify and eventually to supersede the twofold movement of analysis and synthesis in theological method.

The introductory remark to the entire set of class notes says that the work of *Insight* is presupposed, and what these pages contain is a further step for illuminating the problems of method. In this question, theology has a large need for an adequate philosophy. If method is the most fitting adaptation of means to the end, when the end is science, while it is being sought, the end is unknown. Hence, the problem of method is obscure in its origins. The place to begin the study of method, then, is with the earliest sources of science. Since the earliest sources of science begin with questioning, it is not surprising that the first section of *"De intellectu et methodo"* begins with the notion of the question.[6]

On the Notion of the Question

A. On the Question, the Series of Questions, and the Ordering of Responses

A question exists when there are cogent arguments for affirming and for negating one and the same proposition (DIM, p. 1). When one question is solved, another arises. So there is a series of questions. Just as one question leads to another, so one response leads to another, and this series of responses ought to be ordered (DIM, pp. 4-5). Lonergan treats the ordering of responses in four parts: (1) the ordering is logical; (2) the ordering is coherent; (3) ordered propositions ought to have a reference to reality; (4) the same totality can be ordered in diverse ways in equivalent systems. The first three parts prepare the way for the fourth part that bears directly on the twofold ordering of ideas in theology.

THE ROAD TO LONERGAN'S *METHOD IN THEOLOGY*

1. The Ordering is Logical

One way of ordering a series of answers to questions may be logical. Ordering is logical to the extent that it uses a technique of derivation with respect to definitions and propositions, such that once the terms and propositions are posited, other terms and propositions will follow. Terms and propositions are those that are obtained from others by some technique of deduction. Primitive definitions and propositions are not obtained by a deduction.

The first step in logical ordering consists in collecting all actual responses, and in introducing a technique of derivation for separating primitive elements from derived elements. Then, taking the primitive terms and propositions together and using again the technique of derivation, we arrive at all possible derived terms and propositions. In this way we obtain some system.

A system is a particular, virtual totality of propositions -- a totality determined from primitive terms and propositions through the sole mediation of the technique of derivation. Thus, it is not possible through the sole technique of derivation to obtain from the words of scripture the term *homoousion* used in the Nicene Council. It is clear that an intelligent and reasonable person reading scripture is capable of seeing that consubstantiality is involved in scriptural concepts, but this issue is another question, touching intelligence and rationality, not pure logical technique. In a logical system, all primitive terms and propositions and all derived terms and propositions ought to be ordered according to their derivation (DIM, p. 5).

2. The Ordering is Coherent

For a system to be logical, the ordering ought to be coherent. That is, a system should not contain propositions that contradict one another. In addition, there should be coherence in the movement towards system.

Thus, the system of theological theses in the manuals of 1959 derived proofs from the Church magisterium, from patristic and theological arguments. Such a system was adequate before the exigencies of historical consciousness imposed themselves. "Now, however, we experience more the necessity of distinguishing adequately the historical method from the speculative" (DIM, p. 6).

3. Ordered Propositions Ought to Have a Reference to Reality

It is not sufficient that ordered propositions are coherent with each other. That kind of coherence can obtain as well between pure *entia rationis*. Ordered propositions ought to have a reference to reality. A reference to reality occurs in any system when it can be determined that to affirm some proposition and at the same time to affirm its contradiction will have some consequence in the real world. Hence, in order for a system to have this reference to reality, it must take the step from logic to metaphysics (DIM, p. 6).

4. The Same Totality Can be Ordered in Diverse Ways in Equivalent Systems

This possible multiplicity of ordering in different ways in equivalent systems is of the greatest importance to Lonergan. St. Thomas distinguishes between ordering according to those things that are *priora quoad se* (and then systems are obtained), and the ordering according to those things that are *priora quoad nos* (and then we begin from sense data). Thus, for example,in natural sciences we begin with observations from sense data, from which hypotheses come and theories are conceived. But in the manuals of these sciences, we start from the theories themselves. Hence, we see that the same totality can be ordered in diverse ways in equivalent systems (DIM, pp. 6-7).

119

THE ROAD TO LONERGAN'S *METHOD IN THEOLOGY*

This advance beyond the purely logical ordering of systems has implications for theology. Lonergan saw that St. Thomas ordered theological elements in diverse ways. In theology, the articles of faith are the *priora quoad nos* that are immediately available to believers in the fonts of revelation. But in the *Summa Contra Gentiles*, for example, that is not the procedure. In that work, it is only in Book IV, and not always there, that the argumentation begins from those things that are contained in scripture. On the contrary, most often the mention of scripture occurs only at the end of the chapters. This happens because really there is given a twofold way of proceeding, the "way of discovery" (or analysis, or resolution to causes) by which one proceeds from those things that are *priora quoad nos* to those things that are *priora quoad se*. In this process, we begin from what is available to us from the sources of faith and arrive at the *priora quoad se* elements that are revealed and revealable, at the truths as they relate to one another. The other way of proceeding, however, is the "way of teaching" (or synthesis or composition). Both ways are found in the *Summa Contra Gentiles*, but throughout the entire *Summa theologiae*, the ordering of the theological data proceeds according to the second way. Here the arrangement is not simply logical, but is based on that act of understanding that is the foundation of further understanding. Hence, the ordering of data in the way of teaching begins from those things that must be understood first so that other things may be understood afterward. And different ways of arranging ideas does not mean that there are two different theologies. The same totality of propositions can be ordered in at least two ways (DIM, p. 7). Lonergan then elaborates the now familiar trinitarian example to show that the entire *Summa theologiae* is composed according to the "way of teaching" whereas the way of historical discovery proceeds in a way opposite from the way of theological composition.

The important factor in the total process is a "turning point" (*punctum inflexionis*). From the inquiry about truths that must be believed (understanding seeking faith) there is a turning to the task of understanding those same truths (faith seeking understanding). Thus, in the chapters of the *Summa Contra Gentiles*, there is a turning point when toward the end of individual chapters it is often said: *"Hinc est quod dicitur..."* followed by scriptural quotations. This idiom is no longer used to establish a biblical proof-text, but to ground understanding of the text. True, the understanding sought is not historical or exegetical, but theological. Theology is not more theological to the extent that it attends to what is revealed (for that is the role of faith), but it is more theological to the extent that it cultivates understanding of what is revealed (DIM, p. 8).

If theology is conceived as if it were a complex of conclusions taken either from biblical, patristic, or rational arguments, then no properly theological principles can be admitted. On the contrary, properly theological principles are those very ones at which the analytic process arrives as to its proper conclusions, and from these the turning begins, from which the synthetic process starts out. Theological principles not only can be admitted, but are pivotal. They are last in the way of resolution and first in the way of composition. As an example of this, in question 27 of the *Prima Pars*, St. Thomas takes the notion of God given in revelation, and having brought to bear the psychological analogy already used by St. Augustine for the divine relations, he obtains some principles by which he can return to the understanding of revealed data. Examples of properly theological principles are such notions as processions, relations, persons, names of persons and of essences, properties. Thus, when human reason proceeds from revelation and from those things that natural truth adds, it arrives at theological conclusions from which it can begin a return to the task of understanding those same truths (DIM, p. 8).

This innocent appearing procedure used in the way of teaching that seeks properly theological understanding became a prime battlefield for Thomistic theologians about the nature and notion of theology. Lonergan noted that among classical Thomists, theology is only a science of conclusions at which one arrives from revealed data. Thus Capreolus wrote, "Theology is not a science of the articles of faith, but of the conclusions that follow them" (DIM, p. 8). Lonergan's contention, however, is that properly theological principles are those at which the analytic process arrives as to its proper conclusions, and from these principles the "turning" begins from which the synthetic process sets out.

B. On the Series of Orderings of Responses

We have been dealing with the notion of the question, the series of questions, and the ordering of responses. Now we consider a series of such ordering of responses. When one series of questions has been solved, there arises another series. With the multiplication of the series of responses, these very series ought to be ordered. Thus, the First Vatican Council, quoting the words of Vincent of Lerins, exhorts:

> Let there be growth...and all possible progress in understand-
> ing, knowledge, and wisdom whether in single individuals or
> in the whole body, in each person as well as in the entire
> Church, according to the stage of their development...(DB
> 1800, DS 3020).

This progress will be possible, however, only if new questions always arise and new responses are given. So it is certainly required that there be a successive and progressive change in the ordering of responses. The encyclical, *Humani Generis*, teaches that

> ...the source of divinely revealed doctrine contains so many
> and so great treasures of truth that really it will never be ex-
> hausted.   Therefore, the sacred disciplines are always
> rejuvenated by study of the sacred sources...(AAS, 42 (1950),
> 568).

Therefore, at least some progress is possible as there arise new questions and new responses, and equally as there arises a new series of ordered responses (DIM, pp. 8-9). In what does this series of ordered responses consist?

There are three ways given that this progress can occur. First, subsequent matters relate to preceding matters according to the mode of a simple conclusion from a prior ordering. For example, as a Jew, St. Paul could make deductions about Christ from the Hebraic scriptures. Hence, to new questions there are given new responses. This comes about easily enough through the application of a technique of derivation to the old ordering. The old ordering suffices for responding to the new problems.

Second, progress can occur when to new questions there is no sufficient response from the ordering already existing, and response is had only with some development of the existing order. So for example the use of the term *homoousion* is a development of the scriptural order. Thus, while before there were as many primitive propositions as there were primitive terms, now there are extra terms, introduced easily and in a hidden way through new distinctions imposed by now problems. Therefore, within the earlier ordering there is present the new ordering, but this ordering does not appear openly (DIM, p. 9).

Third, progress can occur when the evolution of the preceding ordering alluded to above is not sufficient for solving new problems. When an exigency of this sort arises, then there come about schools of method. New questions can be solved only by changing the way of ordering responses according to a new method that is not found in already existing works. For example, we can order the questions relating to the Trinity either with attention to or without attention to the historical perspective. If we set aside the historical consideration, then the notion of mission as systematically conceived is not different from Paul's conception of mission as it is found in the epistle to the Galatians; and "mission" which is the last notion in the synthetic series of questions and answers is perfectly equivalent to "mission" which is the first notion in the analytic series. On the other hand, if we pay attention to the historical viewpoint, then there is a great difference between the respective notions as conceived in the synthetic process and as conceived in the analytic process, and the same divine mission is conceived in different ways by Pauline Christianity and by successive theological systematizations. The historical consideration, however, is needed because the causes of knowing are different from the causes of being. This problem receives a fuller treatment in the section that deals with the issues of historicity (DIM, pp. 9-10).

C. On the Criteria for a New Ordering

A new totality of propositions demands a new ordering, and likewise new primitive propositions, and a new technique of derivation or a new principle of evolution. Using symbolic logic, Lonergan demonstrates the difference between an open and a closed system. While these points are not germane to our topic, there is an important reference here to disputed questions. If the scholastic method were to use the technique of symbolic logic, and no one would doubt the need for a new ordering, and things would become clearer. Because there are among many students insolvable questions, doubts rise up about the validity of one system and then of all systems. And not rarely such doubts act to the detriment of the faith, and to avoid this, solid doctrine is sought outside every system, scholasticism is bitterly resisted, and against it there is undue praise for positive and historical investigations (DIM, pp. 10-11).

The point here is that Lonergan recognizes the weakness of the scholastic system that uses logic rather than the act of understanding. The closed logical system that generates disputed questions needs to be opened by further understanding. And while the processes of analysis and synthesis deepen understanding, it is the discoveries of positive, historical scholarship that force the opening of systems to accommodate new evidence and fresh issues for understanding.

D. On the Threefold Problem: Of Foundations, of Historicity, of the Chasm

In this last section of the first major division of "*De intellectu et methodo*", Lonergan deals with the threefold problem arising from the development of a series of questions and answers. His order of treatment is as follows: (1) the problem of foundations; (2) the problem of historicity; (3) the problem of the chasm; (4) the possibility of the solution. We have already seen that the four contemporary problems of 1954 stretch the twofold way of ordering theological ideas according to the way of discovery and the way of teaching. Now we see Lonergan scrutinizing the way a system works and what the problems are in constructing a systematic approach to theological understanding. We will examine here how he views the three aspects of the single methodical problem for theology.

1. The Problem of Foundations

The foundational problem occurs within any system when a new kind of problem appears on the scene whose solution does not seem available within that system itself. Hence, there rises up the transitional problem -- the movement from some ordering that does not solve the present question, to an ordering that perhaps will provide the solution. How will that transition be accomplished, and by what criteria will the new ordering be selected?

The problem is posited in a particular way when one asks what has been the specific foundation of any particular ordering done by such and such an author, in such an environment, at such a time, and then goes on to ask if in different times the same author held different opinions. Thus logically speaking, many St. Thomases ought to be distinguished.[7]

The problem is posited in a general way when there is a transition due to new questions, but the dogmas remain the same (and this happens in fact, if there is any meaning in the words of the First Vatican Council, DB 1800, DS 3020). The whole history of philosophy and theology can be conceived as a series of orderings and transitions from one arrangement of ideas to another. It is in this sense that we speak of "perennial philosophy" and "solid catholic doctrine". But many different theories and opinions claim these same descriptions. What is to be the criterion for selecting what is authentic? This question leads us to the foundational problem. When there is a leap from one system to another, that leap cannot be obtained through a pure deduction from the first system; otherwise we would not have two systems, but one. In both, the premises, terms, and primitive propositions would coincide (DIM, pp. 11-12).

2. The Problem of Historicity

As in the natural sciences, so also in theology, the "cause of knowing" is one thing, the "cause of being" is another. Thus we see phases of the moon and we infer from them the sphericity of the moon (phases are the "cause of knowing" of sphericity). But the reality of sphericity of the moon is the "cause of being" of the phases of the moon. Because the moon is spherical, it has phases. Therefore, we must distinguish in syllogisms between explanatory middle terms that designate the "cause of knowing" and those terms that designate the "cause of being".[8]

The "cause of knowing" is what we experience (*quoad nos*) such as the phases of the moon or the scriptural narratives. So the cause of our knowing is first in the "way of discovery". The "cause of being" is how things relate to each other (*quoad se*), such as the sphericity of the moon or truths expressed as theological principles. So the cause of something being what it is constitutes what is first in the "way of teaching". We have seen that St. Thomas used different arrangements of the data in constructing the treatise on the Trinity. In some chapters of the *Summa contra Gentiles*, he followed the way of discovery that seeks *an sit* (IV, 3 -- whether the Son is God); in other chapters, the way of teaching that seeks *quid sit* (IV, 11, 13, 14 -- on the way of conceiving the Trinity). The *Summa theologiae* contains the pure *ordo doctrinae*. In the "way of teaching", every step presupposes a preceding step, not according to a pure presupposition of fact, but of understanding. In the *Summa theologiae*, where the way of teaching is fully developed, we can easily see that theology not only begins from the articles of faith (which are the "cause of knowing" of theology), but also that theology actually ends up at the articles of faith -- advancing to them from the "causes of being". It is clear, then, that the ordering of theological data in a tract does not arise automatically from logical deduction, but requires the act of understanding to discover what is the "cause of being" (DIM, p. 12).

Lonergan now makes a key point. If we omit a consideration of history, then the "way of discovery" and the "way of teaching" give splendid results. But history shows that St. Thomas did not understand the divine missions in the same way as scripture or the Fathers understand them. So history raises problems for theology that do not occur in the natural sciences where humankind itself -- whose thought is always evolving -- does not enter constitutively among the objects of science.

This problem of historicity is enormous and it has disturbed theologians from the time of the Renaissance. It was then that was born and gradually evolved the so-called "positive theology" under whose rubric we gather treatises of history, religion, exegesis, literature, archeology, philology, geography, liturgy. According to positive theologians, these treatises are handled not in the scholastic mode, but "scientifically", and this according to infinite subdivisions. What are examples of these subdivisions? Positive biblical theology examines the Old and New Testaments, individual books and individual parts of any book of either testament. Positive patristic theology scrutinizes individual patristic periods, any given Father and different periods of any Father's productivity. Positive conciliar theology studies individual councils, and single sessions of any given council. Huge bibliographies multiply so that not even a specialist of the smallest field can read all the pertinent materials of his area (DIM, p. 13).

Why is the introduction of positive studies a problem for speculative theology? To answer this question we need only consider one point. If St. Paul conceived the divine missions in the same way as St. Thomas did, then the two theological processes mutually correspond, their respective notions are equivalent, and so development of positive studies is absolutely equivalent to the development of theology. But because St. Paul and St. Thomas do not conceive the divine missions in the same way, because the divine missions are not conceived in the same way systematically and historically, then there is no possibility of using some kind of logical deduction by which to move from one ordering of ideas to another (DIM, p. 13).

What seems required in order to achieve a continuity in doctrine is to make some kind of leap. But if the only connection between various

127

historical modes of conceiving doctrine is some kind of leap in an absolute sense (*simpliciter*), then the foundation of systematic speculative theology is undermined in an absolute sense, and all continuity between various conceptions of dogma is swept away. For these dogmas are not only conceived in diverse ways in different times, but absolutely one thing seems to be conceived by biblical writers, another by the Fathers, another by medieval theologians. Hence, nothing remains except for us to admit a "transformational evolution" of dogmas according to the meaning of that term asserted by rationalists and modernists. The problem of historicity seems to sweep away the foundation of speculative theology, leaving it without direction, form, purpose, or substance. So there is a need not only to find an integration between positive and speculative theology -- the kind of integration that concretely, *de facto* the Church always embodies -- but also to discover and to explain its theoretical foundation and justification (DIM, pp. 13-14).

3. The Problem of the Chasm

Taken from the word "chaos", the name "chasm" is found in the parable of Dives and Lazarus in Luke 16:26. This chasm or gulf between systematic presentations of doctrine and the belief of simple people appeared when St. Athanasius defended the introduction of the word, *homoousion*, into the symbols of faith in order to vindicate the divinity of the Son against the Arian opponents. The gulf widened when the Council of Chalcedon introduced the definitions of "person" and "nature". Medieval theologians used technical terms systematically. Indeed, the controversy of the thirteenth century between the Aristotelians and Augustinians was radical. Although there were still disputes about particular issues, the real question was whether they could introduce into theology the logical and metaphysical categories that Aristotle used in natural sciences (DIM, pp. 14-15).

The *Devotio Moderna* gave too little praise to systematic definitions and theological disputations. It widened the gulf even further between understanding the faith and simply believing it with such statements as "It is better to feel compunction than to know its definition" (*Imitation of Christ*, I, i). The more that theology becomes systematic, and the more that it gathers questions, responses, orderings of responses, to that degree does it move further away from a scriptural way of speaking in general, and not just from the immediate, concrete needs of humanity. Therefore, there is a reaction against systematization. To the degree that theology becomes scientific, to that degree it lifts itself beyond the horizon of the simple faithful, causing the gulf between systematic theology and believers (DIM, pp. 15-16).

So far we have seen in this last section three important problems that are not solved by applying some logical technique of derivation within the same system. There is the problem of making a transition from one way of ordering to another, or the foundational problem. There is the problem of continuity from one way of ordering, which likewise always becomes more remote from the sources, and this is the problem of the chasm. A solution is not obtained through deduction because the later way of organizing ideas always contains more than what preceded it. Finally, there are not really three problems, but three aspects that are logically distinct of the one real problem of method, and this requires a more profound treatment (DIM, p. 16).

4. On the Possibility of the Solution

Lonergan now deals with the problem of finding some initial step toward the solution of the problems mentioned above. The material is organized thus: (a) on the foundational problem; (b) on the problem of the chasm; (c) on the problem of historicity. Note that in the exposition of the three aspects of the methodological problem, Lonergan treated the foundation first, historicity second, and the chasm third. In this section on the possibility of a solution, he reverses part of the order of his exposition, taking the chasm before the problem of historicity. We will see the reason for this change after the treatment of the problem of the chasm.

THE ROAD TO LONERGAN'S *METHOD IN THEOLOGY*

(a) The Solution to the Foundational Problem

Lonergan says that the solution to the foundational problem can be posited in knowledge, in understanding, or in wisdom, depending upon the genus in which we posit the foundation. We can posit the foundation (1) in names, propositions, and terms (an external foundation); (2) in concepts, internal judgments of mind (an internal foundation manifesting itself externally); or (3) in intelligence itself with its speculative powers of knowledge, understanding, and wisdom. It is here, in intelligence, that Lonergan will posit the foundation. However, intelligence as a faculty is a potency to be completed by the three "habits" of science, understanding, and wisdom. It is important to see wisdom as the crowning development of intelligence. Hence, after a short exposition of science and understanding, he turns to wisdom.

First, wisdom is the principle of ordering and of judgment about terms and about first principles. As St. Thomas says in the *Prima Secundae*, 66, 5 ad 5, the function of wisdom is to know the meaning of being and non-being, of whole and part, and of other consequences to being, which are the terms that constitute indemonstrable principles, since universal being is the proper effect of the highest cause, God. Thus, wisdom makes use of indemonstrable principles, which are the object of understanding, not only by drawing conclusions from them, as other sciences do, but also by passing its judgment on them, and by vindicating them against those who deny them. Hence, it follows that wisdom is a greater virtue than understanding.[9] Second, it is the principle of judgment about understanding. Wisdom judges about the intelligibility of the connection existing between terms, whether it is *de facto* true. Third, wisdom is the principle of judgment about whether any one argument proves something by itself, how all the arguments fit together, and whether they likewise attain probability or certitude. Fourth, wisdom is the principle of judgment about the ordering of a virtual totality of multiple orderings. It judges about the end of the ordering; whether, when, and how the old ordering is to be retained or amplified or replaced by a new ordering.

Hence, wisdom is a principle of ordering and of judging, making judgments about everything (DIM, p. 17).

Conclusions About the Foundational Problem

The first kind of foundation (in names, propositions, and terms) is sufficient only if a question arises between those who agree about primitive terms and propositions, and only if they do not ask why they agree. It is sufficient only if questions do not arise which cannot be solved within the system. Therefore, this first type of foundation is exceedingly limited.

The second kind of foundation (in concepts, in internal judgments of mind) is sufficient only when terms are always conceived in the same way. For example, there was only one concept for the triangle in geometry until the nineteenth century. But this is not sufficient when some term is conceived in a variety of ways. This second kind of foundation does not suffice if one attempts to sort out the problem about judging diverse concepts of being which occur in the history of philosophy. There are no means of comparison to use. This second kind of foundation is sufficient when questions are posited respecting the intelligible connection about things that are only empirically true; also, when a judgment has to be made about the very postulates themselves, as in the example of the non-intersection of parallel lines taken from Euclid. Likewise in theology, the Thomist "suitable arguments" (*argumenta convenientiae*) treat of intelligibility when the connection between terms is not necessary, but is *de facto* true. If one opposes these arguments and says that they do not prove anything, then all knowledge that is not necessary collapses, whether theological or empirical. Hence, the question is really about the conception and notion of knowledge. Therefore, the second kind of foundation is not sufficient when questions exceed systems, or if it solves problems, does so only by abandoning the system (DIM, p. 18).

The third kind of foundation, namely, wisdom, is a principle of terms and connections, and it suffices even when the first and second kinds of

131

foundations are deficient. Terms and their connections are in turn the principle of words and propositions; hence, with the advancement of wisdom, orderings become more perfect.

This third kind of foundation has its own difficulties. Wisdom really would suffice if people were wise. On the contrary, however, the number of fools is infinite. Therefore, the question arises whether this third kind of foundation is possible. Using the technique of the question found in St. Thomas, Lonergan proposes to pay attention to the difficulties that can be brought against the foundation placed in wisdom (DIM, p. 18). He lists five objections, gives eight initial indications of the real problem raised by these objections, and offers five solutions to the five objections (DIM, pp. 18-22). Since wisdom is the foundation for moving from one system to another, and since moving from one system to another is at the heart of the analytic/ synthetic process, then seeing how wisdom evolves and functions as the foundation for correct judgment is important. Suffice it to say -- germane to the topic of the analytic/synthetic procedures -- that insofar as there is present in all people the natural notion of being and the natural desire of knowing and the natural movement of wisdom, there occurs as well the foundation for moving from one system to another.

Recall that we have been dealing with the basic problem of method in its three aspects: foundations, historicity, and the chasm. Now that we have seen that the foundation of moving from one system to another is posited in wisdom, we can turn to the two remaining aspects of the basic problem of method.

(b) About the Problem of the Chasm

The consideration here is especially about the chasm between theology as a systematic science and as it is known by the simple faithful. Inasmuch as the simple believers are such, their faith is simple. But the believer is a human being as well, naturally endowed with intellect, who continually asks not theological but his own questions. Insofar as the simple believer is an intelligent person, he has some understanding of the faith. "Believe that you may understand" is surely different from "believe that you may prove"; nevertheless, even for the simple faithful there is an understanding of the faith which although analogous and imperfect is really most fruitful (DB 1796, DS 3016). New problems arise for providing believers with an understanding of the faith because universal mandatory education means that more people can ask questions now. In order to meet new demands, two things are required: that theologians themselves be occupied with an understanding of the faith; that the chasm between understanding and sensation be eliminated.

For the first point, theologians must not simply occupy themselves with deductions from the articles of faith as theologians have done for the past three centuries. They must recognize the existence of the two processes outlined as the movement from revelation to truths derived from revelation, and the movement from truths derived from revelation to revelation itself. They must not omit the "turning" back to revelation in order to gather the fruit of understanding the faith. Theologians are not able to communicate to the faithful an understanding of the faith unless they have it themselves.

As for the second point, theologians must eliminate the chasm between understanding and sensing. Just as understanding enters into sensitive life and sensing enters into intellectual life, so theologians can preach in a popular vein to ordinary people communicating both what must be believed and an understanding of the articles of faith. Hence, theologians must fill in the chasm not by rejecting or by changing the understanding of the faith, but by transposing it from one way of understanding to another. And a theologian ought to know these diverse modes of thought and their mutual relations. Many investigations have already been conducted in our time in every field of human science that express these various modes of thought.[10]

(c) About the Problem of Historicity

We noted that Lonergan made his exposition of the three aspects of method's problem starting with foundations, then moving to historicity, and ending up at the chasm. In this part, which has to do with the solutions of these three aspects, he reverses the order of treating the last two, working first on the chasm and ending up with historicity. The reason for this reversal seems to be that the solution to the problem of the chasm sheds light on the solution of historicity. The solutions to foundations, the chasms, and historicity are three parts of a whole. The solution to foundations, however, derives from the progress of human understanding -- insofar as it is connected with the *intellectual* part of the human person. The solution of the chasm comes from human understanding -- insofar as it is connected with the sensitive part of our human composition. As we shall see, the solution to historicity depends on the more or less evolved syntheses between intellectual and sensitive life.

If we view concepts as fixed and immutable and analogous to Platonic ideas, then we rule out the possibility of an evolution of under-standing. If we see concepts as unconscious reproductions of things, as that which is imprinted by things necessarily and mechanically in the mind, then there is no evolution of concepts and no problem of historicity. But if concepts are considered concretely as they exist in the human mind, then they appear with endless variety because concepts are not independent from the intention and intelligence of the individual human person. According to Lonergan's viewpoint, which follows that of St. Thomas, the concept is only the expression of our understanding of things. So as there is a greater or less evolution of understanding, there is a greater or less evolution of concepts. To acknowledge this is to acknowledge the fundamental point for finding the solution to the problem of historicity (DIM, p. 24).

The act of understanding holds a middle place between sense and concept, and because the act of understanding can always advance and become more profound and more comprehensive, so the historical

134

progress of science is possible. Nonetheless, there also exists the possibility of regression. Authors of the fourteenth century were most acute logicians, but they cultivated understanding too little. Logical dexterity does not increase understanding but gradually diminishes it (DIM, p. 50).

An example of the solution to the problem of historicity is given. There can be advances in any field while other areas decline. So from the sixteenth century, positive science and mechanical science have particularly advanced while philosophy has regressed. We must distinguish, therefore, fundamental stages in the evolution of the human mind. And we should make these distinctions of stages not just from an historical but also from a systematic consideration. Bultmann enumerates the various ways of conceiving reality according to Hebraic, Greek, gnostic, primitive Christian and subsequent mind-sets. What causes the differences in understanding are different ways of conceiving, judging, and so on. Much is said about the Pauline of Johannine or Hellenistic mentality. But this is no more than a somewhat useful enumeration and naming of phenomena unless it assigns the causes of these mentalities -- for example, that the Hebraic notion of thinking is such because it lacks a clear distinction between understanding, will and appetite. Therefore, systematically to distinguish the diverse stages of the human evolution means to state the causes from which derive the different human ways of conceiving, judging, deciding. Without a cognitional theory that has worked out the stages in the process of human development of understanding, the solution to the problem of historicity remains meaningless (DIM, pp. 24-25).

5. On the Unity of the Solution

Lonergan summarizes his preliminary steps for the solution of the problem of method in its three aspects by commenting on the unity of the solutions. The unity of the solution consists in the potential human understanding. First, insofar as human understanding is potential, its habits of science and wisdom can grow, and from the progress of human understanding derives the initial solution to the foundational problem.

135

Second, insofar as human understanding is human, it is intimately connected with the sensitive part of man, and from this connection emerges the solution to the problem of the chasm. Third, insofar as human understanding both advances in knowledge, understanding, and wisdom, there arises diverse syntheses between intellectual and sensitive life. As science, understanding, and wisdom are less evolved, what has the ascendancy is sensitive life and the way of conceiving according to the sensitive mode. Different modes of evolution in science, understanding, and wisdom lead to various crises and transformations, which lead to ever changing solutions. The need to sort out these various solutions introduces the problem and notion of method (DIM, p. 25).

On The Notion Of Science

The second main heading of the "*De intellectu et methodo*" is on the notion of science. This problem, too, besides those of foundations, of history, and of the chasm, requires methodical response. Not only does science evolve, but the very notion of science does as well. This affects our topic, for analysis and synthesis are procedures of science. Further, since Lonergan was so influenced by St. Thomas, it is especially important to see how he understood St. Thomas' notion of science. Where Aristotle and St. Thomas used to speak about science, moderns speak about method.

That the notion of science is evolving is not immediately known at the beginning of science, when it is not known in practice what science is. Scientific practice, however, evolves more rapidly than does the notion of science itself. For this reason, conflicts can arise that cause serious problems. The conflict between the developing scientific practice and the notion of science raises once again the problem of method. After a brief introduction, Lonergan gives five illustrations of different notions of science. In order to see the context for his discussion of the notion of science where the twofold way occurs, we will examine the first, second, and fifth examples, and pay particular attention to the second one as it bears on the twofold process used by St. Thomas.

PROBLEMS OF THEOLOGICAL UNDERSTANDING

A. Illustrations from Different Notions of Science

1. Science can be conceived as "knowledge of the essence of a thing, by which knowledge of essences are known the properties of the thing" (DIM, p. 26). The foundation of this notion is logic and supposes the divisions of the Porphyrian tree. This notion contains part of the truth, but it is not able to found an adequate notion of science.

2. Science can be conceived as "certain knowledge of things through their causes" (DIM, p. 27). This is the Aristotelian notion of science. Science in this definition comprises the ten categories of being (things) and the four causes (as applied to these categories): formal, material, efficient, and final. Aristotelian science consists in determining how the categories pertain to things.

This same notion of science as certain knowledge of things through their causes can be understood in another sense, that is, insofar as it supposes a twofold process: analysis and synthesis. Now when St. Thomas applied this concept of science to the exposition of trinitarian doctrine, he did not presuppose the notion of science as used in the Aristotelian sense (DIM, p. 27).

3. After an explanation of the other notions of science, namely, that science is about the laws used in any system, and that science is a deduction from analytic principles, Lonergan turns to the fifth notion. Science can be conceived as about necessities. This concept is entirely true if one treats of Aristotelian science. For Aristotle, the causes of earthly things are accidental, so the whole world is penetrated by contingency. No science is possible concerning accidental things, so for Aristotle, there is no science of historical matters. St. Thomas, on the other hand, holds that science concerns accidental things because not all agents are natural agents; there are those that act through understanding and will, as for example, God.

Although St. Thomas often repeated the Aristotelian definition of science, he understood something different from the notion that science is about necessary things. So, for example, in the *Summa Contra Gentiles* 2, 28-30, he distinguishes many times the difference between absolute and hypothetical necessity. Yet the fact remains that we have almost nothing by St. Thomas on history (DIM, pp. 29-30).

We have already noted that problems with the notion of science have a bearing on the twofold way because in his own theological writing, Lonergan initially used the scientific model of St. Thomas. Unlike the Aristotelian model, the analytic/synthetic procedures used by Aquinas could include history's concern for the *de facto* and contingent. So even until 1959, Lonergan was upholding the Thomist scientific procedure of arranging speculative theological ideas according to analysis and synthesis.

B. The Conclusion Concerning the Notion of Science

Lonergan summarizes this section by stating that sciences are evolving and with them the very notion of science. So a clearer notion of science is obtained only with the fuller working out of scientific practice. The theological practice of St. Thomas was the systematizing by which he tried to reduce everything to some fundamental principles. The difficulty with his systematization is that he never explained what he did, but he only did it. That he used the analytic/synthetic procedure is clear, but how St. Thomas understood them we can only detect from a careful scrutiny of his work.

Before we turn to the fourth major division of "*De intellectu et methodo*", we can note in passing that the third major division examines the way by which people experience, conceive, judge, think and know: the symbolic and the theoretical ways of human knowing. These two modes complement each other because alone they are imperfect. Only a further, dialectical development generates a third, more perfect mode of thinking that Lonergan calls scientific, methodical understanding. Already in the section on the development of dogma in the *Divinarum personarum*, Lonergan had adverted to the stages of human consciousness that move from the commonsense apprehensions of the *prius quoad nos* to the scientific apprehensions of the *prius quoad se*. We have already seen that this movement from commonsense apprehension to scientific knowing is the heart of the analytic/synthetic process. Lonergan's thought in this third section provides a careful look at the elements that compose these different stages of consciousness, and this section is important for students of Lonergan's thought on intentionality. But we can turn our attention to the next major division of the 1959 doctoral seminar, on method and its precepts.

On Method and Its Precepts

The fourth major division of the "*De intellectu et methodo*" comprises over a third of the material of the course. Five rules are given for a general method pertaining to any and all sciences. The sections of this part correspond roughly to the five rules, with another part given to theological examples of these rules. The five rules are: (1) understand; (2) understand systematically; (3) reverse counterpositions; (4) develop positions; (5) accept responsibility for judgment.

After extensive explanation of each of these rules, Lonergan applies the five precepts to theology. When someone understands something but does not know how to say what is known, there occurs unformulated understanding that is not systematic (as in the artist). An instance of systematic understanding happens when someone knows something and knows what it is he knows. The third and fourth rules, inasmuch as they seek the coherence of things thought and spoken, postulate the reflection of subsequent judgment. The fifth rule is an exercise of rational conscious-ness by which one seeks the difference between astrology and astronomy, alchemy and chemistry, legends and history (DIM, pp. 45-46).

THE ROAD TO LONERGAN'S *METHOD IN THEOLOGY*

In order to apply the rules given above, Lonergan insists on stressing the importance of development of intellectual habits. At first blush, theology seems to be what we read in theological authors. Then, in a refinement of that idea, theology appears to be what is understood in those works. Principles are acquired from which others are deduced. Only if theology arrives at the intellectual habits of the theologian (and does not consist in the mere reproduction of single theses, but in this -- that he can formulate from himself the definitions sufficient for his proper ends) will that theologian be able to judge well and to communicate to the Christian people what he has understood. When the theologian arrives at this versatility, then fundamental theology (apologetics) and dogmatic theology will only appear as two usages of the same habit (DIM p. 49).

Before moving to Lonergan's application of the five rules to theology and noting their relevance to the analytic/synthetic process, it is worth setting forth the notion of theology found in *"De intellectu et methodo"* in order to understand what he thought about the various branches of theology in 1959. Generally speaking, theology is divided into speculative (more cultivated in the Middle Ages) and positive (evolved since the Renaissance), into apologetics (fundamental) and dogmatics. The distinction between dogmatic and apologetic theology is in no way methodical. In dogmatics, there are not lacking considerations about objections, for example, of rationalizations opposed to the Trinity, so the apologetic problem remains. On the other hand, apologetics is occupied with dogmatic questions such as about the reasonableness of faith. Fundamental theology deals with the Church, which is the mystical Body of Christ, a spatio-temporal reality. Therefore, just as technical concepts such as procession, relation, and person are required for trinitarian theology -- without which we would have no systematic thesis on the Trinity -- so a systematic conceptualization of the historical reality is required to obtain a tract on the mystical Body of Christ. While there is plenty of material available for a dogmatic tract on the Church, no tract has appeared to date because there is a defect in systematic conceptualization. The defect is that there have been many disputations about the concept of history, but no definitive systematic theory about history has been elaborated (DIM, pp. 48-49).

The five rules given above may equally be applied to fundamental and dogmatic theology, positive and speculative theology. These rules are based on the nature of human understanding, so people who proceed in the sciences observe them, even when they do not explicitly think about them. Method, however, ought only to make explicit what is implicit in the structure of the intellectual process (DIM, p. 49).

What follows are five sections that illustrate each of the five rules as it applies to theology. These examples are important because they show the basic movement of the analytic/synthetic process which is from unsystematic to systematic understanding. After the fourth section, which is a theological illustration of the rule, "develop positions", there is a lengthy treatment about points that must be noted about the particular history of any discipline. It is in this context that we shall see Lonergan's comparison between historical and speculative theology. This comparison is especially germane to our topic in light of the introduction two years earlier in the *Divinarum personarum conceptio analogica* of a "third, historical process" to the twofold procedure of analysis and synthesis.

A. A Theological Illustration of the First Rule: Understand

The desire for understanding was present in the primitive Church and the patristic Church. But questions at that time were posed by chance. Questions did not arise systematically but only when occasioned by heresies (DIM, p. 49).

What was only casually accomplished in the primitive and patristic Church the medieval theologians tried to do in a universal and systematic way. The importance of Abelard's *Sic et Non* was that any one assertion could be affirmed or negated on the basis of scriptural or patristic authorities. This shows that it is not always sufficient to cite a Father or scripture to determine a question (DIM, p. 49). After Abelard, the notion of the question was developed by Gilbert of Porree and was perfected by St. Thomas. Before St. Thomas, Peter Lombard had prepared historical investigations and positive collections that were read in the schools all the way until the seventeenth century. Nevertheless, it is typical of the commentaries on the *Sentences* of Lombard that they treat of questions that Lombard had not posited and had not understood. Because concepts arise from acts of understanding, new concepts always emerge from new understanding. So all of scholasticism is a verification of the first rule (DIM, p. 50).

B. A Theological Illustration of the Second Rule: Understand Systematically

Although there can be and are preludes to science before a system is sought, still a science properly speaking exists only when the system exists that specifies all the relations proper to that science. In every science, the preparatory period is one thing, the explanatory period is another. In science, before form there occurs the development toward form. With systematization, science begins to have form, hence its own unity, its own laws and proper concepts that distinguish it from everything else, even from its own method. So theology was born as a science around the year 1230 (DIM, p. 50).

In the twelfth and at the beginning of the thirteenth centuries, many inextricable questions used to torment theologians. One massive question concerned the correct conception of grace and liberty. Philip the Chancellor discovered the solution to the problem of grace in the entitative distinction between the natural and the supernatural order. This distinction was made all along the line: faith is above reason, grace is above nature, charity is above human love, merit is above the debt of nature. The discovery of this fundamental distinction was the key to solving the controversy about grace and nature (DIM, p. 51).

In this entire question, the fundamental word is order. Order is some relation or complex of relations of many intelligible things. Hence, with the discovery of the supernatural order, theologians detected the proper object of theology, or the complex of intelligible relations encompassing within themselves everything pertaining to theology (DIM, p. 51).

"Understand systematically" means understand in such a way that fundamental concepts proper to any science will be determined through reciprocal relations with one another that arise only with the passing of time. Systematic understanding means obtaining a unified conceptualization of the whole field of any science so as to obtain all the propositions of that material, to generate disputations about that material, and to answer difficulties raised against that discipline. Because the natural goal of understanding is to apprehend the entire concrete universe, partial systematization of one field does not achieve this end. St. Thomas wanted to obtain a systematic understanding by integrating it with systematic understanding of the rest of the universe. While St. Bonaventure saw in natural things only signs and symbols through which the human mind could be elevated to God, St. Thomas did not attend only to theological systematization, but aimed at the systematizing of the universe, whether physical, psychological, metaphysical, or ethical. Only then was theology able to be truly systematic (DIM, pp. 51-52).

C. A Theological Illustration of the Third Rule: Reverse Counterpositions

Systematic understanding gradually arises in history and in the life of the individual. Only a later era discloses the ideal of understanding. So questions that Parmenides had already discovered received their systematic solution only with Aristotle and ultimately in Aquinas. Interpersonal symbols are objectified in art, but this objectification differs from what is obtained through universal concepts. Commonsense understanding evolves within some specific horizon for concrete situations. It is in such an evolution that the transition to universals comes about (DIM, p. 43).

143

This transition signals a conversion in the subject, who moves from care of himself and of his own world to orientate himself toward the universe. A person ought not to lay aside all commonsense and symbolic understanding, but only inasmuch as one turns to scientific knowing, to its mode of thinking and of judging. The scientific mode, moreover, ought not to be specified by intersubjective categories. The crowd seeks utility, so it sees in science what is useful because science deals with what is particular and concrete. Such a utilitarian criterion ought to be put aside in scientific thought.[11]

Assertions made by those who discover ideas must be tested. Some are coherent with intelligent and rational activity (and are *positions*) while others are not coherent with what Lonergan will later call authentic subjectivity (and are *counterpositions*). For correct method, therefore, we should make a transition from counterpositions to positions by breaking out of the horizon of bias, while we should develop positions further. This is the way the Fathers acted, "despoiling the Egyptians", or taking for their own the truths of pagan authors while omitting their mistakes. This is what Newman did when undertaking a criticism of universal doubt. He asserted that if it were necessary to choose, one ought to decide for universal credulity. With the passing of time, errors would pass away and truth remain, while for universal doubt, nothing would remain for understanding (DIM, pp. 44-45).

A theological illustration of the third rule about reversing counterpositions can be seen in the Thomist-Augustinian conflict of the thirteenth century. St. Thomas was a great innovator, so a bitter reaction arose in the thirteenth century pitting the Friars Minor and the anti-Aristotelians generally against the Dominicans and those who wanted to perfect systematic theology by using Aristotelian science. The conflict was ambiguous. Inasmuch as the reaction rejected Thomist positions that assumed Aristotelian science, it was equivalent to a counterposition. But inasmuch as the reaction intended to reject errors contained in Aristotelianism, we should think of it rather as a position. Had there not been a most bitter resistance in the Church to Thomism, then Aristotle would have had an

144

inevitably exaggerated authority, and it would have been much more difficult afterwards to accept the truer conclusions of natural science in subsequent centuries. But the reaction also had grave defects: Augustinianism wanted to appropriate from Aristotle only what was evidently certain and logical. They rejected notions fundamental to obtaining systematic understanding, and in the place of the more or less scientific vision that Aristotle had about everything, they aimed at a pure, abstract, logical systematization (DIM, p. 52).

St. Thomas, on the other hand, conceived science as the under-standing of real things, of the concrete universe. He cared little if at all for hypothetical worlds about which we know nothing. Since the Augustinians wished to take from Aristotle only logical systematization, and likewise maintained the notion that science is about what is universal and necessary, about things somehow known *a priori* as pertaining to science, it is no wonder that their constructs were empty, and that the fruit of their labor was the general skepticism of nominalism (DIM, p. 53).

D. A Theological Illustration of the Fourth Rule: Develop Positions

St. Thomas and the entire theology of the thirteenth century do not constitute the conclusion of theology, but its beginning, and so its perfection is not to be sought in them. Conspicuous in them was a defect of what today is called "a sense of history". In order to eliminate contradic-tions that appeared among the sayings of Augustine or some Father or of scripture, they used a logical solution. Rather than inquire what scripture or the Fathers or Augustine *de facto* had said over the centuries, the logical solution selected from all possible senses of any text the one that could agree with the other senses and the rest of the truths, caring little whether this was the true sense of the author or not. An historical sense pre-supposes that concepts vary over time, and when they proceed from acts of understanding, they evolve when there is a greater evolution of understanding, and grow poorer when there is an involuntary regression of understanding. While medieval theology was deficient in a sense of history, all of subsequent theology has been increasingly occupied with a critique of the origin of Christian doctrine and with the question of the evolution of dogma. So the issue that the medievals did not pay attention to has become prominent in more recent theology (DIM, p. 54).

The application of the fourth rule, "develop positions", is seen precisely in the systematic application of the categories of history to our systematization in theology. After distinguishing between the application of the categories of history to science generally and to theology in particular, Lonergan sets aside a whole section in *"De intellectu et methodo"* for illustrations of the systematic application of the particular categories of theological history. Since the introduction of the historical consideration of recurrence of the twofold analytic/synthetic process is key to Lonergan's developing thought on theological method, this next section is especially relevant to our discussion (DIM, p. 54).

Some Points About the Particular History of Any Discipline

Pure historical competence is not sufficient for composing special history. Everything that makes a person an historian is indeed required -- collection of data, textual criticism, knowledge of sources and manuscripts. But if one is writing a special history of mathematics, physics, or medicine, it is required that such a person have a special knowledge of that discipline, a knowledge that the historian does not have *qua* historian (DIM, p. 55).

If we ask why a special knowledge of the discipline is required to write special history, the answer is simple. In actuality, the history of any particular discipline is the history of the evolution of the discipline itself. The evolution, however, which was accomplished in history, is not something simple and compendious, but something carried out through many diverse steps, errors, deviations, corrections. Inasmuch, however, as we study this movement, we learn this evolving process. We already have in ourselves an example of this very evolution, which perhaps was protracted in our ancestors throughout centuries. This is only possible if we ourselves understand both the discipline and our learning of the discipline. Only then would we understand as well what elements in the evolved historical process we must apprehend before the others; what were the causes of progress or of retardation in understanding; what elements pertain to this science, which not; what elements contain errors. Only then would we be able to discern when new visions of the whole science arose in history; when the first true system emerged; when the transitions occurred from earlier to further systematic ordering; what system was only an amplification of the earlier one, and what was radically new; which ones allowed progressive transformations of all the material; how through new systematizations we have the double fact that those things which were explained by the old system are still explained by the new, and, beside that, many others are explained that were not explained in the old. Only then would we be able to understand what things favor progress and what things would impede it, and why they would favor or impede it, and so forth (DIM, p. 55).

The historian of any discipline ought both to know and to understand profoundly his whole subject area. Moreover, it is fitting that the historian understand systematically. When this is said of history, it means that successive systems ought to be understood that progressively evolved in time. This systematic understanding of the evolution ought to use the analogy of the evolution that occurs in the mind of a researcher learning something, and this internal evolution of the researcher ought to be compared with the historical process by which the discipline evolved (DIM, p. 55).

Further, a theologian writing theological history does not ignore these differences between ways of thinking and understanding. For before anyone was a theologian, he was a Christian who had some understanding of the faith, although inchoate. Furthermore, if the theologian teaches, it ought to be in such a way that others who do not yet have systematic understanding may acquire it. In order to teach well, it is fitting to know both the term to which we tend (systematic understanding) and the term from which we set out (commonsense understanding). Moreover, if the theologian is a preacher, he ought to translate his systematic understanding into popular, intersubjective understanding. When Christ spoke to the people about the Incarnation, he did not speak of its formal constitution, but of the intersubjective dimensions of that order. So a true and good theologian will not only be capable of doing the job of the specialist, but will also be capable of exercising best the ministry of the Word (DIM, p. 56).

So if anyone wants to write the history of Christian doctrine and of theology, one ought to be not only an historian but a theologian as well, and one who can use personally acquired experience both of systematic and non-systematic understanding. Hence, it is not correct to hold that less speculative understanding is required for doing historical work than for cultivating speculative theology (DIM, p. 56).

In a more concrete fashion, in order to illustrate the role of the historian of theology, we can now turn to a comparison between systematic understanding and other understandings. In the fourth century, an enormous tumult took place over the one word, *homoousion*, when it was introduced into the symbols of faith. The sense of this word was not intersubjective, or symbolic, or proper to popular understanding. The sense of *homoousion* was technical. This word signified a transition to the systematic mode of thinking. Because this transition was taking place for the first time, it generated a whole spectrum of opinions throughout the Church. Even those who defended the introduction of this word did not consider it a wholesome innovation, but as a novelty bad in itself but accidentally good and necessary. But with the transition from the popular to the systematic way of understanding, the peace and unity of the Church again was preserved. So progress occurred with its introduction. And this example is not unique. The whole history of doctrine illustrates the transitions from a non-systematic to a systematic way of thinking (DIM, p. 57).

If the entire history of doctrine is a series of these kinds of transitions, how are they to be understood? The answer is that in the history of the period in which a transition occurred, a bridge will be found between the two ways of understanding, the earlier one and the later, systematic one. What we need to scrutinize well is the situation that obtained before the transition, with all of its scriptural, patristic antecedents. Obviously, chronology is not sufficient to obtain an understanding of these transitions (DIM, p. 57).

Further Notions Concerning the Investigation of This Transition from the Non-Systematic to the Systematic Way of Understanding

Lonergan provides an example of the investigation of the transition from the non-systematic to the systematic by looking at mechanics. In his systematization of mechanics, Newton often repeated the phrase, "I am not inventing hypotheses". This statement is highly important for the historical understanding of science. While in one sense a theory (for example, of universal gravity) is *de facto* an hypothesis, there is another sense in which this is not the case, and that is the sense which is now our interest. Lonergan explains in three steps the sense in which the theory of universal gravity is not an hypothesis, and by which Newton contended that he did not invent hypotheses. Lonergan gives these three points to explain what we must avoid when we seek an historical understanding of the transition from a non-systematic to a systematic way of thinking (DIM, p. 58).

First, do not begin your investigation by looking for an efficient cause (in this case, what will make a body fall). Indeed, it is quite useful for obtaining knowledge of anything to investigate what influences it. But in the beginning, one ought to prescind from this consideration. Before one examines the influence of the cause on the effect, both the cause and the effect ought to be understood in themselves. It is not possible to investigate this influence until one establishes the *id ex quo* and the *id in quo* of this influence. Otherwise we would be able to discover nothing solid and could not avoid a process to infinity. So in historical matters, what we must ask before all else is the intrinsic intelligibility of the text itself that we are examining (DIM, p. 58).

Second, do not speak of hidden causes. It was thus that Descartes solved the problem of planetary motion by supposing some invisible matter which revolved exactly as the planets seemed to move. This solution was indeed exceedingly secure because it was impossible to refute.

This happens in theological material when people appeal to a "mentality" that is Hebraic, biblical, medieval, Palestinian. We do not assert that all of these notion lack sense, but we must proceed in another way so that they have sense. If instead of appealing to these notions as to a kind of *deus ex machina*, we try to obtain intrinsic intelligibility about the documents themselves, and we join this understanding with the evolution of the total human understanding, then instead of speaking about the Hebrew mentality, for example, in a vague and obscure way, we may speak of the evolution of the human mind and culture, which since it consists in the progressive distinguishing and specialization of individual elements constitutive of human life in the proper sense, the Greeks had perfected more than the Hebrews. For the Greeks used to distinguish both understanding and desires, both affects and praxis which the Hebrews did not yet distinguish. So neither their vocabulary, nor notions, nor life itself denote any specialization. Therefore, if we have obtained the understanding described above, then by appealing to these notions, we not only describe a pure fact, but understand something as well (DIM, pp. 58-59).

Third, do not inquire about final cause or about value. On this point Newton especially opposed Aristotle. In Aristotle, motion ultimately is produced by the final cause, because anything at all is moved toward its natural place, and this is the task which the final cause performs. On the other hand, Newton limited his investigation primarily to those things that are presented, so that he would find intelligibility in them, the intelligible relations immanent within those things that are apparent, so that -- in an Aristotelian way of speaking -- he might know the form of things. Many thinkers before Aristotle had spoken of final, efficient, material causes, but the originality in the Aristotelian consideration was the notion of form. Before Newton, indeed, many philosophers disputed about form, as happened not rarely among scholastics. But with the impetus of Newton, there emerged again a seeking of what we can call the Aristotelian notion of form, or of seeking intelligibility in those things that are given sensibly.

If the historian is not supposed to seek efficient causes, hidden causes, final causes or value, what is he supposed to do? The historian of theology has for his first task the discovery of the internal intelligibility of a transition. One obtains this when one expounds all the historical data in their successions and all the diverse positions, any one of which is illumined by an opposed position (DIM, p. 62). An historical understanding of what transpired in the Councils of Nicea or Chalcedon is not obtained by considering the truth defined in these councils (because this pertains to dogmatic inquiry), but by seeking the intelligibility of what was done, the reason it was done, and who were the ones contradicting it. Once this intelligibility has been obtained, the judgment about the truth and usefulness of these definitions will be much easier because it is a subsequent judgment. Furthermore, understanding of these transitions occurs easily in this sense, that when we learn theology, the transition from the popular way of understanding to the systematic way occurs in us (DIM, p. 59).

Recall that the historian of theology's first task is to understand systematically. The historian's second task in theology is to give a judgment on and the reasons for diverse tendencies. We can do this easily after we obtain the intelligibility of the transition. So what explains the multitude of positions is the complexity of the question. The question of Nicea really was not only speculative (how the Son is really from himself and from another), but also exegetical (it was difficult to select texts of scripture and their interpretation for proving the divinity of Christ) , and terminological (the various senses of the words used -- *hypostasis*, being), and methodological (whether it would be legitimate to introduce into the creeds a word that was not found in scripture), and dogmatic-disciplinary (the question was being treated by the first ecumenical council and there was as yet in the Church no clear doctrine about the validity of such a council). To these intrinsic factors, add those that pertain to the environment, whether it be the imperial interference in theological questions and ecclesial matters, or the very organization of the Church (DIM, p. 62).

How can one provide for criticism of the diverse interpretations given about the same historical facts by diverse historians, whether idealist, empiricist, existentialist or catholic? The only intrinsic means is to attend to the intelligibility of things given and to make a judgment on them. This diversity of interpretation certainly does not come from the facts but from other headings. A critique of the diversity is possible inasmuch as we not only pay close attention to documents but also understand the aprioristic element belonging to the mind of the historian himself. Thus, an interpretation may be clearly distinguished which best agrees with the data and always remains the same. But there are other interpretations that continually shift because they never arrive in any absolute sense at an understanding of things. So historians criticize not only deeds but other historians as well. This criticism of other historians can be established with the mediation of a dialectical argument. The dialectical argument differs from a logical argument because, while a logical argument presupposes notions and common propositions, the dialectical argument transforms some false original assertion by starting out from that very assertion.[12]

By the use of the dialectical process, it is possible to show the aprioristic elements of diverse historical theories. An intrinsic understanding of these data is the foundation for dialectical arguments against aprioristic interpretations, in which is manifested the latent opposition between the *a priori* historians and the data which intrinsic understanding seeks to comprehend. This is not possible if we seek after efficient causes, or final causes, or hidden causes, or after giving a judgment of value (DIM, p. 63).

A Comparison Between Historical and Speculative Theology

In this section, we see Lonergan explicitly addressing the methodological issues he raised in the 1954 article, "Theology and Understanding". The treatment here is not about two theologies, for historical theology is speculative theology as it develops (*in fieri*), while speculative theology is historical theology as it exists at its term (*in facto esse*). Terms and categories proper to speculative theology (such as Church, supernatural, sacraments, *homoousion*, person) have arisen within the historical theological movement. Moreover, these terms have been assisted by that historical movement when it arrived at those transition points that are the key of the entire theological movement. Furthermore, these key transitions are especially connected with the great heresies and with the most celebrated disputations (DIM, p. 63). So one who wishes to know speculative theology ought to know the historical movement as well. And one who wants to know the historical movement ought to know speculative theology (DIM, p. 64).

Lonergan argues that the special history of any science can only be done by one who is expert in that science. Thus, the history of theology can be written only by one most expert in theological matters, hence, by a speculative theologian. If speculative theology and historical theology are separated, then big problems are created for both fields.

If speculative and historical theology are separated, then positive theology loses its proper method. The history of theological thought is not just some indistinct element in the history of philosophy, literature, or religion. It ought to be singled out as some determinate movement. When speculative theology is omitted, however, the delineation of historical theology's realm is eliminated. Similarly, if we want to study the stages preceding scientific systematization in the history of some physical science, we obtain the criterion for figuring out what belongs to the earlier stages of the science by using the categories that we know from later stages of the science's evolution (DIM, p. 64).

Another result of the separation of historical and speculative theology is that the very nature of speculative theology is corrupted. Theology is not any kind of understanding at all, but an understanding of faith. If contact with revealed data is lost, some understanding can be arrived at, but not an understanding of faith. When positive theology is eliminated, speculative theology is separated from its proper origins, and if this does not happen, origins often are falsified through anachronism that projects later categories into earlier stages.

153

True, without positive theology, speculative theology would be able to rely on the Church magisterium. Thus, it will be able to demonstrate what is *de fide*, what is not, what is theologically certain, what is probably safe, what is not, and what is presumptuous. But in this way a judgment will be given only about faith or about what must be believed, and no understanding of the faith will be obtained. This "inquisition" theology is more useful for discerning heresies and avoiding errors than for generating further understanding (DIM, p. 64).

From these observations Lonergan distilled some initial notions about the question that in 1959 caused agitation regarding biblical and patristic theology, namely, the question about method. What are the correct procedures for doing biblical or patristic theology? In fact, these disciplines are not a treatment of philology, or of the history of literary types of human thought, but of scripture and the Fathers inasmuch as they precede any theology. Biblical theology wants to make a transition from the study of history, philosophy, culture, or literature to another genus of study that is named theology. But theology only became "scientific" from the thirteenth century with the systematization of all the theoretical material on the supernatural (DIM, p. 64). It is only in this century that theologians acknowledge the existence of a prescientific stage of theology. For the distinction between theology's prescientific stage and scientific stage to become clear, theologians need to acknowledge the difference between the systematic and the symbolic-popular way of thinking. Up to now, there has been no attention paid to this difference in the theology manuals (DIM, pp. 64-65).

The first step toward understanding the prescientific stages of any science is to describe them, and later to investigate them systematically according to an understanding of later scientific age (only a doctor can investigate the history of medicine). It is obvious that one who does not understand systematic theology and wants to write about theology in its prescientific stage is dealing with matters he does not understand. He is bound to omit much that is essential and to give prominent attention to much that does not pertain to the issue (DIM, p. 65).

PROBLEMS OF THEOLOGICAL UNDERSTANDING

Theological science is bound more than others to investigate its own prescientific stage. This is not essential for natural sciences, although such an historical recounting of development could be useful for the pedagogy of these sciences. But theology is an understanding of the faith; objective faith that is believed, however, is first proposed in scripture, by the Fathers and the first councils, so the exposition of revelation took place instead in the prescientific stage of theological science (DIM, p. 65). Since the very elements that theology seeks to understand systematically were conceived in its prescientific phase, there is raised the serious problem of historicity that we have already seen.

Since we must understand not only in a commonsense fashion but also systematically, theology must evolve its own categories for investigating its own prescientific stages. But what systematic elements must be assumed in the understanding of the prescientific stages? Some indications of what these elements are can be obtained inasmuch as the prescientific stages are conceived as a movement to speculative theology. How can we understand faith, revelation, inspiration and other elements that occurred before the transition came about when we obtained these notions explicitly? This is the fundamental methodological problem Lonergan faced in 1959, and its solution, to his mind, depends upon an intimate cooperation among biblical, dogmatic, patristic, and conciliar theologians (DIM, p. 65).

E. A Theological Illustration of the Fifth Rule: Accept Responsibility for Making a Judgment

The fifth rule is supreme in any science and is fundamental in theology. While theology presupposes both faith and an understanding of faith, it does not simply repeat beliefs. Theologians believe that in a providential way God preserves revealed truth through his Church. Theologians obtain faith from God and direction about the faith from the Church magisterium. Nonetheless, even theologians ought to make their own judgments since understanding increases through the ages. Moreover, a new, fuller apprehension of revealed truth does not derive as a necessary deduction from concepts already available. New apprehensions require an extension of the principles and an amplification of concepts. So simple deduction does not suffice for deeper understanding. Rather than deducing something, theologians perceive something new with the understanding, and judge responsibly whether this fuller understanding is true or not (DIM, p. 67).

Judgment comes about according to some wisdom. But the only wisdom proportionate to judging about the understanding of faith is the divine wisdom, which we as theologians do not have. Therefore, we judge according to our thinking, our opinion, and are prompt -- since we know the insufficiency of our own wisdom -- to submit our judgment to the Church's judgment. We know that the Church magisterium is directed by the Holy Spirit for guarding and declaring the dominical doctrine. So as theologians, we do not judge definitively about the validity of our understanding, but humbly propose our opinion and accept the judgment of the Church (DIM, pp. 67-68).

Lonergan's Concluding Section

The fifth and final section of the "*De intellectu et methodo*" summarizes the points that Lonergan has made previously in the body of his lectures. The key problem for him in 1959 was how to join systematic and historical thinking. Only an expert in a special science can complete a history of that science. In theological history, special attention must be paid to the transition points where occur the concrete historical connection between the systematic mode of thinking and the prior, intersubjective mode. To discover how the truth of dogma is implicit in scripture, we must seek an empirical and a theoretical specification. The empirical specification comes from an investigation of the transition as it was prepared from the second and third centuries and accomplished in the fourth. The theoretical specification seeks to make explicit what before was implicit. It means apprehending in a systematic way what was understood before in an intersubjective way. So the central point of the problem of historicity is found empirically in crucial points of this transition; it is found theoretically, however, in the movement from an unsystematic way of thinking to asystematic way of thinking (DIM, p. 72).

Positive theology is speculative theology in its evolution, and speculative theology is positive theology as it exists in its term. The present difficulty in 1959 between the two is the way that manuals propound theology. The end of the manuals is both scientific and pedagogical, and these two ends conflict. The difficulty is in making a systematic tract of diverse orderings of responses at the same time in any one thesis. So there is the practical problem -- how to teach, how to examine; and the scientific problem -- how to join systematic and historical thinking. And Lonergan says that as of 1959, no solution has been found to these problems (DIM, p. 72).

Concluding Overview

We have seen that from his first days as a dogmatic theologian, when Lonergan spoke of theology, he meant speculative theology in the strict sense, the operation of faith seeking understanding. In speculative theology, there was a twofold process for organizing the material in systematic fashion. The first process began with the analysis of truths of faith so as to arrive at principles properly speaking (for example, in the trinitarian tract, at notions such as procession, relation, person). The second process was called synthesis because it began with the theological principles themselves, and after further understanding, returned to the original truths and arranged them in an intelligible organization that revealed more fully the connection between the truths than was discernible when the truths were first being assembled in the prior analytic process.

As we have noted, the context in which the analytic/synthetic process operated was within the boundaries of speculative theology. So while Lonergan traced the development of ideas in the analytic process, it was a development devoid of concern for an historical context -- it was merely the evolution of ideas without concern for the ones thinking them, in what circumstances, for what ends. But in the 1954 article, "Theology and Understanding", which thematized his understanding and use of the *via analytica* and the *via synthetica*, he introduced the problems for speculative theology imported by the rise of historical scholarship in positive theology.

By 1957, in the *Divinarum personarum conceptio analogica*, Lonergan not only introduced a third, historical process in addition to the twofold analytic and synthetic ways, he addressed as well the problems connected with the evolution of dogma. The development of dogma was seen as being an historical unfolding of transcultural, theological, and dogmatic processes in which the same, unchanging revealed truth was understood and progressively expressed in diverse patterns of consciousness. Yet in 1957, he was content simply to refer to the fact of dogmatic development without explaining it because the main objective of the introductory chapter of *Divinarum personarum* was to explain his current notion of theological understanding, and the reference to dogmatic development was incidental to that explanation. But serious questions were raised by the fact of dogma's evolution. How do we make the transition from the prescientific stage of theology to the scientific phase that uses technical terms and procedures? What is the systematic explanation for an increase in understanding of the same truth? What is the foundation for systematic understanding itself?

The 1959 *"De intellectu et methodo"* addresses the questions just cited. Instead of talking about four methodological problems as he had in 1954, or even about the twofold way of ordering theological ideas in its own right as he had in 1957, Lonergan now speaks about three aspects of the one methodical problem of how to join historical and systematic theology.

True, there are echoes of the four earlier methodological problems in these three aspects of the one methodical problem. For example, the 1954 first problem about the patterns of human experience (how to integrate a commonsense and a theoretical way of knowing) is repeated and elaborated in the third aspect of the methodical problem here (how to fill in the chasm between ordinary belief and its systematic communication). Instead of focusing here on one way of arranging ideas or another, he concentrates rather on systems -- how they are constituted, how they evolve, and most importantly, how we can move historically from one system to another.

Lonergan posits the solution to the methodological problem of maintaining the continuity of truth among various successive systems by adverting to the evolving stages of human understanding. This evolution of the human mind derives from wisdom, the foundation that integrates the sensitive and the intellectual part of the human person. This integrating work of wisdom makes possiblo the solution to the other two aspects of the methodical problem, the chasm and historicity. First, it solves the difficulty of the chasm between ordinary believers and speculative theologians. Because the theologian attains the development in human understanding that embodies familiarity with both commonsense and systematic apprehensions of the faith, he contains in himself the bridge needed to join the two sides of the chasm. Second, it solves the problem of historicity. Because the theologian embodies in himself the sensitive and intellectual parts of human development, he solves the problem of historicity (how to achieve a continuity of the same truth as expressed in successive systems) in that he recognizes in himself, and so in others, distinct stages of development of the human mind. It is clear, moreover, that theology's methodological problems require a correct cognitional theory for their solution. The principle that generates and discloses the development of dogma, so far as Lonergan is concerned, is the dynamism of our intelligence illumined by faith to understand what has been revealed to be true.

What explains this movement from faith to understanding is not logic, but the dynamism of intelligence that, through stages developing from symbolic, intersubjective consciousness to scientific consciousness, makes the transition from commonsense apprehensions of revealed truth (as expressed, for example, in scripture) to scientific apprehensions of the same truth (as formulated in the technical language of the councils). This principle is only implicit, however, since Lonergan does not set out in any explicit fashion to propose a theory of dogmatic development.

Lonergan's main concern is to answer the question of foundations, historicity, and the chasm that posit the one problem of method. And his solution to the problem of method is given in his five methodical rules for any science. While he places the solution to theology's foundational problem in wisdom, the principle of correct ordering, still the dynamism by which wisdom works is the dynamism of intelligence inquiring *quid sit* and *an sit*. While the solution to the problem of foundations derives from the progress of human understanding, the solution of the chasm comes from human understanding insofar as it is connected with the sensitive part of human experience. The solution of historicity depends on the more or less evolved syntheses between intellectual and sensitive life. So the solutions to foundations, the chasm, and historicity are three parts of a whole.

In the material of "*De intellectu et methodo*" covered in this chapter, we see Lonergan stressing the need for systematic understanding generated by the twofold way, but now there is the further insistence on including the historical perspective. The dynamism of intelligence is still primary -- what is sought is an understanding of the transitions in history from non-systematic to systematic ways of understanding. While adverting to the problem of interpretation that underlies the correct understanding of the transitions, he posits the remedy to the problem in the dialectical argument. Instead of seeking the answer to historical problems by looking for efficient causes, or final causes, or hidden causes, he recommends the primacy of formal cause, of seeking intelligibility immanent in those elements that are sensibly given. But the only reason that systematic understanding is possible is that the evolution of the human mind and culture consists in progressive differentiation and specialization. And this is the role performed for theological science by the analytic and synthetic processes.

A lingering problem remains. What is the connection between this last chapter and the twofold ordering of ideas? The connection between this last chapter on joining historical and systematic theology and the twofold way enunciated earlier in the 1954 "Theology and Understanding" and the 1957 *Divinarum personarum* is that the function history plays in theology is still not clear for Lonergan in 1959. Analysis and synthesis (to Lonergan's mind) still belong to speculative theology, not historical theology. But if analysis/synthesis are his ways of ordering theological ideas, what do we do with history, which is yet another way of ordering ideas? Lonergan adverts to this issue in *"De intellectu et methodo"*, but he has not figured out at this time how to include within systematic theology the historical perspective that investigates theology's prescientific stage.

NOTES

CHAPTER V

[1]Bernard J.F. Lonergan, S.J., "Theology and Understanding", *Collection*, ed. F.E. Crowe, S.J. (New York: Herder and Herder, 1967), p. 136.

[2]*Ibid*., pp. 137-139.

[3]*Ibid*., pp. 139-140.

[4]*Ibid*., pp. 140-141.

[5]Bernard J.F. Lonergan, S.J., *"De intellectu et methodo"* (mimeographed edition, Rome: St. Francis Xavier College, 1959). This is a *reportatio* edition taken down in Latin by students who attended the lectures. It is important to remember that these notes, while a careful account of Lonergan's content and structure of presentation, do not come directly from his own hand. Since there are frequent references to this text, the citations will be noted directly in the body of the chapter with the abbreviation (DIM) and the page number.

[6]The first main section of *"De intellectu et methodo"* is on the notion of the question. It contains six divisions: (1) on the question, pp. 1-4; (2) on the series of questions, pp. 4-5; (3) on the ordering of responses, pp. 5-8; (4) on the series of arrangements of responses, pp. 8-10; (5) on the criteria for a new ordering, pp. 10-11; (6) on the threefold problem: of foundations, of historicity, of the chasm, pp. 11-25.

[7]The *reportatio* notes are somewhat cryptic at this juncture. The point seems to be that St. Thomas held different opinions at different times. Is it possible to go from one of his opinions to another by logical deriva-

tion? If not, and Lonergan's view is that we cannot, then logically we have to postulate many St. Thomases.

[8]Lonergan, "*De intellectu et methodo*", p. 12. See *Insight*, pp. 246-257.

[9]W.D. Hughes, O.P., trans., *Virtue*, Vol. 23 of St. Thomas Aquinas, *Summa Theologiae* (New York: McGraw- Hill, 1969), p. 217. This citation is a paraphrase of the Blackfriars edition's translation.

[10]Lonergan, "*De intellectu et methodo*", pp. 22-24. Many examples are given from fields as varied as philosophy, the theory of art, psychology, the history of religions, phenomenology and liturgy. Lonergan's solution to the problem of the chasm -- increased theological understanding -- derives from the twofold process of the way of discovery and the way of teaching, with special emphasis on the latter process that "turns" back to the truths of revelation.

[11]*Ibid*., p. 44. See *Insight*, chapters XI through XIV; these chapters contain a fuller treatment of the notions of knowing, of reality, and of objectivity.

[12]*Ibid*., p. 62. There follows in Lonergan's lecture an example of a dialectical argument that while illuminating is not germane to our topic.

CHAPTER VI

THE CONCERN FOR THE PLACE OF HISTORY
IN THEOLOGICAL DEVELOPMENT AND THE TURN
TO THE SUBJECT IN "*DE METHODO THEOLOGIAE*"

In the "*De intellectu et methodo*" of 1959, we saw Lonergan's emerging concern for the place of history in a theological procedure. In the theological illustration of his five rules pertaining to a general method for science, his focus in the fourth rule was on the use of categories of history in the systematization of theology. Guidelines were given for reaching an historical understanding in any science. There also arose a comparison between historical and speculative theology. If we separate these two, then positive theology loses its proper method, and the nature of speculative theology is corrupted.

"The Philosophy of History"

In an introductory lecture for the year at the Thomas More Institute, Montreal, on September 23, 1960, Lonergan gave an address titled, "The Philosophy of History".[1] This lecture is important for us to consider because it reveals his thinking about history as of 1960, and because here we see him wrestling with the issues generated by historical scholarship for theology that prompts his alterations in the analytic/synthetic procedures. The first part of the lecture is on the subject, "history". The second part is on the topic, "philosophy of".

By history two quite different things can be meant, the history that is written, and the history that is written about. There are three kinds of history that is written: occasional, technical, and explanatory. Occasional history bears on a particular issue. So Herodotus wrote his nine books to explain why the Persians fought the Greeks; Gibbon wrote on the decline and fall of the Roman empire.[2]

Technical history, as a scientific subject, had its principal development in the nineteenth century. History begins as belief. As conflicting testimonies arise, history shifts from a collection of beliefs to something analogous to an empirical science. This kind of historian is not simply a shrewd believer sizing up testimonies, but something like a scientist seeking an understanding of all the traces of the past that are existing in the present.[3]

Technical history differs from the empirical sciences. Historical understanding is not of general laws, but of the particular and concrete. So the historian cannot check his understanding of a case by appealing directly to other cases, as for example, the physicist can. On the other hand, the historian does achieve understanding analogous to empirical science's understanding insofar as the historical interpretation of a period presents something of a coherent picture. Lonergan illustrates this point from doctrinal history, from his own historical work on operative grace in the writings of St. Thomas. While this work does not give an absolutely certain conclusion about the views that St. Thomas held when he finished writing on operative grace, it does provide an interlocking of data that is difficult to interpret in a different way.[4]

Technical history has a weakness. When there is not enough data regarding some era, the abiding temptation of the historian is to fill in the blanks. The attitudes of historians to this weakness of technical history differ. Some say that history is a limited undertaking, that we do not try to answer all questions. A second view is that of relativism, that there are several histories insofar as history is not simply the strict technical history, but depends upon the point of view of the historians. A third view comes from Bultmann who maintains that a person's interpretation of history depends upon his philosophic assumptions.[5]

Explanatory history seeks to overcome the weakness of technical history. The method of empirical sciences is like a pair of scissors with a lower blade (proceeding from the data) coming together with an upper blade (the theoretical understanding expressed in a system). Explanatory history asks whether it is possible to go beyond the sure points where the data interlock in technical history to a systematic type of bridge between these points achieved by the introduction of an upper blade into historical method. In particular fields, that is not only possible but already achieved. For example, it is possible in a limited field such as chemistry, biology, or medicine to write an explanatory history because these are sciences on which everyone agrees. So as developments occur, consensus about the developments will emerge within the history of fields where everyone accepts the developments in the empirical sciences themselves.[6]

The problem becomes more complex when we ask about the history of philosophy. Any sufficiently developed philosophy will supply an upper blade for the explanatory history of philosophy, creating a philosophy of the philosophies. The trouble is that there are many of these philosophies, and the debate here obviously shifts. It is not to be settled so much by historical criteria as by the debate between the philosophies themselves.[7]

There is a further complication when you come to the history of religions, of arts, of cultures, of literatures. The further complication is not only that there are many types of religious beliefs, but that the concreteness of the beliefs sets up a resistance to systematic conceptualization which is the essence of such subjects as mathematics and physics.[8]

Given these problems about providing an upper blade for some kinds of history, is it possible for there to be an upper blade for general history? Sociology and its statistical procedures could provide a higher level control, but at times it uses categories that are philosophical rather than sociological in the proper sense. Toynbee suggested that the unit of historical study be "civilization" as an upper blade in explanatory history. The trouble with Toynbee is that he does not use categories belonging to the systematic conceptualization that exists in explanatory science. The difficulty that has been conspicuous for explanatory history, then, has been a problem of relativism. This relativism becomes apparent in dated history ("That was a fine historical work, but for 1850; it doesn't count any more"), or in national history.[9]

Lonergan now leaves his discussion of history to focus on the notion of philosophy as it relates to history. Ordinarily philosophy is considered as something in its own right, such as logic or epistemology or ethics. When we speak of philosophy *of* history, it is one member of a species or genus. What is this "philosophy of"? In a general way, philosophy means love of wisdom. Wisdom is the ordering of all. So wisdom as such is concerned with universal order and judgment, but it has applications to particular fields. Precisely because it is universal and ultimate, it will have its participation in such fields as science, nature, religions, history. Hence, there arises philosophy of various subjects.[10]

If philosophy is incorrectly conceived, then it is difficult to reach the kind of wisdom that finds its applications in particular fields. The problem with a deficient notion of wisdom is that it affects the notion of a system. Lonergan's model for constructing a system is not Euclid but St. Thomas. Euclid starts from a set of definitions and axioms. St. Thomas sets up an ordered series of questions and responses. This difference in approaches explains what Lonergan was doing in the *"De intellectu et methodo"*. For Aquinas, a system consists in a basic group of operations that can be combined and recombined in various ways, and the various combinations can handle all the questions that arise. Far from the static notion of system found in Euclid, this notion of system can be applied to concrete, human developments, as Piaget has done in child psychology. Philosophy can be conceived as a basic group of operations, and the basic group of operations is experiencing, understanding, and judging. The understanding can be differentiated and you get different kinds of combining experiencing, understanding, and judging.[11]

The problem is to bring the two discussions together, the first on history that is written (occasional, technical, explanatory), the second, on philosophy as a reflection on the history that is written and the history that is written about.[12]

Several notions emerge when reflection on history occurs on the philosophic level. The first of these is the notion of historicity. Just as a human being is a subject known and constituted by consciousness, so also a human being is known and constituted in his humanity by historicity, by the historical dimension of his reality. This is the shift that transfers the focus of philosophy from substance to the subject. A person's memory of himself is constitutive, a fundamental determinant, of what a person does. So history becomes an objectification of the existential memory of a people, of their self interpretation.[13]

Another notion coming from philosophic reflection on history is dialectic. Dialectic is the working out of a fundamental opposition between what are called positions and counterpositions. Positions express the dynamic structure of the subject *qua* intelligent and *qua* reasonable. Counterpositions contradict that structure. Whenever a person holds something at variance with his intelligence and judgment, it involves a tension that is a principle of change. The effect of dialectic is not simply a matter of changing affirmations about propositions, but a development in the subject himself. Dialectic takes place not only within an individual, but between individuals, as in the Platonic dialogues, and when dialectic has its relevance to the total field of human development, then that is history.[14]

A third notion stemming from the philosophic reflection on history is of stages of consciousness. In order to have some exact knowledge of the movement from undifferentiated to differentiated consciousness, one has to draw on philosophic concepts. The movement from symbolic to discursive use of language, from mass society to the breaking forth of individualism are indications of the growth toward historicity. If differentiated consciousness is itself a product of the historical process, it becomes evident in a clear way that there is a dimension of human nature contained in historicity itself.[15]

At the end of the lecture, Lonergan reflects briefly about the theology of history. Theology, insofar as it is a science and is systematic, follows a basic group of operations. The basic group of operations are experiencing, understanding, and judging. The judging is of a different type from ordinary science because it involves beliefs. The understanding is a new type of inverse insight because of the mysteries. Just as there is a basic philosophic set of operations, so there can be a specialization into a basic set of theological operations. And then we proceed as before to have a mutual illumination of philosophy, theology, and history. The lecture concludes with the statement that there is a huge development within theology concerned with the evolution of dogma and the evolution of theology from history.[16]

What bearing do these reflections in 1960 about history have for the twofold analytic/synthetic procedures? We have seen that the 1959 *"De intellectu et methodo"* revealed the need for a linkage between history and systematic theology. But there Lonergan could only indicate the three aspects of the one methodical problem of theology (foundations, historicity, chasm). Here he took a closer look at the different kinds of history that is written, and showed that explanatory history is what theology needs to use for its prescientific investigations. When reflection about history occurs on the philosophic level, there emerge such notions as historicity, dialectic, and stages of consciousness, and these notions help explain what is going on in the development of dogma.

But some important questions now need to be answered. How does history perform its task for theology -- as part of the analytic process only, as part of the synthetic process only, as part of both, or as the 1957 *Divinarum personarum* would have it, as a separate way of ordering ideas alongside analysis and synthesis? Further, who is to perform the task of historical investigation for theology? Is it the job of dogmatic theologians, or of specialists such as exegetes and patristic scholars, or of the magisterium as it exercises its teaching role? Obviously, the task of history in theology raises serious questions about the function of the twofold process and the aims and procedures of the dogmatic and positive theologians. We see Lonergan addressing these problems as he further differentiates the role of the *via analytica* and the functions of the dogmatic and positive theologians.

THE PLACE OF HISTORY

The *De Deo Trino: Pars Analytica* of 1961.

In 1961, Lonergan published "for the use of students" his *De Deo Trino*, subtitled, *Pars Analytica*.[17] This work opens with an eight-page preface (pages 5-12) in which he distinguishes the aim, the proper object, and the method of the analytic process for theology. He has already stated in *Divinarum personarum conceptio analogica* of 1957 the aim, the proper object, and the method of the synthetic process. Here he wishes to explain that the analytic process is not only the "way of resolution" and the "way of discovery", but it is also an "historical way" in a special sense.

The analytic way is called a *via historica* inasmuch as it narrates not any discovery whatsoever, but only the discovery that a specific author makes according to the circumstances and particular influences attendant upon his work. What is significant here is that other sciences relegate the history of the science to an auxiliary discipline which is used by way of introduction to the science as it is taught in the synthetic process. Theology, on the other hand, treats its historical development in a different manner. Because divinely revealed truths contain something implicitly, no one can determine what is implicitly present except the one who has wisdom proportionate to this revelation, namely God. And this divine judgment is not left to exegetes or philosophers, but to the Church magisterium whose job it is to judge about the true sense and interpretation of sacred scripture (DB 1796, DS 3016). Finally, the magisterium exercises its office over the course of time, on specific occasions and in opposition to heresies, or in response to the love for truth that stimulates the promulgation of a new definition *de fide*. The mode of operation of the magisterium is historical. It is historical objectively inasmuch as within the historical process either heresies have arisen, or their refutation and condemnation, or the definition of the opposite truth, or that pure love of truth which without stimulus of an opposed error sometimes leads to definitions. It is historical subjectively inasmuch as all of these elements are investigated by the historical method. So the mode of operation is historical by which the magisterium is exercised, and equally is the mode of operation historical by which we determine how the magisterium arrives at the dogmas that the divinely revealed truths implicitly contain (DDT:PA, pp. 6-7).

The history that is spoken about in theology's analytic process is both doctrinal and sacred. It is doctrinal because this history evolves from revealed truths to dogmas; it is sacred because the process is governed by divine providence and by the special assistance that enables the Church to make infallible declarations in matters of faith and morals (DB 1839, DS 3073).

Doctrinal history must conform to all of the rules and precepts that guide a true work of history. Any historian collects, selects, orders, and judges his materials and thereby understands the matter he treats. The historian who sets out to write the theological history of doctrine must understand doctrine. The historian of doctrinal development would have to know how all of a doctrine's elements fit together, what opposes individual parts of a doctrine, and what would happen if this or that element had been ignored until the present.[18]

The history treated in theology's analytic way is also sacred history because the entire development of doctrine evolves from God's providence. It is true that everything mankind does is under the providence of God and is accomplished by God's intention. In other realms, however, we cannot understand clearly what God's intention is except in a general way. In doctrinal and sacred history, however, this obscurity is obviated. Since God does not permit evil except for a greater good and does not want heresies but permits them, then it follows that heresies are allowed in order that the greater good of Church dogma may emerge with its explicit expression of what is implicit in revelation (DDT:PA, p. 8).

Lonergan explains that his aim in the *De Deo Trino: Pars Analytica* is to expound the chief principles of trinitarian doctrine according to the analytic way. Because the theological analytic process proceeds through reason illumined by faith, it examines what the Word of God implicitly contains. It recognizes that the Word is not to be judged by any wisdom but divine wisdom. It accepts that this divine judgment is only manifested through the Church's magisterium. It proclaims that the magisterium only exercises itself within history and under historical conditions. So doctrinal and sacred history do not seek endless proofs, but easily collect and judge what elements are proper to theological history (DDT:PA, p. 9).

This understanding of the analytic process for theology says nothing other than what theologians down the ages have said and done. Theologians receive doctrine from four sources: scripture, Fathers, theologians, magisterium. They receive doctrine from scripture, not as understood in any fashion, but as it has been and is understood by the Church. They receive doctrine from the Church Fathers -- not as the Fathers discoursed about any matter, nor as one or another of them uttered a private opinion, but as they taught with moral unanimity. In a manner similar to that recounted about the Fathers, they receive doctrine from theologians praised by the Church. Finally, theologians receive doctrine from the magisterium that acts as a kind of ultimate and infallible judge in these matters. Although theologians receive doctrine from four sources, they do not receive four doctrines but one. For two millennia, theologians have received the same dogma communicated in the manner of expression used in their own day, and they have discovered underlying all of the various expressions the same meaning, the one view, the same dogma. The real issue, of course, is to discover how these dogmas that have unity and identity are consistent, mutually coherent, and can be investigated through the process of a single investigation.

In footnote six of page ten, Lonergan adverted to the problem of integrating biblical theology as it pertains to this doctrinal and sacred history. In order to integrate biblical theology with doctrinal and sacred history (instead of opposing it to traditional theology) we must understand what constitutes a mentality that is differentiated or undifferentiated. Even more, we must appreciate that the process of moving from undifferentiation to differentiation obtains as much from the side of the subject as from the side of the object. People who stress biblical categories as if they were sufficient for explaining doctrinal and sacred history do not understand these distinctions about differentiation. If the analytic process in theology is to accomplish its task, moreover, it must come to grips with the problems raised by positive studies whether they be biblical, patristic, medieval, or contemporary (DDT:PA, pp. 9-10).

The analytic process of theology is not all but only part of theology. Lonergan next outlines how the synthetic process uses an order inverse to that of the analytic process. The synthetic process described here is the same as outlined in the *Divinarum personarum*. It is called the "way of composition", the "way of teaching" and the "theoretical or speculative way". This last set of terms is new here and is not found in the explanation of the 1957 *via synthetica*. The synthetic way is called the "theoretical or speculative way" because it begins from the *priora quoad se*, proceeds according to its own proper principles which are not understood except by the learned and not learned except by the docile. It promises to the docile and confers on the learned this advantage, to be able to contemplate intelligible truth in a single view, when there would otherwise be only a certain multitude of truths that order does not unite and intelligibility does not illumine (DDT:PA, p. 11).

Lonergan completes his introduction to *De Deo Trino: Pars Analytica* by summarizing the differences between the analytic and synthetic ways. It is one thing to analyze, another thing to compose; one thing to discover, another thing to teach what was discovered; one thing to search through the history of discovery, another thing to stretch to that contemplation that perceives the fruit of the whole enterprise. Both of these processes have the same object: to attain an imperfect understanding of mysteries (DB 1796, DS 3016). Such is the goal and term of the analytic way, and the principle and beginning of the synthetic way. This imperfect understanding of mysteries is the proper object of theology. So people would gravely err who think that theology is not defined by its own proper object, that it does not possess its own kind of field, or that it invades, confounds, and corrupts studies that are philosophical, biblical, conciliar, medieval, or contemporary. Furthermore, we may conclude that biblical studies pertain to doctrinal and sacred history and constitute part of the analytic way to this extent -- that they are ordered and regulated for attaining the proper end of theology (DDT:PA, pp. 11-12).

Because the analytic and synthetic ways differ from each other, they should not be mixed together to the confusion of each. Indeed, it seems useful to treat them together at the same time. But a disputation about this usefulness would require an investigation into the whole theological method. Lonergan remarks that enough has been said, however, to conclude that it is an error to invert the synthetic way and then propose it as a continuation of the analytic way (DDT:PA, p. 12).

"De Methodo Theologiae"

The next work covered in this exposition is the graduate course, *"De methodo theologiae"*, which Lonergan taught in Rome in 1961-1962 and in 1963-1964. In the summer of 1962, he presented the same material as he had taught at Rome earlier in the year. The summer class was given at Regis College in Toronto with the title, "Method of Theology", and he taught not only what was presented in Rome, but added sections on positive and systematic theology, on meaning, on hermeneutics, and on history.[19] While this course contained nothing explicit about the analytic/synthetic process, it revealed Lonergan's thought that accounts for his move away from the earlier ways of conceiving theology's procedures.[20]

The absence of any explicit mention of doing theology according to analysis and synthesis is surprising in light of the earlier, extensive treatment given to the procedures -- and his later use of them until 1964 in the introduction to the trinitarian works that we will review in the next two chapters. Instead, there is a whole new range of concerns and questions that flow from the account of the development of dogma. Here we see him dealing with the problems he raised earlier: theology's foundations, its historical aspect, its practical need to bridge the gap between systematics and commonsense apprehensions. In addition, he remained true to the exigencies of the analytic/synthetic way while transposing these processes to a new level under the pressure brought to bear on theology by historical consciousness and by the findings of positive theology. Here he answered the problem of method, which is to join the commonsense apprehension (*priora quoad nos*) of revealed truth to the theoretic apprehension (*priora quoad se*) expressed in Church dogma. The way he accomplished this shift was by turning to the conscious subject and to the world of interiority that integrates the worlds of common sense and of theory.

In "*De methodo theologiae*", the concern of method was not simply the classical interest in the object of theology -- God and all things in their relation to God. The concern of method was for the subject operating in the worlds of community, theory, interiority; for the subject as intellectually, morally, and religiously converted; for the subject whose horizon is authentic or unauthentic.

The methodical consideration of objects is only through the subject's operations. Insofar as method considers objects, it is comparative, genetic, dialectical. Objects commonly are divided into material and formal. There are two ways of viewing the formal object, *de jure* and *de facto*. If one considers the formal object as it is *de facto* reached, then it is the object as reached through such and such a group of combinations of differentiated operations. This concrete consideration of the formal object is the methodological way (DMT I, pp. 29-30).

The *de facto* notion of theology makes room for an historical consideration. In an historical consideration of theology, there is the subject who in his differentiated operations makes statements that belong in a dogmatic-theological context. The problem of moving from the static arrangement of ideas according to analysis and synthesis into the dynamic, methodical ordering is the problem of working out some sort of a classification of a development.

Because the analysis of development in terms of operations is cumbersome, Lonergan put the matter of development on a new basis by reflecting on the human good, value, and meaning.

THE PLACE OF HISTORY

According to Aristotle and St. Thomas, the good is in things and is completely concrete. In virtue of social mediation of the human good, operation becomes cooperation (DMT I, pp. 57-66). Values in Lonergan's analysis are either originating or terminal. By orientation is meant the direction in which the use of liberty heads. The object of orientation and personal relations are terminal values. The orientation of liberty is the originating value. As Kant remarked, "The only thing that is simply good is a good will". In that sense, the orientation of the person is what is simply good because it is insofar as one has good will that the whole process will function. Finally, there are interpersonal relations that may arise from one's role in society. With this analysis, one has a concrete notion of the human good that can be specified and adapted to any particular situation (DMT I, pp. 67 60).

According to St. Paul, all people have sinned, introducing the surd into the human good. Sin heads for the breakdown of the human good. It operates by introducing the supernatural, faith, hope, and charity, that as elevating grace heads us toward eternal life, as healing grace counteracts the influence of sin in the social order. If we add one fundamental reflection to the outline above, we come to the basic problem that Lonergan was wrestling with in 1962. The additional reflection needed was about meaning (DMT I, p. 69).

Meaning is the formal element in the process of the human good from the originating value to the terminal values. Without meaning, there is no human cooperation except in the most elementary forms, not merely linguistic meaning, but symbolic, aesthetic, intersubjective meaning. Further, meaning develops. Human activity is constituted formally by the intentional, by meaning. When one moves to the point that the understanding of human activity is the understanding of these developing meanings, then one arrives at the viewpoint called *historical consciousness*. The viewpoint of historical consciousness has a tremendous importance in any effort to deal fundamentally with the problems of contemporary theology (DMT I, pp. 69-72).

THE ROAD TO LONERGAN'S *METHOD IN THEOLOGY*

As theology has been inundated with historical studies over the past fifty years, it has been increasingly disturbed by questions of meaning. For example, what is revelation? It is a new meaning added into human life. By bringing a new meaning into this process of the human good, one transforms something that is formally constitutive of that human good. This outline gives an indication of the human good and value, their formal constitution by meaning, and the problems posed for theology by the emergence of an historical consciousness that seeks an understanding of developing meanings (DMT I, pp. 72-73).

The second chapter of "*De methodo theologiae*" is on two problematics. The first problematic pertains to theology as a science with the root of the problem based in three pairs of antithetical worlds: between the sacred and the profane, the subject and the object, common sense and theory. A "world" is a field of possible objects. By introducing the notion of mediation, Lonergan shows that when the analysis of human development runs into the limits exemplified by these antithetical worlds, then the classification of development can be made in terms of the dynamism, structure, and specialization of human consciousness.

Lonergan introduces the notion of mediation as a means of classifying development. An example of mediation occurs in the writing of history. Writing history is the commonsense type of understanding -- a specialization of intelligence that deals with the particular and the concrete. If the historian also knows economics, he will be able to understand elements in the historical data that otherwise he would miss. So the historian's knowledge of history becomes more full simply by the co-presence of another development. This is the fundamental meaning of the word, mediation. We know the visible world, the world of community, by living in it. But insofar as we know the human sciences and philosophy, we can have our knowledge of community mediated by theory. Again, our theory can get into ultimate problems. We can mediate theory by interiority, reaching down to the fundamental operations involved in knowing anything. In theology, we can mediate our theory by interiority, and then we are raising the question of method in theology (DMT I, pp. 96-99).

THE PLACE OF HISTORY

The analysis of human development in terms of spontaneous operations runs into a limit, and then we must investigate the dynamism, structure, and specialization of consciousness. The *dynamism* of consciousness leads to a differentiation between operations that regard the ultimate, and on the other hand, ordinary activity. The *structure* of consciousness leads to a distinction between the purely objective world and the subject as subject. Whenever one is operating, one is present to oneself. The subject as present to himself is not present as object. And when he objectifies himself, he is not only present to himself as object but also as subject. A *specialization* of consciousness leads to a differentiation between the world of common sense and the world of theory. It is through the dynamism, structure, and specialization of consciousness that we are able to reach a classification of development (DMT I, pp. 100-102).

The second problematic is for theology to explain the transition from the world of community to the world of theory in the evolution of dogmas. In order to meet the challenges posed by the three antitheses, the theologian must obtain a coherent set of basic terms. There are limits to the Aristotelian approach. Modern human sciences, moreover, seek the empirical intelligibility of things human as *de facto* they occur. Furthermore, historical consciousness is opposed to classical culture and shifts from man as substance to man as subject, from the ideal order to what *de facto* is. This transposition, from the classical way of seeing science and philosophy as related to theology, to the empirical scientific model and intentionality analysis of *Insight*, was pivotal to the emerging changes in theology's procedures (DMT, pp. 140-153).

The part of the course that compares and contrasts theological operations to all other operations is extensive. After some preliminary distinctions about common sense, the systematic exigence, the critical exigence, and the self-correcting process of learning, there are comparisons between theology, faith, and human knowing. Germane to our topic are the transition from faith to theology (a process that illustrates nine sets of opposites); the transition from the exegete's method to the dogmatic theologian's method; the different ways that the exegete and the dogmatic theologian use scripture.

A. The Transition from Faith to Theology

In the transition from faith to theology there are listed nine sets of opposites based on Lonergan's discussion of such thinkers as Husserl and Heidegger, Jaspers, Sartre, Marcel, Nietzsche and Cassirer. The nine contrasts are between the implicit and the explicit. One arrives at the *terminus ad quem* in two steps: *quid sit* and *an sit*. Note, however, that one moves from one world to the other not because of one single question. To effect the movement there is required a whole series of questions. And it is the task of meeting the whole series of questions in one coherent set of basic statements that is the movement from the world of faith to the dogmatic-theological context. So there is an upper circle that represents the dogmatic-theological context, and a lower circle that is the world of faith -- from revelation, the kerygma, the believers in the Catholic Church. Because theologians are also believers, they belong to both worlds, and integrate the two worlds within their own interiority (DMT II, p. 51).

Historical investigations into the development of the doctrine of grace by Landgraf and of freedom by Lottin show that the transition from the world of faith to the world of theory is a transition from the implicit to the explicit. It is one thing for the development of dogma to occur; it is another thing to discover the development. The two are distinct (DMT II, pp. 52-56). Examples of the process of going from what is implicit to what is explicit are given by comparing the patient and the doctor, the witness and the judge. The doctor and the patient are in two contexts: the systematic context learned by the doctor in medical school, the commonsense context of the man who is ill. This example shows that one and the same reality can be transposed from the commonsense mode of apprehension to the theoretic mode. Thus one can use another type of knowledge to attain a more accurate type of knowledge in a different world (DMT II, pp. 56-59).

B. The Transition from the Exegete's Method to the Dogmatic
   Theologian's Method

The exegete gets his questions from the scriptures themselves. He
wants to tell us as much as John or Matthew has to tell us about our Lord.
The exegete's purpose is to remain within the world in which the text was
written and to tell us about that as much as possible in the terms of the text
itself (DMT II, pp. 64-70).

The dogmatic theologian gets his questions from the later dogmatic-
theological context. He is out to understand problems such as how we
should conceive the consciousness of Christ. When one is transposing
from one world to another, then one's questions come out of the world one
is heading for. And the criteria for what an answer is come out of that
theoretical world. And one's appeal to scriptures is an appeal to what may
be very fragmentary and minute points in scripture. But it has to be
decisive. And the decisive point is not in terms of experience, something
that gradually builds up as one understands John's way of talking. The
appeal to scripture is decisive if we can make a judgment based on
sufficient evidence. So the dogmatic theologian's question comes from the
contemporary dogmatic context, but the answer is sought in the sources
of revelation -- not by attempting to reenact the experiences, thoughts, or
sensibility that lie behind the words of the scriptures, but in taking the
scriptures as true, and finding in them precise elements that settle one way
or another the questions arising from the dogmatic-theological context
(DMT II, p. 70).

We can now ask where the dogmatic-theological context comes
from. It is a matter of summing up, putting together all the little transitions
that have occurred for the last nineteen hundred years. The dogmatic-
theological context that has gradually built up is the development of dogma
and of theology. And each phase of that development consists in a
transition from the world of faith to the world of theory. The best way to
understand the dogmatic-theological context and its development is to
study questions at the time they were new. In going through a question

historically, studying the time at which the transition was made from the world of faith to the world of theory is the best way to understand what exactly is contained in the world of theory, what is the exact content of dogma, and what were the problems left over for the theologians later to solve (DMT II, pp. 72-76).[21]

C. The Dogmatic Theologian's Use of Scripture.

The dogmatic theologian presupposes that the exegete has arrived at the meaning of the author in the sense intended by the sacred writer. He then makes use of heuristic definition. That is, the dogmatic theologian starts out with a definition that is constituted by a question, or as is said algebraically, "let the unknown be 'x'". For example, in John's Prologue, the word "*Logos*" appears four times. By substituting "x" for the word, *Logos*, we can run through a series of assertions that occur in the Prologue about the *Logos*. The advantage of the heuristic type of procedure is that it escapes revision by the future developments of biblical scholarship. Moreover, the obscure is reduced to the clear (DMT II, pp. 87-89).

D. New Material in the 1962 Regis College Lectures

The last six lectures of the 1962 Regis College tapes contain new material not presented in the Latin notes reported in "*De methodo theologiae*". In this new material, there is a lecture on positive and systematic theology, one on meaning, two lectures on hermeneutics, and two on history.

Positive theology as conceived here is concerned with the relation between the contemporary context and the sources of revelation, as well as with the further development of the contemporary context. Systematic theology as methodical relates the contemporary context to theology's end -- increased understanding. Insofar as systematic theology is methodical, it says that theologians not only have minds and faith, but know exactly what that mind is and what its faith is (DMT II, pp. 110-115).

The next lecture treats four types of meaning: linguistic, intersubjective, aesthetic, and symbolic. We have already seen that Lonergan wanted to work out a way of classifying development that would handle methodically theology's problem of the evolution of dogma. Instead of basing his classification on operations, he turned to the human good, value, and meaning to account for the development of dogma. While these preliminary statements on meaning are interesting to the historian of Lonergan's thought, particularly because they are used so extensively later in *Method in Theology's* chapter three, "Meaning", we can omit further consideration of them because they do not contribute directly to our topic of Lonergan's use of the analytic and synthetic processes in theology.

The next two lectures are on hermeneutics (that deals with the general principles of the meaning of a text) and exegesis (that deals with the application of those principles to particular cases). The three basic exegetical operations are described: (a) understand the text; (b) judge how correct one's understanding of the text is, and (c) state what one judges to be the correct understanding of a text. After an explanation of the components of each of these operations, the lecture ends with some remarks about basic context.

The final two lectures are on history. After distinguishing between the history that is written about and the history that is written, Lonergan explains existential history (the commonsense knowledge of the past that makes social continuity possible) and narrative history (that thematizes many partial views about the past into a unity -- and so is explanatory, artistic, ethical, apologetic, prophetic, and existential). Critical history revises narrative history by proceeding from the sources critically, that is, by scrutinizing them for authenticity and trustworthiness, and by understanding them. The understanding of sources can be mediated by science and by a philosophy, a theology, a religion. This understanding is communicated not abstractly but in the concrete narration of events. So the historian does not operate on any theoretical level, but his type of intelligence is the common-sense specialization of intelligence in the concrete and particular and practical (DMT II, pp. 175-177).

E. The Methodical Classification of Historical Studies

There are various ways in which history is done and the results of these various methods need to be distinguished. The methodical classification of historical studies breaks into eight divisions: (1) common historical research; (2) historical essays; (3) history and science; (4) history and philosophy; (5) history and tradition; (6) history and religion; (7) history and apologetics; (8) theological mediation of history.

After defining common historical research, the historical essay, and after examining their relationship, Lonergan shows the mutual dependence between history and the human sciences. Human science studies human data, and most of the data are in the past, so historical data are invoked. With this we have a mutual dependence, namely, the development of human sciences depends upon historical knowledge, and inversely, the history of the science can be written only by a person who knows the science (DMT II, pp. 192-195).

There is a mutual dependence between history and philosophy. The basic context of our starting point is that there are worlds of community, theory, interiority, that each person in the world of community is an instance of interiority. Insofar as a person has arrived at self-appropriation, one knows the potentialities of anyone. Such a person knows that knowing is a compound of experiencing, understanding, and judging, and that there is a further dimension added on by divine faith. One knows just what the effects of horizon and unauthenticity and the need of conversion are and how the whole outlook is changed just by varying one of these factors in the subject (DMT II, p. 196). Insofar as one thinks of history as simply a collection of data, then it remains just a collection of data. What is the methodological possibility of doing more than that? It is that we possess a fundamental understanding of man. Anyone who writes the history that is written about has to be human. Anyone who is human has some knowledge of man from self-appropriation. But the purely positive inquiry by itself does not take one beyond enumeration (DMT II, p. 197). The upper blade of method is the contribution of a critical philosophy to historical method. What one knows through self-appropriation is relevant to understanding the people who are written about by historians. It is relevant to understanding the historian who does the writing and to understanding the critics of the historian. Critical philosophy adds a normative element all along the line, the normative element that is implicit in such notions as horizon, authenticity, and conversion (DMI II, p.198).

The 1962 Regis lectures contain additional comments on the relationship between history and tradition, religion, apologetics, as well as reflections on the theological mediation of history. While not directly germane to the topic of analysis/synthesis in theological method, they reveal Lonergan's full attention to the historical dimension that had been passed over in the way theologians of an earlier era had theorized about theology's aims and procedures.

In the 1954 article, "Theology and Understanding", Lonergan asked four contemporary methodological questions that demonstrated his awareness of the wide range of data and methods of positive theology. He distinguished between speculative and positive theology, but he did not functionally interrelate them. Functional interrelation took place in the realm of speculative theology in its twofold *via resolutionis* and *via compositionis*. While the functional relationship in speculative theology came from the faith of the theologian, still the resolution/composition procedures moved along the Aristotelian track of premises to conclusions.

In the 1957 *Divinarum personarum conceptio analogica*, there was no mention of positive theology. Instead of linking up positive and speculative theology, Lonergan added to the analytic/synthetic processes the "third, historical process". Because the twofold way operated in a

185

speculative context devoid of concern for history, analysis and synthesis were seen as linear. At any given moment, synthesis explained what had already been understood, and analysis set out to gain further understanding. The movement was from truth to understanding and back to revealed truth. The historical process added the notion of recurrence to the analytic/synthetic movement.

The *Divinarum personarum* not only introduced the idea of recurrence in the historical process, it expressed an increasing attention to the historical dimension of the human. In the physical sciences, the *quoad nos* is univocal. But in the human sciences, there are as many instances of the *quoad nos* as there are cultures. We see here as well a shift from the concern for reaching understanding by moving from premises to conclusions. The turn is to a concern for moving from *problems* (such as those generated by the desire to understand the development of dogma) to their *solutions*, whether transcultural, theological, or dogmatic. This shift to a more holistic procedure indicated the evolving awareness of a need to attend to historical consciousness.

In his 1960 lecture, "The Philosophy of History", Lonergan showed his expanded interest in the role of history, examining both hermeneutical problems and three notions stemming from the philosophic reflection on history: historicity, dialectic, and stages of consciousness. These reflections germinated the further inclusion of history in theological method that showed up in 1961.

In the 1961 *De Deo Trino: Pars Analytica*, the primary focus shifted from the synthetic procedure spotlighted in the 1957 *Divinarum personarum* to the analytic process. Here the *via analytica* is also designated as the *via historica*. The addition of this designation indicated a shift toward a fuller integration of the original historical dimension and function with the analytic/synthetic movement. The *via analytica* used to be formulated as the work of the individual theologian or school that passed from the revealed truths to the imperfect understanding that was available at the time. Here the *via analytica* became much more the movement of history itself. Now called for the first time a *via historica*, it was seen as the several culturally conditioned exercises of the magisterium in concrete historical circumstances. It was now the role of the *via analytica* to discover "the same dogma, the same meaning and the same view" (DB 1800, DS 3020) that is present in the cultural diversity of dogmatic formulations. Still, the earlier view of the *via analytica* was not entirely abandoned, so its function as recounted here was ambiguous. The problem that remained was how to differentiate and distinguish the aims, proper object, and methods of positive and dogmatic theology.

In the 1961 *"De methodo theologiae"*, Lonergan makes what seems like a quantum leap in his methodological thinking when he turns his attention to the subject, who in differentiated operations dwells in a dogmatic-theological context that makes possible a *de facto* notion of theology that empowers an historical consideration of theology. When one realizes that the understanding of human activity is the understanding of developing meanings, it becomes clear how the viewpoint of historical consciousness finds the analytic/synthetic account of theology's tasks to be too abstract, too undifferentiated and static to work out a classification of development, too broad to distinguish the methods of positive and dogmatic processes.

In order to understand more fully how Lonergan understands the theory of history during this period as it relates to theology, we can examine his critique of Emerich Coreth in the 1963 article, "Metaphysics as Horizon."[22] The critique challenges Coreth's view of metaphysics in its subjective pole, but the substance of the argument pivots on the issue of history. According to Lonergan's account of intentionality analysis, the structure of human consciousness, particularly as based on the pure and unrestricted desire to know, generates a pure metaphysics, or a pure account of what it means to be a human person -- hence, he agrees with Coreth about the objective pole of the horizon of metaphysics, as about being. But the account is abstract. It is abstract because it does not take into account what is concretely going on in the human person. Lonergan wrote that "Metaphysics, as about being, equates with the objective pole of that horizon . . . ."[23] The horizon referred to here is the pre-thematic, underlying horizon of all horizons which generates a tension between present achievement and the desire toward the future. And this tension is the source of new questions. We notice a gap between the horizon of being itself, which is always unthematically co-posited, and the particular horizon which is always limited, in which any person at any given moment is operating -- and this tension is the source of new questions. Transcendental method provides the thematization of this gap as the source of new questions.

Lonergan says that the subjective pole of metaphysics as science can quite legitimately be abstract when one is mediating the immediacy of latent metaphysics, "but is to be removed when one is concerned with the total and basic horizon".

> In the concrete, the subjective pole is indeed the inquirer, but incarnate, liable to mythic consciousness, in need of a critique that reveals where the counterpositions come from. The incarnate inquirer develops in a development that is social and historical, that stamps the stages of scientific and philosophic progress with dates, that is open to a theology that Karl Rahner has described as an *Aufhebung der Philosophie*. The critique, accordingly, has to issue in a transcendental doctrine of methods with the method of metaphysics just one among many and so considered from a total viewpoint.[24]

When Lonergan refers to history, it is not the consideration of history as a discipline, but rather the whole notion of historical consciousness, that the human person, when considered according to the method of dialectic, is constituted as a particular inquirer within a horizon which is both fraught with bias as well as with a manifestation of the authentic spirit of inquiry that constitutes the normative achievement of human progress. So the concrete reality of the person is always in tension between the tendency toward authenticity and withdrawal from authenticity. Dialectic refers to two co-equal principles that are united in the single subject, but are not necessarily correlated in any way. For example, people notice in themselves a principle of spontaneous intersubjectivity, on the one hand, an orientation by our biology so we seek in the outer world the satisfaction of our largely biologically based needs. On the other hand, we recognize a principle of intelligence, the pure, unrestricted desire to know. Both of these principles are characteristically human, and they generate a kind of dialectic such that they give two characteristically human ways of knowing. The tension between spontaneous intersubjectivity and the intelligent, self-transcending dynamic of intentionality that takes us into the world of being, a world mediated by meaning and motivated by value -- this tension is the source of history.

History is precisely the account of the interrelationship of these two principles that are operative and that generate the concrete reality of historical inquiry. Lonergan's contention is that authenticity is achieved as a withdrawal from unauthenticity, so that the basic human reality is reality as a dialectical mixture where the tendency toward biological extroversion and the need to secure our well-being in the world interferes in some measure with the intelligent, self-transcending dynamic of questioning. The human subject is concretely caught in bias, so that authenticity, then, is achieved as a kind of withdrawal from the biased state that humans find themselves in. And it is the tension of withdrawal and giving oneself over to the cycles of progress and decline which are the concrete source of history.

In order to take account of the concrete reality of this dialectic, there is a need to examine authenticity in subjects as well as in historical structures, an authenticity or withdrawal from authenticity which is the source of progress as well as decline. And an account of the history of theological ideas is going to have to take account of the possibility of dialectic, that people are falling into counterpositions such that when they articulate their own interior life, their account is biased. Lonergan observes that differences in articulations can be grounded in a fourfold set of methodological heuristics: the classical, genetic, statistical, dialectic. Thus differences can be genetic (one position can be related to another as earlier to later); they can be classical (differences can be related as an ideal expectation); they can be statistical (actual occurrence might in fact diverge, but in a non-systematic way, from ideal occurrence); they can be dialectical (differences can be grounded in the fact that people are living out of an unauthentic subjectivity, therefore, out of an unauthentic world view which has not fully moved into the world mediated by meaning and motivated by value). So dialectic has to be part of every account one gives of the history of ideas, otherwise it would be possible to take contradictory positions as genetically related.

To round off this section on the theory of history, it is noteworthy that counterpositions, in Lonergan's view, are intrinsically contradictory, they are always caught in a tension between intelligence and unintelligence. So intelligence is always working in some fashion to reverse counterpositions. Usually counterpositions reverse themselves by generating such internal tensions within the individual or society that the tensions can no longer be held together, therefore the counterposition collapses, and a new one has to be built up. Hence, Lonergan distinguishes between the longer and shorter cycles of decline. The point is that eventually counterpositions, unauthentic subjectivity, are going to tend toward their own self-destruction. These insights about the issues for theology generated by historical consciousness now find their application in Lonergan's observations about the analytic and synthetic procedures in the revised 1964 trinitarian texts. In dealing with historicity and the account of the development of dogma, we will see the reflections of the 1961 "*De methodo theologiae*" transpose the *via analytica* into dogmatics, and the *via synthetica* into systematics -- a clear anticipation of what eventually becomes functional specialization in *Method in Theology*.

NOTES

CHAPTER VI

[1]Bernard J.F. Lonergan, S.J., "The Philosophy of History", mimeographed edition (Montreal: The Thomas More Institute for Adult Education, 1960). These notes were typed from a tape recording and are available in xerox form at the Lonergan Research Institute of Regis College, Toronto.

[2]*Ibid.*, p. 1.

[3]*Ibid.*, pp. 1-2.

[4]*Ibid.*, pp. 2-3.

[5]*Ibid.*, pp. 3-4.

[6]*Ibid.*, p. 5.

[7]*Ibid.*, p. 5.

[8]*Ibid.*, pp. 5-6.

[9]*Ibid.*, p. 7.

[10]*Ibid.*, p. 8.

[11]*Ibid.*, p. 9.

[12]*Ibid.*, pp. 9-10.

[13]*Ibid.*, pp. 10-11.

[14]*Ibid.*, pp. 11-12.

[15]*Ibid.*, p. 13.

[16]*Ibid.*, p. 14.

[17]Bernard J.F. Lonergan, S.J., *De Deo Trino: Pars Analytica* (Rome: Gregorian University, 1961). Since there are frequent references to this text, we will note the citations directly in the body of the chapter with the abbreviation (DDT:PA) and the page number.

[18]*Ibid.*, pp. 7-8. See *Insight*, chapter XVII on the nature and truth of interpretation.

[19]Bernard J.F. Lonergan, S.J., *"De methodo theologiae, notae desumptae ab alumnis"*: (Rome: Gregorian University, 1962). The twenty lectures for the 1962 summer course at Regis College were transcribed from the tapes by John Brezovec and made available to the Lonergan Research Institute of Regis College, Toronto, in 1980. Lecture 15 is on positive and systematic theology; lecture 16 is on meaning: lectures 17 and 18 are on hermeneutics; lectures 19 and 20 are on history. References will be to the lectures of the 1962 summer institute, Regis college, "Method of Theology", as they were transcribed by John Brezovec. Since there are numerous references, they will be made directly in this text with the abbreviations (DMT I) or (DMT II), to indicate the first or second volume of the Brezovec transcript.

[20]The 1961-1962 Latin notes from *"De methodo theologiae"* contain two chapters. The first chapter is on method in general. The second chapter contains two sections. The first section is on theology as science and three fundamental antithetical worlds. The second section is on the theological problems based in these antithetical worlds. We will follow the organization of the Latin notes as we analyze the transcript of the 1962 Regis tapes of the first fifteen lectures on the method of theology.

²¹This was what was recommended in *"De intellectu et methodo"*, p. 8, when Lonergan noted that the important factor in the way of historical discovery for discerning development is a "turning point".

²²Bernard J.F. Lonergan, S.J., "Metaphysics as Horizon" in *Collection*, ed. Frederick E. Crowe, S.J. (New York: Herder and Herder, 1967), pp. 202-220.

²³*Ibid.*, p. 219.

²⁴*Ibid.*, pp. 219-220.

CHAPTER VII

THE 1964 REVISION OF THE *DE DEO TRINO: PARS ANALYTICA* THAT BECOMES THE *DE DEO TRINO I: PARS DOGMATICA*

Thus far we have seen that Lonergan's interest in theology and understanding was thematized in his 1954 review article, "Theology and Understanding". Although theology was seen as having two phases, the *via resolutionis* and the *via compositionis*, the former phase was viewed as only a preparation for the latter, more central task of theology. There were four methodological issues, however, that seemed to strain the capacity of the twofold way to carry the burden of theology's task. Central to these contemporary methodological issues was the place of history in theology.

In the Introduction to the 1957 text on the Trinity, *Divinarum personarum conceptio analogica*, Lonergan still saw the goal of theology to be achieved by a twofold process, now called the analytic and synthetic way. He tried to include history in the theological process by identifying a "third, historical process" by which analysis and synthesis accumulated theological understanding over the years. In the Introduction's consideration of the evolution of historical understanding in theology, an explanation was clearly needed to show how theology moves from the commonsense apprehension of revealed truth (*priora quoad nos*) to the theoretic apprehension achieved in Church dogmas (*priora quoad se*).

The 1958-1959 doctoral seminar, "*De intellectu et methodo*", continued Lonergan's treatment of his concern for theological understanding. There he transposed his concern into the context of methodology generally speaking and as it applied explicitly to theology. There he studied questions and responses, the series of questions and responses. This led him to a consideration of systems and to the criteria for a new ordering, as for example, when in theology the historical perspective is added to systematic procedures. There was identified a threefold problem of method arising from the development of a series of questions and answers: (1) foundations; (2) the chasm between simple faith and systematic presentations; (3) historicity. The solution to the problem of method was posited in wisdom. Yet the only meaningful solution to the problem of method arises when a cognitional theory has worked out the stages in the process of the development of human understanding. In a section that compared historical and speculative theology, he showed that if we separate these two, then positive theology loses its proper method, and the nature of speculative theology is corrupted. It is only the development of intellectual habits of the theologian that will integrate the various branches of theology rather than what is contained in diverse tracts of fundamental, apologetic, or dogmatic theology. Yet the key problem for him in 1959 was how to join systematic and historical thinking.

Although the key problem of 1959 was joining systematic and historical thinking, it is clear from Lonergan's reflections in the 1961 "*De methodo theologiae*" that the turn to the subject made possible an account of the development of dogma, and this account of historicity for theology generated new attention to the relationship between positive scholarship and dogmatic theology, focused new interest in the *analytic* part of theology regarding the transition from the exegete's method to the dogmatic theologian's method, and the dogmatic theologian's use of scripture. Just as a human being is a subject constituted by consciousness, a human being is also constituted in his humanity by historicity, by the historical dimension of his reality. Historical consciousness shifts from a consideration of the human person as substance to the human person as subject, from the ideal order to what *de facto* is. What makes the evolution of dogma possible is the transition from undifferentiated common sense to the intellectual pattern of experience. Once he had worked out such notions as horizon, authenticity, and conversion in a critical philosophy, he was able to show the transition from the commonsense apprehension of revealed truth to the theoretic apprehension enunciated in Church dogma by turning to the conscious subject and to the world of interiority that integrates the worlds of common sense and of theory. His work on the connection between history and theology, moreover, allowed him to explain what are some of the significant differences between the methods of positive and dogmatic theology. It is now possible to show how the seeds of thought sown in "De methodo theologiae" issued in new attention to dogmatics and the development of dogma.

The 1964 De Deo Trino I: Pars Dogmatica

In 1964, Lonergan published a second edition of the De Deo Trino: Pars Analytica and he changed the subtitle of the revised edition from "Analytic Part" to "Dogmatic Part".[1] The main difference between the revised and the first edition of this analytic part are found in pages 3-28, which contain the preface, the introduction, and the section on the dogmatic development. In the first edition, which we have just outlined, Lonergan distinguished and contrasted the aims and methods of the analytic process and the synthetic process in theology. In this second edition, he identifies the analytic way with dogmatic theology and the synthetic way with systematic theology. The development in his thought here is that he now includes the task of historical studies for theology within the function of dogmatics. But if historical investigation for theology is to be accomplished within dogmatics, then a differentiation is needed between the aim, the proper object, and the method of dogmatic theology and positive theology strictly speaking. We will study how he works out this differentiation first, and then return to a new section introduced in the revised 1964 edition, the one on dogmatic development, in order to see the implications for the analytic/synthetic procedures implicit in the joining of historical and systematic theology.

As Lonergan wrote in the 1964 edition of De Deo Trino I: Pars Dogmatica, theologians did not explore the distinction between dogmatic and positive theology much before this century. By the end of the sixteenth century, theology was called dogmatic in distinction to moral, and it was called positive as it was separated from speculative (systematic) theology. Of course this distinction does not adequately acknowledge the positive investigations of scholastic theology nor adequately distinguish positive from dogmatic theology. But Lonergan does not want to impugn his predecessors, as if they had spoken ineptly, since positive studies of medieval theology are rather recent. Those who not many decades ago spoke of positive theology sought an end that is dogmatic or at least apologetic rather than strictly positive (DDT:PD, p. 7, footnote 4).

In our era, after *Deus Scientiarum Dominus*, ecclesiastical studies flourished that intended not a dogmatic or a systematic end, but a positive one. But because realities change more rapidly than the names of realities, it frequently happens that either disputes arise in a confused way about realities or disputes are about mere names. Some seem to blame positive studies because they are not dogmatic. Others, from an opposite point of view, think that dogmatic studies ought not to use their own method but a positive method. And all of these viewpoints seem to miss a central awareness, namely, that evolution or progress consists in differentiation and integration. So in effect, from the common dogmatic-positive root there ought to spring up two kinds of study -- one more strictly dogmatic, the other more strictly positive. Indeed, these two kinds of study first evolve before being distinguished exactly, and are distinguished before they can be arranged in a mutually supportive way (DDT:PD, p. 7, footnote 4).

A. The Aim of Dogmatic Theology

Although Lonergan has already written about the aim of dogmatic theology in *De Deo Trino: Pars Analytica* of 1961, he wants to elucidate here the special sense in which what he has been calling the analytic process is different from the aim and method of positive theology. Dogmatic theology in the strict sense has one aim: to show how the dogmas defined by the Church are contained in the sources of revelation (DB 2314, DS 3886). The dogmatic theologian seeks the implications according to which dogmas are said to be implicitly revealed. But the approach must not be abstract -- that is, it must not attend to a doctrine as if it were pure, well-defined, changeless, and somehow existing independent from the human mind. Instead, the approach must be concrete, that is, organic, genetic, and dialectic. What is significant here after "*De methodo theologiae*" is that dogmatic theology's task is not solely concerned with a correct arrangement of ideas, but with an investigation of the ones thinking the ideas and the context out of which their thinking arose.

For the dogmatic approach to be *concrete*, it must take into account both those doing the thinking in a doctrinal development as well as the content of their thought. The approach is *organic* if in those who apprehend there are discerned many interconnected insights that modify and elucidate one another. It is *genetic* if the thinkers under consideration are arranged according to places and times so that as their apprehensions increase and evolve, they exhibit that understanding of faith, knowledge, and wisdom that the First Vatican Council praised (DB 1800, DS 3020). It is *dialectic* if the approach tracks down what is the doctrine opposed to the position being treated. And the approach is dialectic in the wider sense if it considers various authors opposed to one another, and in the narrower sense if it traces opposing views within the same author (DDT:PD, pp. 5-6).

The dogmatic approach must be concrete because doctrines do not evolve as some bare series of propositions, but are formed and perfected as they respond to questions, remove difficulties, and resolve problems. Since these questions and problems are not known except in the concrete, historical course of events, it follows that the doctrines corresponding to them ought to be investigated and learned according to the circumstances of their time and place. So the theologian who removes doctrines from their historical context to consider them abstractly makes a grave mistake because this abstraction creates other, new and difficult problems. For example, too many students have been misled into thinking that by a marvelous intuition they can see immediately in scripture something that emerged originally only with the passage of time and with huge effort; something that many resisted and many denied; something that is not grasped except by a few great minds, and that only gradually found acceptance in the Church (DDT:PD, p. 6).

B. The Aim of Positive Theology

The aim of positive theology is to provide a precise, detailed understanding of individual authors. Its goal is not to discover what individual authors have in common, but to set forth the meaning, mind, and doctrine of authors as individual, with their separate backgrounds, styles, interests, and temperaments.

The positive part of theology deals with documents and monuments of the faith; hence, it is biblical, conciliar, pontifical, patristic, medieval, and and contemporary. These major divisions are further multiplied by subdivisions as to time and place, relative authority of each author, and similar specific considerations. The positive inquiry is not designed to set forth what the researcher believes, but only to relate what sort of theology others once had. It does not write its monographs as if it would determine what the Church ought to teach or what the faithful ought to believe. The positive inquiry does not seek a picture of the whole culture -- but only an intimate knowledge of all the particulars of a given culture (DDT:PD, pp. 7-8).

The inquiry is called positive because of the method proper to it. It does not ask questions except those that arise from the evidence. It wants only the intelligibility perceived in the same evidence. It rectifies and accumulates its understanding only by the addition of new evidence or by a more careful scrutiny of the evidence it has. It asks about an individual document, who wrote it, what he wrote, where, under what circumstances, why, how, when.

It does not pass over the uncertain, the obscure, the exceptional in order to concentrate on the certain, the clear and the ordinary. Rather it gives greater attention to those points which show need of clarification. Its end is that the sense, the mind, the teaching of any author being studied should some day be brought to light in all its parts, according to all its aspects -- some day, not right now. And if, as the skill of investigators grows and enough time passes by and if almost innumerable studies should be made so that finally all the authors of some one past age would come to be known thoroughly, then indeed the particular spirit and almost the living image of that culture would seem to be reconstituted before our eyes. But the positive theologian wants that kind of overall view of the whole thing only if it arises from an intimate knowledge of all the individual facts.[2]

It is important not to confuse the part of positive theology's method with the whole method. What is proper to positive theology are only those things that made it both distinct and self-superintending. But these distinctions about positive method are not meant to be understood in an exclusive sense, as if positive theology were separate from the method common to dogmatic and systematic theology. These points distinguishing what is proper to positive theology are made to create a prior differentiation so as to make possible a later integration (DDT:PD, p. 8, footnote 5).

The proper object of positive theology is the intelligibility residing in individual historical events. The ancients have said that history cannot be a science since history is about single events, whereas science is about universals. But the positive scholar seeks in history the intelligibility that is present in single events. There exists a kind of global aspect of understanding and intelligibility that is indeed immersed in particularity, but in such a way that it can be perceived and described in particulars without excluding the possibility of its being removed from them and defined by universals. So the positive scholar seeks intelligibility residing in individual matters. The object of the positive method, then, needs to be carefully distinguished from the universal that is investigated in human sciences such as psychology, sociology, or economics. But there is a subtle difference between the proper object of positive theology and the proper object of the human sciences. These other disciplines seek principally laws that have universal validity and laws that are so cohesive with one another as to form a kind of system. This distinction is not obviated because the positive theologian can speak in generalizations, nor because human sciences use historical documents for discovering laws, nor because laws already discovered and established can be applied with great profit to understanding and interpreting historical documents. But the generalizations which the positive scholar expresses (like grammatical rules that undergo numerous exceptions) are not properly universals. For this reason, the empirical method is more wide open than the positive method. Both methods begin from evidence, understand through evidence, are confirmed in evidence. But the empirical method used by the human sciences goes on to laws and systems that must be formulated; positive method wants only to reach the intelligibility residing in particulars (DDT:PD, p. 9).

What about dogmatic theology? Dogmatics only draws its doctrines from the documents and monuments of the faith. But it is not interested in the particular meaning of this or that author. It deals with individual authors, events, works, but only as they are objects of faith. And the faith meant here is not solitary, the faith belonging to some individual, but it is the universal faith. This difference between positive and dogmatic theology as each relates to individual documents in different ways raises the problem of singularity. It is necessary to distinguish between two kinds of singularity: of the thing apprehended, of the one act of apprehension. Positive theology pays attention to both -- to know not only the particular items narrated by John or Paul, but also to penetrate the particular genius of Paul and understand how it differs from John's. Dogmatics only seeks the singularity of the apprehended thing. So dogmatic theology does not seek the singularity of an author as an end but only as a principle from which it can advance to its end. Dogmatics, moreover, does not want individual catholics to discard their own mind-set so as to clothe themselves in the mentality of Paul or John. But it does want all catholics to believe with their own mentalities the faith that John and Paul believed with their mentalities (DDT:PD, p. 10).

C. Difference Between the Methods of Positive and Dogmatic
    Theology

Differences in the ends and objects give positive theology a different
method from dogmatic theology. There are six differences that Lonergan
lists.

1. The positive method posits questions only as they arise spontaneously from the evidence itself. It does not proceed to a wider consideration
of its elements but limits its inquiry to sifting through the same evidence as
new insights gradually accumulate.

Dogmatic theology presupposes a wide scope for its consideration
of its elements. Its total problematic arises because different meanings are
what seem to be collected from scripture, the Fathers, the councils, the
theologians. Hence, positive and dogmatic theology each raise different
questions.

2. Positive theology exhibits extensive subdivisions because each
different genus or species of document requires a new specialization. This
is clearly necessary for the positive scholars since they only seek what is
particular to individuals.   It follows that positive theologians devote
themselves to narrow fields with strict boundaries which they are loathe to
violate. Thus the positive method seeks what is individual, what requires
narrow specialization, and what remains in a narrow category with strict
territorial limits.

Dogmatic theology seeks what is common and leaps over the limits
imposed by positive theology upon itself. It examines individual documents
not for themselves but to see connections, implications, consequences that
may reveal the common faith residing in diverse documents.

3. The positive method seeks to elucidate obscure, rare issues and
matters that are doubtful and uncertain.

Dogmatics seeks foundations for the definitions of faith from what is clear, ordinary, and certain. So the two methods usually investigate different materials. But even if they study the same evidence, the methods are different. Positive method seeks to attain at least sometime the meaning as fully determinate whereas dogmatic method seeks the lowest common denominator of meaning, but a meaning that is certain and clear.

4. This point has to do with anachronism. Positive method only uses categories contained in the documents under scrutiny. So it does not want to impose a contemporary mind-set or language on the materials it examines.

Dogmatics compares many authors, different eras and cultures, so it renders explicit what was implicit. Furthermore, Lonergan asserts that there are categories common to all people. The cultivated use these categories reflectively, explicitly, distinctly -- as St. Thomas used the categories of metaphysics to extend his understanding of theology. Primitives, on the other hand, use these categories indirectly, implicitly, and in a commonsense mode. Thus the sacred authors used images and parables, and symbolic, rhetorical language. So dogmatics is truly an interpretation and not the imposition of an alien mentality.

5. The positive method seeks that intelligibility which is found in the particular and not in the properly universal apprehension. While not seeking the laws and systems generated by the empirical method, it does not reach more unity than what is already present in the objects that it studies.

Dogmatics manifests in the evolution of a doctrine a particular process of universalization. Dogmatics does not purposely ignore the singularity of its objects, but because a common confession of a common faith surpasses the singularity of this or that apprehension, it pays more attention to what is common. So dogmas mutually intertwine both because all dogmas pertain to the one God and because the question to which they respond reveals a series, the solution of one question raising another. This is especially evident in trinitarian work. After the consubstantiality of the Son is defined, spontaneously there is a question whether the Holy Spirit is consubstantial to the Father. Therefore, after having acknowledged three who are consubstantial, there is a question about their real distinction which nonetheless does not take away that very consubstantiality. And after this distinction has been explained through processions, a question must be asked about the procession of the Holy Spirit. In all these points, questions concerning mystery come up that do exceed the created mind but in such a way nonetheless as to admit some imperfect, analogous, obscure understanding. And this understanding the dogmatic theologian leaves to the systematic theologian to discover and to develop (DDT:PD, pp. 11-13).

6. The positive method leaves some questions unanswered and some problems unsolved. It is patient and seeks only eventually to arrange all matters in a clear light.   Other questions it reduces to probable conclusions so that eventually it can arrive at which is certain.

The dogmatic theologian does not use the positive method that can be content with what is probable. For the dogmatic theologian, faith is most certain right now. The objects of faith have already been drawn from the sources with the assistance of the Holy Spirit. But what has already been done can hardly be said to be possible only in some very remote future. For this reason, the dogmatic part of theology needs its own proper method, a procedure that differs from the method of the positive part (DDT:PD. p. 13).

The method proper to dogmatic theology requires it to (1) posit its own questions; (2) distinguish its own specialization which is to gather into a unity that which for a different end may be divided into diverse fields by positive theology; (3) examine documents its own way; (4) use its own right to render explicit what was implicit; (5) move away from scrutiny of individual texts so as to say what is common, definitive, coherent, certain (DDT:PD, p. 14).

THE ROAD TO LONERGAN'S *METHOD IN THEOLOGY*

If the dogmatic part and the positive part are not distinguished from one another as to their end, object, and method, then confusion arises. Since the two methods are mutually opposed in many ways, it is clear how calamitous it would be to seek the dogmatic goal with a positive method or the positive goal with the dogmatic method. Through confusion they mutually destroy one another, yet through distinguishing one from the other, they can and ought to enrich each other (DDT:PD, p. 14).

Before we examine the section on dogmatic development to see the impact of these differentiations between dogmatic and positive theology, some observations are in order. Theology's use of history is different from that of other sciences because theology's prescientific stage contains something implicitly -- revealed truth in its commonsense expression. So history has the special task in theology of determining what is implicitly present in the sources of revelation. The office of judging the true sense and interpretation of these sources belongs to the magisterium, whose mode of operation is historical both objectively and subjectively. Because the magisterium exercises its function historically, equally is the operation historical by which we retrieve how the magisterium arrives at dogmas. And the task of discovering how the magisterium has reached its teachings belongs to dogmatics.

The important differentiation here is that dogmatics and positive theology have different aims and procedures. Once positive theology through biblical, patristic, conciliar scholarship has achieved its goal of probable conclusions about intelligibility in particular, specialized studies can show how the dogmas defined by the Church are implicit in revealed sources. Instead of dogmatics using an abstract approach, there is a new focus in the description of the dogmatic approach -- as concrete, organic, genetic, dialectic. The focus is on the thinkers instead of merely on their thought. This approach shows an awareness of the existential dimension to the function of dogmatics that seeks more than propositional truth in a vacuum, but the discovery of doctrines implicit in the sources of revelation, that evolved in response to human problems.

THE REVISION OF THE PARS ANALYTICA

D. Dogmatic Development

The 1964 edition of *De Deo Trino I: Pars Dogmatica* contains a new first section that is not present in the original, 1961 edition of the *De Deo Trino: Pars Analytica*. This new first section treats of dogmatic development. There are three parts to the section: (1) the four aspects of dogmatic development; (2) the relationship of these four aspects with one another; (3) six implications of these relationships. We will concentrate on the first and third parts where Lonergan ties in his differentiations about positive and dogmatic theology with the methodological problems raised in *"De intellectu et methodo"* in accounting for the development of dogma.[3]

Dogmatic development has four aspects: objective, subjective, evaluative, hermeneutical.

The objective aspect of dogmatic development contains two kinds of transition: (1) from one literary genre to another -- the scriptures aim at the whole person whereas the councils only want to enlighten the intellect; (2) from multiplicity to unity in the order of truth -- the scriptures present many truths whereas the councils express a single truth that is the foundation of many truths of scripture.[4] These transitions and how to make them were the domain of the foundational problem in *"De intellectu et methodo"*.

The subjective aspect of dogmatic development has to do with the many different patterns in which our conscious acts emerge. A basic distinction between undifferentiated consciousness (where the whole person is involved) and differentiated consciousness (where the person can operate on a single level) is operative here. The gospels correspond to the former level, dogma to the latter.[5] Corresponding to this subjective aspect is the notion of historicity in *"De intellectu et methodo"* that shows how the connection between various historical modes of conceiving doctrine depends upon a development of consciousness.

The evaluative aspect of dogmatic development arises from the human characteristic not only to act but also to reflect and to judge actions. So Lonergan comes to the question of the value of dogma. That value is sometimes challenged, for the gospels seem clear while dogmas seem obscure. But really the gospels are endlessly interpreted whereas dogmas, like Euclid's Elements, are so precise as to present almost no problem of interpretation. What explains this is that scholars, advanced in the intellectual pattern of experience, find the meaning of a dogmatic definition clear. But ordinary living is so tied to particular circumstances and human intentions as never to be reducible to the clarity of a definition of a theorem.[6] The problem of the chasm in "De intellectu et methodo" was how the theologian could bridge the gap between commonsense and theoretic apprehensions and maintain the value of theoretical consciousness.

The hermeneutic aspect of dogmatic development considers how a person's views about dogmatic development will influence his investigation. Since the human mind is not equally open to all ideas, correct apprehension must await conversion.[7]

There are serious disagreements among historians of dogma. These disagreements stem from erroneous cognitional theory, epistemology, and metaphysics that render dogmas unintelligible or unacceptable. Dogma emerges from the revealed Word of God when that Word is considered precisely as *true*. After some illustrations taken from the gnostics and some heretics, Lonergan says that the meaning of technical terms in expressing religious belief only makes sense to one who has correct cognitional theory and epistemology.[8]

If it were the Word of God, considered precisely as true, that led from the gospels to the dogmas, then it was the same Word from the same point of view that brought about the differentiation in consciousness. The bond that unites the subject's patterns of consciousness so that we can remain in the same world but shift from one pattern of consciousness to another is the Word as true. But different patterns of consciousness are bounded by different horizons. So there will be different expressions of the same truth. Just as the subject remains the same who moves in various states of consciousness, so the truth is the same that is expressed within one or another pattern of consciousness. The one simple remedy for dealing with the apparent discontinuity between the gospels and the dogmas is to pay attention to the Word as true.[9]

After a section on the relationship of the objective, subjective, evaluative, and hermeneutical aspects to one another, Lonergan outlines six implications of these relationships. Since our interest is in the functional connections between positive and dogmatic theology as they relate to the arrangement of ideas in the development of dogma, we will summarize the six implications of these relationships.

1. The movement of thought before the Council of Nicea has two distinct although related developments. One development is of doctrine; another is of the notion of dogmas, an implicit development. It could only be implicit, for in the field of intellect, something must first be accomplished before it can be methodically reflected upon and explained. These distinctions provide the foundation for the difference between positive theology (that investigates the specific elements of the development) and dogmatic theology (that originates as a discipline only after the notion of dogma has been thematized).

2. There are two types of doctrinal development: from obscurity to clarity (as was the emergence of the very notion of dogma), or from one kind of clarity to another (synoptic gospels about Jesus, conciliar definitions, historical investigations of dogmas -- all needed before the dogmatic development itself could be established). For this reason, the question of dogmatic development is in itself a rather recent one.[10]

3. An investigation on the pre-Nicene development requires distinguishing two developments not of the same kind, yet related as generic to specific (the development of the notion of dogma itself as related to the development of a specific dogma). Not all dogmas are equally relevant for understanding the two developments: the most relevant

dogmas are the ones that show how differently various authors understand the same thing.[11]

4. The two types of development require two different methods of inquiry. It is one thing to ask an author what he knew and quite another thing to ask what he did without knowing it. To answer the first question, you admit as evidence only what an author actually said; to answer the second requires a different method. Lonergan omits at this time a discussion of the various methods needed, and is content to say that no one is equipped to study dogmatic development whose understanding of dogma and of development is little better than those of the pre-Nicene authors themselves.[12]

5. The whole crux of the matter lies in the development of a new mode of understanding. It cannot be grasped by one who has never experienced a similar kind of development. Those who want only scriptural use of categories and language will agree with the earliest Judaeo-Christians in their expressions. Those perceptionists who see knowledge as a matter of looking will be in agreement with Tertullian instead of finding the root of their error in him. Those afraid of intellectually developed consciousness will brand propositional truth as nominalism or a product of a mythic mentality.[13]

6. Those not sufficiently helped by philosophical studies to develop, purify, and perfect their own capacity for understanding can be helped by a concrete historical investigation of the emergence of dogma as concretely understood at the time of its origin, and this may suggest how it can be properly understood now.[14]

THE REVISION OF THE PARS ANALYTICA

Concluding Overview

In the 1954 article, "Theology and Understanding", Lonergan asked four contemporary methodological questions that demonstrated his awareness of the wide range of data and methods of positive theology. He distinguished between speculative and positive theology, but he did not functionally interrelate them. Functional interrelation took place in the realm of speculative theology in its twofold *via resolutionis* and *via compositionis*. While the functional relationship in speculative theology came from the faith of the theologian, still the resolution/composition procedures moved along the Aristotelian track of premises to conclusions.

In the 1957 *Divinarum personarum conceptio analogica*, there was no mention of positive theology. Instead of linking up positive and speculative theology, Lonergan added to the analytic/synthetic processes the "third, historical process". Because the twofold way operated in a speculative context devoid of concern for history, analysis and synthesis were seen as linear. At any given moment, synthesis explained what had already been understood, and analysis set out to gain further understanding. The movement was from truth to understanding and back to revealed truth. The historical process added the notion of recurrence to the analytic/synthetic movement.

The *Divinarum personarum* not only introduced the idea of recurrence in the historical process, it expressed an increasing attention to the historical dimension of the human. In the physical sciences, the *quoad nos* is univocal. But in the human sciences, there are as many instances of the *quoad nos* as there are cultures. We see here as well a shift from the concern for reaching understanding by moving from premises to conclusions. The turn is to a concern for moving from *problems* (such as those generated by the desire to understand the development of dogma) to their *solutions*, whether transcultural, theological, or dogmatic. This shift to a more holistic procedure indicated the evolving awareness of a need to attend to historical consciousness.

THE ROAD TO LONERGAN'S *METHOD IN THEOLOGY*

In his 1960 lecture, "The Philosophy of History", Lonergan showed his expanded interest in the role of history, examining both hermeneutical problems and three notions stemming from the philosophic reflection on history: historicity, dialectic, and stages of consciousness. These reflections germinated the further inclusion of history in theological method that showed up in 1961.

In the 1961 *De Deo Trino: Pars Analytica*, the primary focus shifted from the synthetic procedure spotlighted in the 1957 *Divinarum personarum* to the analytic process. Here the *via analytica* is also designated as the *via historica*. The addition of this designation indicated a shift toward a fuller integration of the original historical dimension and function with the analytic/synthetic movement. The *via analytica* used to be formulated as the work of the individual theologian or school that passed from the revealed truths to the imperfect understanding that was available at the time. Here the *via analytica* became much more the movement of history itself. Now called for the first time a *via historica*, it was seen as the several culturally conditioned exercises of the magisterium in concrete historical circumstances. It was now the role of the *via analytica* to discover "the same dogma, the same meaning and the same view" (DB 1800, DS 3020) that is present in the cultural diversity of dogmatic formulations. Still, the earlier view of the *via analytica* was not entirely abandoned, so its function as recounted here was ambiguous.

In the 1964 *De Deo Trino I: Pars Dogmatica*, there was a major recasting of the *via analytica* that eliminated the ambiguity about its function. Here there was the notable evolution of the *via analytica* as indicated by its new name, the *via dogmatica*. The focus now was upon the distinction between positive and dogmatic theology. The dogmatic aim is to show how the dogmas defined by the Church are contained in the sources of revelation, so its method must be concrete, that is, organic, genetic, and dialectical. Positive theology has its own method and aims at the intelligibility immanent in the evidence of particular historical events and documents (and not in revealed truths). Instead of an exclusive concern for understanding the movement of ideas from premises to conclusions, there was a concern for seeing problems and solutions in their historical context.

In the section on dogmatic development in the 1964 *Pars Dogmatica*, Lonergan pointed out the key that made such an evolution possible: a transition from undifferentiated common sense to the intellectual pattern of experience. This development of a new mode of understanding explained the evolution of dogma. And when he distinguished between positive scholarship and dogmatic aims and procedures, he not only relieved some of the ambiguity about their functional connections but paved the way for greater collaboration between positive and dogmatic theologians.

What was constant during the 1940-1964 period in Lonergan? His notion of the primacy and office of the magisterium is unchanged. His desire to explain the legitimacy of theology as a science remains constant. His commitment to Aquinas perdures, but not without some qualifications. Following St. Thomas, he still sees the goal of theology strictly speaking to be speculative -- the imperfect yet fruitful understanding of mystery (whereas in *Method in Theology*, his goal will be to explain the functions of various specialties within theology). And he still follows the Thomist procedure for arranging trinitarian doctrine according to analytic/synthetic processes. But he now more fully differentiates the roles of positive and dogmatic theology within the analytic process. He places the task of historical scholarship within the purview of dogmatics. Yet these differentiations, arising as they do from the explanation required to account for the development of dogma, are still well within the Thomist framework of ordering ideas. What is new here is Lonergan's attention to the approach of dogmatics as utterly concrete, as solving problems instead of merely searching for correct propositions. New as well is the adjustment of viewing history as part of a dogmatic process that is carried out by positive theologians pursuing their proper aims and methods. New, finally, is the increasing focus on the dynamism of human consciousness as it relates to the tasks of theology.

NOTES

CHAPTER VII

1Bernard J.F. Lonergan S.J., *De Deo Trino I: Pars Dogmatica* (Rome: Gregorian University, 1964). References to this text will be made directly in the body of the chapter with the notation (DDT:PD) and the page number.

²This translation of Lonergan's *De Deo Trino I: Pars Dogmatica*, p. 8 is from Quentin Quesnell, "Theological Method on the Scripture as Source" in *Foundations of Theology*, ed. Philip McShane (Dublin: Gill and Macmillan, 1971), p. 248.

³The page references in this section are to the translation by Conn O'Donovan of the *De Deo Trino I: Pars Dogmatica*. Bernard J.F. Lonergan, S.J., *The Way to Nicea*, trans. Conn O'Donovan (London: Darton, Longman & Todd, 1976). Pages 1-17 cover the section, "Dogmatic Development".

⁴*Ibid.*, pp. 1-2.

⁵*Ibid.*, pp. 2-3.

⁶*Ibid.*, pp. 4-5.

⁷*Ibid.*, p. 7.

⁸*Ibid.*, pp. 8-9.

⁹*Ibid.*, pp. 9-11.

¹⁰*Ibid.*, p. 13.

[11]*Ibid.*, p. 14.

[12]*Ibid.*, pp. 15-16.

[13]*Ibid.*, p. 16.

[14]*Ibid.*, p. 17.

CHAPTER VIII

THE 1964 REVISION OF THE INTRODUCTION TO THE 1957
DIVINARUM PERSONARUM CONCEPTIO ANALOGICA

We have seen that in the 1959 *"De intellectu et methodo"*, Lonergan investigated different ways of ordering a series of responses to questions, of ordering the same totality in equivalent systems, and of moving from one system to another by exercising the foundational wisdom of human intelligence. Moreover, the rule of method was not only to understand, but to understand systematically. The question arises whether these new interests had any bearing on Lonergan's formulation of the twofold way in the new edition of his speculative treatment of trinitarian doctrine.

Lonergan differentiated the twofold way in the introductory chapters of his trinitarian texts, first, the synthetic way in the 1957 *Divinarum personarum conceptio analogica*; next, the analytic way in the 1961 *De Deo Trino: Pars Analytica*; and finally, the revisions of the analytic and synthetic ways in the 1964 *De Deo Trino: Pars Dogmatica* and *Pars Systematica*.[1] We have already examined the evolution that occurred in the dogmatic part. Now we focus our attention on the revisions that took place in the systematic part.

In the dogmatic context, when Lonergan faced the problems connected with accounting for historical consciousness in the development of dogma, he differentiated the aims and procedures of positive and dogmatic theology. Here, in the systematic context, there are similar problems that call for a greater differentiation of the twofold way of ordering ideas, particularly the synthetic procedure. For example, what should be the source of the systematic theologian's work, the words of scripture or the dogmas of the magisterium? What difference is there between the aims and methods of the exegete and the systematic theologian? What are the stages and limits of the evolution of theological understanding? How are we to judge the consequent truth of theological understanding? Is there any difference between the way we judge theological understanding and the way we make other theological judgments? Finally, if we neglect to differentiate the procedures for doing theology according to analysis and synthesis, what happens to systematic theology? Our procedure in this chapter will be to list briefly the points of convergence and divergence between the 1957 *Divinarum personarum* and the 1964 *De Deo Trino II: Pars Systematica*, and then see how he differentiated the twofold way in response to these problems.

The preface of the revised edition is the same as the original one. Lonergan related that his concern is with the most fruitful yet imperfect understanding of the mysteries that the First Vatican Council asserted to be the goal of reason illumined by faith. In the first chapter, the first two sections, "On the end intended", and "The act by which the end is attained", are identical in both editions. But the 1964 edition introduces an entirely new third section, "On the question or the problem".[2] In addition to this new section, he revised the 1957 third section, "Further reflections about the same act (of understanding)" and in the fourth section of 1964, gave it the new title, "On the truth of understanding" (DDT:PS, pp. 19-39). Corresponding to the fourth section of 1957, titled "The threefold process by which the end is realized", is the fifth section of 1964, "The twofold process by which the end is realized". Finally, sections six through ten of 1964 substitute the term *via dogmatica* in almost all the places where the term *via analytica* had previously appeared; likewise, in 1964 the term *via systematica* replaces almost every instance where the term *via synthetica* appears in 1957. We will now examine these revisions.

De Deo Trino II: Pars Systematica, Chapter I, Section 3: "On the Question or Problem"

In the 1957 edition, Lonergan wrote about the end intended in theological understanding, about the act by which the end is attained, and then he proceeded immediately to say how theological understanding related to the truth. In this revised edition, he introduced a new topic. Before attaining the end, we *intend* it, and it is that act of intending that he wanted to amplify in his new third section.

This anticipation of the end of theological understanding is called a question or a problem; and it comes about either spontaneously, or explicitly, or scientifically. A question arises spontaneously inasmuch as we experience wonder, which is the origin not only of science and philosophy, but also the source of all theology. Explicitly, our anticipation becomes a question when we state what we are seeking in clear and distinct terms. Scientifically, we posit a question whenever we designate the reasons why a particular question should be asked (DDT:PS, pp. 13-14).

If we pursue this scientific anticipation and inquire what sort of reasons there are for positing the question, then we will discover that not all questions belong to the same class. Some are boiled down to problems of coherence, others to a problem of understanding, and others to a problem of fact.

Although these three kinds of questions are interconnected, still now one type of question, now another, requires more attention than do the others. Thus, it can be useful to posit the problem of coherence at the beginning of a science when people have to be persuaded to engage in scientific work. So it was that Abelard composed his opus, *Sit et Non*, in which he upheld both the affirmative and negative viewpoint on 158 theological propositions (DDT:PS, pp. 14-15).

The quest for resolution to problems brings about the transition from a problem of coherence to a problem of understanding. We quickly learn that questions cannot be posited in any order whatsoever. We cannot resolve some questions unless others are solved first, while as soon as some questions are answered, the way is open to solving others. St. Thomas noted this difference in the Prologue to the first part of the *Summa theologiae* when distinguished between the order of learning and the order required to give a detailed explanation in a book.

THE ROAD TO LONERGAN'S *METHOD IN THEOLOGY*

As in the 1959 "*De intellectu et methodo*", Lonergan adverted here to the role of wisdom in dealing with the problem of understanding. First, the wise person orders things correctly, so it is the work of wisdom to discover the problem that is first in this sense, namely, (1) that its solution does not presuppose the solution of other problems; (2) once it is solved, a second is solved expeditiously; (3) these two solutions immediately solve a third problem, which leads one after another to the solution of all the remaining connected problems.

Second, understanding has to do with principles. But a principle is defined as what is first in any order. So it is the task of understanding to grasp the solution of that problem that is first in the order of wisdom. But this order is of such a kind that, once the first problem is solved, the solution of other problems follows rapidly. Therefore, the understanding ought to be such that it contains in itself virtually all the solutions to the remaining questions.

Third, scientific knowledge is about conclusions. But the questions are to be presented in such an order that once the first question is solved, we can proceed with almost no effort to solve the remaining questions (DDT:PS, p. 15).

The problem of understanding is solved, not because individual responses are given individually to individual questions, but because wisdom orders the total series of questions, because the first question derives its solution through a highly fruitful act of understanding, because all other questions are solved in an orderly fashion in virtue of the first resolution, because a system of definitions is introduced to express the solution of problems, and because a technical terminology is evolved for formulating the defined concepts.

There follow some reflections about systems. There are two proper effects that belong to a system once it has been discovered: (1) that it grow, and (2) that it be perfected. A system grows inasmuch as it extends to all parts of theology and includes within its purposes philosophy and other human disciplines. A system becomes more perfect to the extent that an understanding of its principle increases, and that from this principle conclusions are derived that penetrate the subject matter more profoundly so that solutions of questions abound (DDT:PS, p. 16).

Of course the system can be misunderstood, or rejected entirely, or there can be a denial of the facts which the system seeks to understand. So there are three accidental effects that belong to a system. First, the misunderstanding of a system accords with the saying: Whatever is received is accepted according to the manner of the recipient. When there is misunderstanding, both the initial problem and the consequent connected problems are only imperfectly solved. But imperfect solutions are only partial solutions and also partially new problems. And these new problems only remotely stem from the sources of revelation. Proximately, they arise from poor understanding of the system. What is more, these new problems are ordered not according to the wisdom of wise people, but according to those who misunderstand. The new problems are solved by the same people whose misunderstanding was the origin of the new problems. So a new system arises that is only a pretense of a true system, whose problems are pseudo problems, whose method of arranging materials suffices for the less wise, and whose principle avails for those whose understanding is superficial (DDT:PS, pp. 16-17).

The second accidental effect pertaining to a system is that some people totally reject it for two reasons. First, some people have only known the appearances of a system. And since they know that these semblances are not good but bad, they conclude that every system necessarily deviates from what is proper. Second, there are others who do not grasp what understanding means, so they think that the question of understanding only has to do with a problem of truth or fact. So whenever a systematic understanding of the sacred is achieved, they judge this not to be an understanding, but a new doctrine that relies on philosophical dogmas. Now once a system is completely rejected, the problem of understanding is excluded as well. Then a return to the problem of coherence may occur -- where the discussion becomes the application of logical subtlety to what is absolutely necessary and absolutely possible -- as happened in the fourteenth and subsequent centuries. After these logical exercises are finally abandoned, there is a turn to the problem of fact (DDT:PS, p. 17).

The third accidental effect pertaining to system is a denial of the facts which the system seeks to understand. The various forms of this rejection of facts are manifested in the thought of Protestants, rationalists, atheists, modernists, existentialists, critical historians and historical relativists (DDT:PS, p. 17).

De Deo Trino II: Pars Systematica, Chapter I, Section 4: "The Truth of Understanding"

Thus far the new third section of Chapter I. Now, in section 4, Lonergan returns to the original 1957 third section, "On the truth of understanding", and considers the issue in three parts.

The relevant introductory paragraph of the 1957 edition states that theological understanding has a twofold relation to the truth: the truth preceding it is the revelation we seek to understand; the truth following it is the theological truth arising from the understanding itself (DPCA, p. 13). The introductory paragraph to the 1964 edition says that the present investigation speaks of theological and systematic understanding to ask three questions: (1) is a theological understanding true with respect to itself (*secundum se*)? (2) does theological understanding understand truth? (3) is a theological understanding of a truth true? These three questions give a new organization to the materials of the 1957 section, besides providing a framework for introducing new material.

True, the first question had been discussed in 1957 (although not as one of three). But the second and third questions are new. They are contrasted according to a new distinction, that is, the difference between antecedent and consequent truth, where the former is the truth that precedes theological thinking, and the latter is the truth that follows.

THE REVISION OF THE *DIVINARUM PERSONARUM*

Omitting then the first question, which is unchanged in the 1964 edition, we will study the second and third, noting as we go the differences from the treatment of 1957.

A. 1964, Section 4: Part ii -- How is Theological Understanding to be Compared to Antecedent Truth?

Part ii contains three points, two of which are not treated in the 1957 edition. It repeats the difference between natural or human sciences and theology as to their starting point (DPCA, point 10, p. 17). It adds new considerations about the source in scripture or the Church magisterium for systematic theology to find the mysteries about which it seeks understanding; about the problems that arise from poor systematic understanding.

Of the new considerations, the first questions whether it is scripture or the Church magisterium that the theologian should approach to learn the mysteries he seeks to understand. In one sense, it does not matter. What the Church offers for all to believe as divinely revealed is the same as that which is contained in the source of revelation (DB 1792, DS 3011) and indeed in the same sense as it has been defined by the Church (DB 2314, DS 3886). Nevertheless, while we hold firmly to this identity of truth and meaning, a Church statement pertains far more to the task of systematic theology than does a biblical statement. For biblical categories relate to the customary practice of everyday living as they apply to individual writers, readers, times, places, situations, events, purposes. On the other hand, the categories that can be called transcultural categories have been discovered in the more difficult questions for the use of the Church as dispersed everywhere, as universally valid, as perpetuated in history. Now biblical categories indeed were clearer to the primitive Christians, but we cannot learn their meaning except by arduous biblical studies. But the transcultural categories possess a kind of interior clarity that anyone can realize who has successfully completed a secondary course of study. Biblical categories refer to God in such a way as to communicate simultaneously what we ought to say or think or do. Transcultural categories, however, expound the divine reality with reference to itself. So our hearts are more deeply moved when the Son is said to mirror the glory of God and to bear the very image of God's nature, but we more lucidly grasp the theological problem about the Son's relation to the Father when we determine that the Son is consubstantial with the Father (DDT:PS, pp. 20-21).

It seems obvious, therefore, that systematic theology derives its beginning from Church definitions rather than from biblical studies. But the sources of revealed doctrine contain treasures of truth of such vast wealth as never to be exhausted (DB 2314, DS 3886). Clearly, then, there are many issues in scripture that the Church has not yet defined. Scripture deals with some mysteries, such as the redemption, so completely that disputations about them seldom crop up in the Church. But scriptural sources treat other mysteries, such as the Trinity, more indirectly than directly, and part by part rather than from a single point of view. Because these mysteries generate wonder, doubts, and arguments, the Church has often defined them with precision and clarity. Thus, although the systematic theologian more easily starts from Church declarations than from scripture directly, he cannot always take the easier course (DDT:PS, pp. 21-22).

Moreover, the systematic theologian must be careful not to confound his task with the aim of biblical theology when he seeks in scripture the mystery he wants to understand. The proper goal for the systematic theologian is that he obtain from scripture what would not have to be sought had the Church magisterium defined it. So he wants what is clear in itself. He desires to have the meaning and the meant stated in what above we called transcultural categories. He wants what has been certainly revealed, and so he applies those technical methods that lead not to the probable or more probable, but to the certain. He wants what pertains to the divine reality itself, and so he scrutinizes the mind of Mark, Paul, or John or of any other writer in such a way as to settle not simply for a probable conclusion, but for one that is clear and certain (DDT:PS, p. 22).

Finally, there is the second of the new considerations; that is, we find revealed mysteries not only in scripture and in the infallible Church definitions, we discover them also in what are called the theological sources. So the systematic theologian uses all of these sources. To the extent that misunderstanding enters into theology, to that extent do pseudo problems arise and pseudo systems evolve. But the systematic theologian has a firm foundation when he selects his consequent and connected problems from this fundamental problem, and when he handles in subordinate questions or in appendices the opinions that arise more from human thought than from revealed truth (DDT:PS, pp. 22-23).

B. 1964, Section 4: Part iii -- How is Theological Understanding to be Compared to Consequent Truth?

This 1964 part iii has twelve points where the 1957 edition had ten, but it eliminates points 6,7, and 8 of the 1957 treatment; elaborates the positions given in 1957 as points 5,9,10; and adds new material in the points now numbered 1-4, 7-12.

Why did he eliminate points 6,7, and 8 of the 1957 treatment? The sixth point says that theological understanding of itself, while leading only to an imperfectly understood hypothesis, can acquire truthfulness from three other sources: from natural reasons, the fonts of revelation, and deductions from theological hypotheses. The seventh point outlines the progress in theological understanding that moves from understanding single hypotheses to synthetic understanding expressed throughout an integral system. The eighth point says that the truth of any system is derivative and not equally certain in its various parts -- so we should distinguish what is believed by faith, what is defined by the Church, and what is accepted by theologians with qualifications.[3] It would seem that he changed his focus in 1964 to the truth which follows theological understand-ing. Hence, instead of treating theological understanding as something in its own right, he now concentrated on the function of theological under-standing, eliminating the ambiguity in these points about whether theologi-cal understanding is a true understanding that reaches probable conclu-sions.

Omitting a consideration of the first five points of the 1964 edition because they do not manifest new problems, we turn to the sixth point. There is a correspondence between the 1957 tenth point and this point in 1964 about the continuity in the development of theological understanding (DB 1800, DS 3020).

The sixth point of 1964 makes some important additions to the tenth point of 1957. The First Vatican Council says that there is an increase in understanding, science, and wisdom according to the degree proper to each age and each time (DB 1800, DS 3020). So a certain historical series exists that discloses an evolution of understanding. A most fruitful understanding of mystery develops not only because this growth solves many problems, but also because the earlier and less perfect stages of the process anticipated, cultivated, and somehow nurtured the later perfection (DDT:PS, p. 25).

We can compare the earlier and later stages of understanding in a threefold way: (1) by reason of the object understood; (2) by reason of the analogy used; (3) by reason of the perfection attained. First, by reason of the object understood, both the earlier and later stages belong to the same genus, the same dogma, the same meaning, and the same view (DB 1800, DS 3020). For it is always the same divinely revealed mystery we want to understand. Second, by reason of the analogy used, the procedure moves from a multiplicity to a uniformity so that (a) many different formats are tried; (b) the consensus increases that a certain type of analogy is to be preferred; (c) understanding is upgraded in a more profound, precise expression of this analogy. Third, by reason of the perfection that is acquired, we can compare the earlier and later stages not only as to understanding that more deeply fathoms the principle, not only as to the scientific knowledge that draws conclusions from the principle, but also as to wisdom that orders the totality of the subject matter. An example of this comparison between earlier and later stages of understanding can be seen in the different ways that St. Augustine and St. Thomas sought some understanding of the same trinitarian dogma. Both used the psychological analogy. St. Augustine expressed the analogy psychologically while St.

THE REVISION OF THE *DIVINARUM PERSONARUM*

Thomas explored the same analogy not only psychologically but also metaphysically, so that in him there is a fuller understanding of the principle, the possibility of a wider ordering by wisdom and of a more precise deduction of conclusions (DDT:PS, pp. 25-26).

The seventh point is new to 1964. No limit is to be put on the increase and growing perfection of understanding, science, and wisdom. The object of theological understanding does not pose a limit because divine mystery reveals infinity, and infinity is not limited. The analogy poses no limit because it is based on what reason naturally understands, and human reason does not understand so perfectly as to exclude understanding even more perfectly. The sources of revelation likewise pose no limit because they contain such treasures of truth as will never be exhausted (DB 2314, DS 3886). The part wisdom plays in organizing its materials sets no limit. The more that reason plumbs what is natural and analogous, the more the study of the sources reveals its riches, the more matter there is for a growing and expanding wisdom to order. Finally, theological understanding and theological scientific knowledge do not pose limits. For whenever wisdom proposes a problem, there reason illumined by faith can hope with God's blessing that some understanding may accrue (DB 1800, DS 3020). Furthermore, whenever we attain the understanding of a principle, the conclusions of scientific knowledge spontaneously follow (DDT:PS, p. 26).

The eighth point of 1964 says that just as understanding can grow and expand, so also can there crop up misunderstanding. We have already seen the consequences of mistaken understanding in the discussion of pseudo systems.[4]

The ninth point considers the problem of judging the consequent truth of theological understanding. What are the sources for making a correct judgment here? Lonergan outlines three sources. This point is new to the 1964 edition.

In the first place, the truth consequent on understanding is to be judged on the basis of what *per se* flows from this understanding. Does it solve a certain problem? Is this problem a divine mystery insofar as we can understand it in this life in a mediated way, imperfectly, analogously, obscurely? Is this understanding fruitful in that it solves other connected problems? Is there another analogy that solves equally well or better the same problems? Or is there perhaps no other analogy that we can know in this life?

In the second place, understanding whose consequent truth is in question is to be examined not in its own right, but on the basis of an historical comparison. Has this problem ever been considered before? Has it been done directly or only indirectly? Has it been investigated in the same or another cluster of problems? Has theology used the same or another analogy? If the analogy is the same, is it being plumbed more deeply? Have new dimensions been brought to bear on the problem either from an advance in the natural and human sciences, or from a development in scriptural, conciliar, patristic, or medieval studies? Does the understanding of the principle really ground the deduction of the other conclusions throughout the rest of the work? Are the deductions now both more numerous and more complete than before? Does there emerge a better unifying insight into the material and a fuller grasp of the entire subject matter? Finally, can we grasp additional problems now that both urge and even require a further growth in understanding, knowledge, and wisdom?

In the third place, this same understanding should be compared with the pseudo problems and the pseudo systems that may have cropped up in the subject matter, been disseminated, and not entirely extirpated. Has equal consideration been given to all the questions that were ever asked? Or has there perhaps been a selection process such that certain matters receive the main treatment while others are either handled as ancillary questions or passed over in silence? Does this selection process follow some convention, or is it perhaps determined by some principle? And is this further principle that we are seeking an understanding of divinely revealed mystery, while the problems cropping up from misunderstanding are handled only inasmuch as to omit them would leave untouched the obstacles that prevent understanding of the mysteries.[5]

In the tenth point, there is a comparison between the judgment on theological understanding and other theological judgment -- a point that is new to the 1964 edition.

Judgment on a theological understanding differs from all theological conclusions. Arriving at a correct conclusion is simple enough. Once the premises are posited, the conclusion either follows necessarily or not. If it does not, then it is invalid. If it does follow necessarily, then the conclusion is no less true than the premises. On the other hand, judgment on a theological understanding is difficult because we are dealing here not with a conclusion but with a principle. And a principle can be possible, more or less probable, or at least along the line that solely leads to the understanding that the First Vatican Council praises (DDT:PS, pp. 27-28).

Judgment on a theological understanding diverges from all we know about God through the mediation of creatures by the natural light of reason, and the difference pertains to the problem as well as to its solution. There is a difference in the problem. The problem or question that theological understanding solves emerges only from revelation. If we omit revelation, then we know nothing of problems such as the Trinity, the Incarnate Word, the grace of Christ, the sacraments of the new law. There is a difference in the resolution of problems, for philosophical knowledge of God does not introduce or systematically formulate hypothetical analogies. But what philosophy affirms to be analogously in God it also demonstrates. So a philosopher might say and prove that God is conscious, but a philosopher cannot demonstrate that God is dynamically conscious. And there is no valid reason why he should assume that God is dynamically conscious. A theologian, however, presupposes that God is dynamically conscious, not because he demonstrates this fact, not because he understands it clearly, but because in this one, obscure element he finds the root of all the secret realities to be in the triune God (DDT:PS, p. 28).

229

Judgment about a theological understanding diverges from all dogmatic declarations -- not with regard to the problem, but with regard to the solution of problems. There is no difference in problem because both posit questions (a) that disappear when we exclude revelation, and (b) that pertain to divine realities themselves. But there is a difference in the resolution of problems. A dogmatic declaration stems from a revealed truth or at times from a naturally known truth. But theological understanding adds a further hypothetical element certainly not contained in revelation or demonstrated by reason.

The dogmatic or theological question, then, diverges from the biblical question because the former pertains to divine realities themselves. The latter pertains to the mind of some author about divine matters. An illustration of this difference would be the way we conceive that Jesus of Nazareth is the Son of God. The biblical scholar asks in what sense Mark or Paul or John used the expression, "Son of God", in individual passages. So the different responses of the biblical theologian depend upon the different authors, circumstances, contexts. The dogmatic theologian, on the other hand, has a different understanding of the same question. His intention is not to investigate the expression mainly to ask what this or that hagiographer certainly or probably had in mind when he used the title, "Son of God". Instead, his main question relates to the reality itself, the reality of Jesus of Nazareth, and how all the faithful for all times ought to conceive him (DDT:PS, pp. 28-29).

Furthermore, the dogmatic solution differs from the theological solution. For when the dogmatic theologian specifies that the Son of God is not made but is begotten, he is introducing nothing hypothetical, but is collecting, scrutinizing, and understanding what revelation says. For the name "Son" is predicated of Jesus in a singular sense. This same Jesus cannot be counted among creatures. Yet much that is predicated of him is proper to God. And all of this together but without the addition of any hypothesis implies that the Son was not made but is uncreated, divine, and divinely begotten (DDT:PS, p. 29).

Beyond the dogmatic resolution of a problem, the theological solution properly speaking is another type. For when we ask what kind of nativity or generation would occur within the divinity, then in a single stroke we have posed a virtual plethora of questions. Yet these questions do not all immediately come to mind, but different questions accumulate over the course of time. Revealed truths or naturally known truths solve many questions. Nevertheless, they lead to different additional questions. Soon it becomes clear that we cannot adequately respond to the initial problem unless we consider clearly and distinctly the kind of generation that is utterly unique and entirely unknowable from any other source. Now an hypothesis as such is what is thought out so as to solve a problem. Because what is entirely unknowable from any other source is being thought out, it is properly said to be an hypothesis. Finally, when what is thought out becomes a principle from which flows all that is of faith or a conclusion from faith, and when what is thought out cannot be shown to contradict reason, then we have not merely an hypothesis but a widely verified theory (DDT:PS, p. 29).

In the eleventh point, new to the 1964 edition, Lonergan answers the question about what happens to systematic theology if we neglect to differentiate the procedures for doing theology according to analysis and synthesis. Here we see him exposing the aberrations of "conclusions" theology. Conclusions theology must be abandoned since it (1) differentiates theology both from reason and from faith; (2) permits theology to have no principles except what it receives from faith or from reason; (3) allows theology itself to be simply about conclusions; (4) says that these conclusions are either pure (both premises are received from faith) or mixed (one premise is received from faith, the other from reason).

Conclusions theology seems to ignore the teaching of the First Vatican Council. In DB 1796 (DS 3016), the Council says that when reason illumined by faith inquires earnestly, devoutly, and modestly, it does reach, by God's generosity, some understanding of mysteries, both from the analogy of what it knows naturally and from the relationship of the mysteries with each other and with our final end. Conclusions theology would have

231

it that when reason illumined by faith has drawn premises from the fonts of revelation and perhaps has added to them another premise from reason, it arrives at a most certain conclusion by observing the rules of logic. But it is one thing to inquire so as to understand, another thing to grasp the matter so as to be able to demonstrate conclusions. It is one thing to work out an analogy so as to reach some imperfect understanding of the mysteries, another thing to select premises from scripture or reason. It is one thing to expect an understanding given by God's generosity, another thing to seize upon certitude by correctly observing the rules of logic. Finally, the First Vatican Council wanted a positive exposition of catholic doctrine, so it distinguished two orders of knowledge (faith and reason, DB 1795, DS 3015), and taught the role of reason in cultivating supernatural truth (DB 1796, DS 3016).

Furthermore, the First Vatican Council is clear on how we are to compare this understanding of mysteries to conclusions that are pure and mixed. Deductions from revealed mysteries lucidly indicate problems. The more numerous and exact the deductions, the more plentiful and difficult are the manifested problems. Since these problems arise precisely because the premises themselves narrate divine mysteries, we cannot solve these problems unless we attain some understanding of the mysteries (DDT:PS, p. 30).

Again, when we attain the understanding "from the analogy of what is known naturally", there is introduced a hypothetical element. Even if we were to grant that the same analogy was hinted at, suggested, or clearly manifest in the sources we still could not prove that the same analogy taken formally with all its systematic implications was present in the sources (DDT:PS, pp.30-31).

Since this is the case, we cannot admit the view that theology is simply a matter of pure and mixed conclusions. For problems logically follow from the revealed mysteries, and we can solve these problems only by obtaining an understanding of the mysteries. And when the solution to the problem introduces an hypothetical element -- the very system virtually included in a most fruitful understanding -- then is posited a properly theological principle stemming not from faith alone, not from reason alone, but from reason as illumined by faith and as inquiring with care, devotion, and modesty (DDT:PS, p. 31).

Conclusions theology generates several difficulties for the science of theology. First, it fosters the anachronistic tendency to impose later systematic discoveries upon earlier authors. Second, since systematic theologians do not share one mind and heart, they impose not just one but a variety of diverse systems upon the sources. Third, since the true criterion for establishing the validity of a system does not consist in deduction from the sources, then if we retain a conclusions theology, we cannot refute the more inept systems and provide serious proof for the truer ones. Fourth, when studies flourish in exegesis or other fields, the theologians who deduce systems are customarily criticized as being incompetent scholars. Fifth, since these positive scholars know no other proof for a system beyond that of deduction from the sources, they consider every system as a kind of futile speculation (DDT:PS, p. 31).

If we could stop thinking that theology is only a matter of drawing pure and mixed conclusions, then systematic experts and positive theologians could stop arguing with one another and instead render each other enormous mutual benefit. Clearly, there is no great distance between understanding a doctrine and understanding the history of a doctrine. Indeed, when the doctrine is always the same (that is, when the concern is the same dogma, the same meaning, and the same view), and again, when there increase and advance an understanding, knowledge, and wisdom relative to the same doctrine and according to the degree proper to each age and time, then there can be no valid reason why the positive and systematic theologians should oppose one another. For what the systematic theologian understands now has already had its prior preparation. Therefore, the systematic theologian arrives at a full and exact understanding of his own task from an understanding of history, just as from an understanding of earlier solutions, the positive theologian can grasp and judge with clarity and precision what the earlier solutions were and whither they tended (DDT:PS, pp. 31-32). We omit here the twelfth point of 1964 that emends and elaborates the ninth point of 1957 on how the meaning of a truth is measured by the intelligence from which it proceeds.

In concluding this section, we can observe that although Lonergan worked out the implications of his maturing historical consciousness in dogmatics through distinguishing the roles of positive and dogmatic theology, he adverted to the implications of history for systematics as well. These implications show up in the emergence of systems -- not as a bare series of propositions, but as an evolution of earlier and later stages of understanding. The influence of positive scholarship requires him to distinguish dogmatic, systematic, and biblical questions and solutions to problems. Finally, systematic theology understands its task only if it understands history. And positive theology only realizes its aim if it understands the earlier solutions of problems worked out by systematics.

De Deo Trino II: Pars Systematica, Chapter I, Section 5: "On the Twofold Process by Which the Goal is Attained"

Corresponding to *Divinarum personarum conceptio analogica*'s 1957 fourth section titled "The threefold process by which the goal is attained" is the fifth section of 1964, "The twofold process by which the goal is realized". The revised version no longer speaks about the historical evolution of theological understanding as a third separate process. In the original version, theology was seen as analogous to the natural sciences, and so had a prescientific phase, a synthetic phase, and a third phase that embraced the evolution of knowledge throughout history as the two phases developed. Theology is still analogously a science, but as we have seen, the dogmatic part now is identified with the *via analytica*, and the systematic part is aligned with the *via synthetica*. What the 1957 version called theology's "third process", the 1964 edition considers as "the prior historical process". What accounts for this difference is that Lonergan no longer saw history as a preliminary adjunct to the real work of theology, but as integral to the role of dogmatics (that reduces the truths of faith implicit in revealed sources to dogmatic principles, which systematics seeks to understand more fully).

The topic of this section is the process by which we proceed to the act of theological understanding. Since two goals intended in theological disputations were noted, the one of certitude, the other of understanding certainties, it is obvious that we must distinguish between the two processes for attaining those ends. In the 1964 edition, the two movements received new designations: the dogmatic and the systematic (DDT:PS, p. 33).

Four elements of the process by which we proceed to the act of theological understanding are the same in the 1964 edition as in 1957. Namely, this is the way of (1) analysis; (2) resolution; (3) discovery; (4) certitude. But the 1964 edition adds a fifth point: the way of temporality, because ordinarily causes are not discovered immediately, and not by every investigator, and only with a little luck (DDT:PS, p. 33).

The two versions of 1957 and 1964 agree that the first scientific process is completed by a second that takes its start at the discovered causes and ends up at an understanding of realities in their causes. This process in both editions is called (1) synthesis; (2) the way of composition; (3) the way of teaching or learning. The 1964 edition adds two further points. This process is (4) the way of probability, both because often in this life this process attains only a probability, and because people ordinarily believe that there is no certain discernment of where or when certitude has been reached; and (5) the way of logical simultaneity, because after principles have been posited clearly, then all else is accomplished not over long intervals of time, but by exceedingly brief deductions and applications (DDT:PS, p. 34).

Both the 1957 and the 1964 versions then give an example of the distinctions between these processes by comparing the history of the physical sciences with the manuals in which these sciences are taught.

At this point, the 1957 version says that the twofold analytic and synthetic process is completed by a third. This third scientific process comes about because the analytic/synthetic process described above is never finally completed, but constantly is repeated and revised. So the third scientific process is identical to the history of the sciences. It is the concrete unity of the history of the sciences that comprehends the entire succession of all those truths which over the years analysis has discovered and which synthesis has taught systematically (DPCA, p. 21).

The 1964 version omits the reference to a "third" scientific process, and revises the remainder of the 1957 section that compares the processes of natural science and of theology. Instead of trying to make the evolution of understanding a third historical process for theology, Lonergan conceives in a new fashion the manner in which theological processes are analogous to the movements of the natural sciences.The 1964 version says that since theology is analogously a science, the dogmatic part of theology is not entirely different from the *via analytica*, and the systematic part is not completely different from the *via synthetica*. Just as the natural order has its starting point in a kind of common and prescientific knowledge, so theology takes its starting point from what God has revealed under particular, historical circumstances. Just as in the natural order one proceeds by discovering causes, so theology states universally in the same meaning the same truth as was once revealed in the Bible. Just as one ends up at a knowledge of things through their causes after the causes have been discovered in the natural order, so in theology the divine mysteries, after they have been stated in their catholic sense or even thus defined, can be understood imperfectly and obscurely but nonetheless most fruitfully (DDT:PS, p. 34).

Once these points have been grasped, it follows that since theology is analogously a science, the dogmatic part of theology can be conceived according to a certain similarity it has with the analytic process. The dogmatic process is (1) the "way of certitude". It is the way of certitude that declares the same truth in the same sense as God has revealed it. It is (2) the "way of discovery". It discovers that declaration that regards the needs

236

of a Church that is both universal and perpetual. It is (3) the "way of analysis". It moves from historical and Hebraic particularity to commonly known and well-defined reasons. It is (4) the "way of resolution". It discerns in the multiplicity of revelations the unity of the underlying divine mysteries and gives them expression. And it is (5) the "way of temporality". It is only with the passage of time that the transcultural declarations of the mysteries is achieved (DDT:PS, pp. 34-35).

The systematic part of theology in a similar manner can be conceived according to a kind of analogous relation to the synthetic process. The systematic process is (1) the "way of teaching". This is the process by which professors teach and students learn, and we do not understand except by starting from an understanding that does not presuppose the understanding of any other elements. The systematic process is (2) the "way of synthesis". It explains in an orderly way all other elements from one principle or another. It is (3) the "way of composition". It composes the entire divine mystery from a succession of viewpoints and from a variety of reasons. It is (4) the "way of probability". It does not deduce what is certain from revelation, but it does derive the revealed from a prior hypothetical supposition. It is (5) the "way of logical simultaneity". Once wisdom has discovered an ordering of the questions and understanding has grasped the principle, then the conclusions and applications of the systematic process follow spontaneously. And while these fruits of the systematic process may lack logical rigor, since we are proceeding from a principle only imperfectly and obscurely understood, nevertheless, slowly and over time and with a little luck, we do reach conclusions from the systematic principle (DDT:PS, p. 35).

If we acknowledge in the dogmatic part of theology a process of analysis, resolution, discovery, certitude, and temporality; and in the systematic part, a process of synthesis, composition, teaching and learning, probability, and logical simultaneity, nonetheless we should remember to use these terms analogously. For analysis and synthesis are understood differently in the natural sciences, in the human sciences, and in theological disciplines. Indeed, we do not understand the nature of material realities in the same way as we understand the words of Plato; and we understand Plato so as afterwards to judge whether Plato knew the truth. But what the Word of God teaches we believe to be true before we investigate it. Only in its own way, therefore, is dogmatics the way of analysis, resolution, discovery, certitude, and temporality; and equally in its own way, then, is systematics the way of synthesis, composition, teaching or learning, probability, and logical simultaneity (DDT:PS, p. 35).

We can round out this section by noting that Lonergan's original pairs -- the *via resolutionis/via compositionis* and the *via inventionis/via doctrinae* -- seem to have become features among other features of a larger pair of procedures now called dogmatics and systematics. Moreover, instead of being merely a way of ordering ideas, dogmatics and systematics are "parts" of the entire theological enterprise (as the names in this trinitarian presentation indicate, *Pars Dogmatica* and *Pars Systematica*). As such, these parts are not simply procedures but are tasks of theology with their own goals and methods. Still, Lonergan was not yet trying to relate the tasks of theology in a completely coherent fashion. He is content to figure out the various functions of each part of theology and then to list these features as they pertain to dogmatics and systematics.

De Deo Trino II: Pars Systematica, Chapter I, Section 6: "A Comparison Between Dogmatics and Systematics"

The fifth section of the 1957 *Divinarum personarum conceptio analogica* was "A Comparison of the Analytic and Synthetic Movements". The sixth section in the revised, 1964 edition is "A Comparison Between Dogmatics and Systematics". We have already covered the eight points made in this section, and the treatments are identical in each version except for two important differences. First, what the 1957 edition specified as the *via analytica* is now called "dogmatics", and what was called the *via synthetica* is now termed "systematics". Second, in addition to being the way of analysis, resolution, discovery, and certitude, dogmatics is the way of temporality. Moreover, in addition to being the way of synthesis,

238

composition, teaching or learning, systematics is also the way of probability and of logical simultaneity (DDT:PS, pp. 36-37).

De Deo Trino II: Pars Systematica, Chapter I, Sections 7 and 8: "A Consideration of the Historical Movement; A Further Consideration of the Historical Movement"

The 1957 and 1964 versions of these two sections are almost identical except for the substitution of "dogmatics" for the "analytic process", and "systematics" for the "synthetic process". The only other significant difference is that in 1957, Lonergan conceived the historical consideration as a "third, historical process" in theological understanding. In 1964, he speaks of the historical consideration as "the prior historical process" that must be reviewed now that dogmatics and systematics have been compared (DDT:PS, p. 42).

Concluding Overview

The evolution of Lonergan's thought about the twofold way was less evident in the *Pars Systematica* than in the *Pars Dogmatica* because the chief reformation took place in the latter. We have seen that the *Pars Dogmatica* dealt in a fresh way with a concern enunciated in the 1961 *Pars Analytica*, the need to distinguish between dogmatic and positive theology. In the 1964 *Pars Dogmatica*, there was a movement away from the premise/conclusion expression of theological thought and a shift to a more historically oriented problem/solution formulation.

The shift begun in 1961 toward greater concern for the analytic way had its repercussions in the reformation of this new, 1964 *Pars Systematica* text. Instead of a threefold theological process (analysis, synthesis, history), we have a twofold way (analysis and synthesis) with a "prior historical process" since reason illumined by faith has sought understanding over the centuries with the result that by degrees and in a human manner it has increased and consummated the old with the new. Remember that in 1961, Lonergan called the analytic way "historical" for various reasons. First, the process itself is historical in two aspects: doctrinal and sacred. Then, the mode of operation is historical by which the magisterium is exercised. And finally, the way we determine how the magisterium arrives at dogmas implicitly contained in the revealed sources is historical. Now, however, in the 1964 *Pars Systematica* Introduction, the analytic way is not called a *via historica*. Here for the first time it is called a "way of temporality" because the dogmatic theologian does not discover the causes of doctrinal statements immediately but only after a lengthy investigation blessed with a little luck. The explanation given in 1964 in the *Pars Systematica* for the dogmatic process is that it is the "way of analysis" in the sense that it moves from historical and Hebraic particularity to commonly known and well-defined reasons. Both of these terms indicate Lonergan's heightened sensitivity to the historical dimension of theological development.

One other reversal in terminology in the *Pars Systematica* Introduction indicated the shift from an historical to a more dynamic way of looking at the movement of the "synthetic way". In 1961, the synthetic way was titled the "theoretical or speculative way" because it begins from the *priora quoad se*, proceeds according to its own proper principles, and enables us to contemplate intelligible truth in a single view. Now, in 1964, the *Pars Systematica* does not use the name "theoretical or speculative way" as a predicate of the synthetic way. Instead, it introduces a new term for the synthetic way, the "way of logical simultaneity". Once systematics discovers the correct arrangement of questions and grasps a theological principle, then the fruits of the systematic process follow spontaneously.

Furthermore, until this recasting of the twofold way, both analysis and synthesis sought the same goal, namely, the understanding of mysteries. Nevertheless, there were elements of certitude in the analytic way. In the 1957 *Divinarum personarum*, Lonergan called the analytic way the "way of certitude" because from the common and prescientific knowledge we have of the sacred, which for us is most obvious and certain, we draw up arguments to demonstrate more remote conclusions. However, it was not until the 1964 *Pars Systematica* that he introduced the title correlative to the *via analytica*'s way of certitude, namely, the *via synthetica* as the "way of probability". Here we see that Lonergan designated certitude as the end of the analytic way and probable understanding as the goal of the synthetic way. The synthetic way reaches only probable conclusions because it does not deduce what is certain from revelation, but instead it derives the revealed from a prior hypothetical supposition.

Further, even in the *Pars Systematica*, there was an increased awareness, first indicated in the "Theology and Understanding" article, but one that did not receive much formulation until later methodological schemes, of the historical dimension of theology. Besides the fuller reflections about evolving stages of understanding in the systems in theology, Lonergan clarified the difference between the work of the biblical theologian on an evangelist's mind and viewpoint, and that of the dogmatic or systematic theologian.

Finally, he clarified the difference between the dogmatic and the systematic aims. The systematic theologian sought only probable conclusions while the dogmatic theologian wanted judgments that are certain. And if we fail to distinguish the aims and methods of dogmatics and systematics, then positive studies become aimless and our systems ethereal.

NOTES

CHAPTER VIII

[1]Lonergan's first speculative textbook on the Trinity appeared in 1957 with the title, *Divinarum personarum conceptio analogica*. He published a second edition in 1959 in which he corrected misprints and made two minor additions (pp. 91, 297). And he produced a third, final edition in 1964 called *De Deo Trino II: Pars Systematica* (Rome: Gregorian University, 1964). He retained *Divinarum personarum conceptio analogica* as the subtitle of the 1964 version. This is significant in that it indicates not a repudiation of his former work but an emendation of earlier points in order to meet new exigencies. There is an unpublished, xeroxed translation of this volume by John Brezovec available in the Lonergan Research Institute of Regis College, Toronto.

[2]Lonergan, *De Deo Trino II: Pars Systematica*, pp. 13-18. Throughout this chapter I have used the work of John Brezovec, paraphrasing his translation, with verbatim quotes in many phrases, but in order to avoid the choppiness of frequent quotation marks, I have omitted them, and wish in this note to make full acknowledgment of use I have made of his typescript. Since there are frequent references to this *Pars Systematica* text, the citations will be noted directly in the body of the chapter with the abbreviation (DDT:PS) and the page number. References to the *Divinarum personarum conceptio analogica* will likewise appear directly in the body of this chapter with the abbreviation (DPCA) and the page number.

[3]Theological notes or censures say nothing more than the degree of certitude or probability that is coincident with the individual assertions. Theological notes range from *probabilior* to *de fide definita*. Censures are expressions of disapproval that vary from degrees of mild reproof to serious reprehension in the following order: offensive, scandalous, temerarious, suspicious, erroneous, and heretical. See *Divinarum personarum*, p. 26, and *De ente supernaturali*, p. 11.

[4]This point is new to this section of the 1964 edition, but it is an idea that had been formulated earlier in section three of 1964, *Pars Systematica*, pp. 16-17.

[5]Lonergan, *De Deo Trino II: Pars Systematica*, p. 27.

CHAPTER IX

A CRITICAL REVIEW OF
THE EVOLUTION OF THE TWOFOLD PROCESS

The analytic and synthetic procedures dominated Lonergan's thinking on theological method from 1940 till 1964. After 1964, there is only brief mention of the two ways of doing theology. Now that we have followed the evolution of his thought on the twofold way of ordering ideas, we can review five elements that made up the intra-Lonergan dialectic that led after 1964 to the further differentiation of the aims and methods formerly accomplished solely by analysis and synthesis.

Elements of the Problematic

There are five elements that comprise the problematic connected with Lonergan's development of the twofold way of ordering ideas according to analysis and synthesis: (A) the medieval horizon; (B) the Thomist horizon of wisdom; (C) theology as analogously a science; (D) the role of history in theology -- accounting for the development of dogma; (E) methodical theology's shift to the subject that transposes the twofold way. Our study has shown that Lonergan's use of the traditional procedures for doing theology according to analysis and synthesis underwent a series of differentiations caused by the need to meet the requirements of historical consciousness. Connected with each of the five elements listed above is a movement of the intra-Lonergan dialectic: (1) from one notion of development to another; (2) from one notion of wisdom to another; (3) from one notion of science to another; (4) from one notion of analysis to another; (5) from one notion of theology's procedures to another. We will now review each of the elements of Lonergan's development and see in summary fashion the pressures that prepare for the differentiation of the analytic/synthetic procedures into what eventually becomes functional specialization.

THE ROAD TO LONERGAN'S *METHOD IN THEOLOGY*

A. The Medieval Horizon

At the beginning of Lonergan's theological career in 1939, the paradigm for doing theology was doing what St. Thomas did. Hence, there were two concerns for theologians -- the presentation of dogmatic truth, and speculation that sought to understand that truth. But there were weaknesses in the medieval world view that the manualist tradition inherited. The weakness that most affected the twofold arrangement of ideas according to analysis and synthesis was that medieval theology lacked the dimension of time, that is, it overlooked the problems raised by history for theology.

This weakness set up a dialectic in Lonergan between his early work, where he conceived theological development as equivalent to the systematic expression of ideas, and his later writings on the development of dogma that explored the joining of speculative and historical theology.

It is not that Lonergan disregarded history and development, for his own thesis was an historical study of a development in Aquinas. But he seemed to regard history and development as lying somewhat outside, as being just a condition for, the real work of theology.

As we have seen, Lonergan's initial work was to do historical interpretation of the development of Aquinas' thought on *gratia operans* and on *verbum*. While the 1940 *Gratia Operans* dissertation was an historical study, it contained an underlying interest in the nature of theological speculation. While he was obviously concerned about the conclusions of the investigations themselves, of prime interest as well was his method -- to explain the procedures of his historical interpretation in order to insure objective, scientific results.

Lonergan's interest in theological method and his conscious attention to his procedures continued after his initial explanation of his aims in the

Introduction of his dissertation. The primitive expression of the twofold way of ordering ideas occurred in his use of the "way of composition" in organizing the entire little work, *De ente supernaturali*, his speculative treatment of grace. The "way of composition" is the descent from an intelligible principle of organization to the matter that is organized. That is, there is a correspondence between the scholastic metaphysical notions of potency, form, and act (from which structure derives the intelligible organization) and the arrangement of the five theses (the material that is organized). Just as what something is (essence) appears from what it can do (form), so what something can do appears in what it does (act). This structure was implicit, however, and Lonergan did not explicitly advert to his own organizing principle other than to say it was the "way of composition". In this speculative treatment, there was no particular interest, moreover, in filling in the historical evolution of different modes of thought or of accounting for the changing climate of human questions and problems. The arrangement of ideas here was strictly in the context of a speculative development, so the focus was on ordering a series of ideas, prescinding from a consideration of the milieu in which they evolved.

Why did Lonergan use the "way of composition"? Writing in the manualist tradition as a dogmatic theologian, he tried to ease the burden of learning for his students. While still teaching tracts composed in the framework of theses, propositions, and proofs from reason, he tried to organize his material according to a unifying principle from which would flow all the other theses and propositions. His job as teacher was to work out the unifying idea that would bind together a variety of points culled from various sources. It was an admirable procedure since it helped students learn from the thrill of insight rather than from an endless accumulation of examples. But it was difficult for other teachers to emulate. It presumed a breadth of learning that became increasingly impossible for a professor, however brilliant, to achieve. Moreover, it neglected to inquire where the ideas came from, who were the people who thought them, and what accounted for changes. But it is impossible to do everything at once. We must remember that Lonergan presupposed the historical part of a treatise already was covered in the dogmatic presentation of a course on grace or

Trinity or Christology. He used the "way of composition" to expedite learning, to deepen understanding, and to focus strictly on ideas in the pristine context of speculation (without getting bogged down in the particular concrete, almost messy milieu of history).

When in the *Verbum* articles (1946-1949) Lonergan drew a contrast between two kinds of development -- the historical way a science may be studied (*via inventionis*) and the systematic way a science may be examined (*via doctrinae*) -- there was confusion about what exactly constituted development. It would not be correct to say that he was uninterested in theological history or that he neglected correct procedures in writing his historical works. But in this last section of the *Verbum* articles, he paid only scant attention to the way of historical discovery, simply noting what was "needed to make Aquinas' *via doctrinae* possible".[1] His real interest was with the procedures of speculative theology. So the confusion about development arose when he treated trinitarian ideas as taking place in the context of systematic ordering of thought with its two phases -- development in process (*in fieri*), and development at its term (*in facto esse*). At least in the trinitarian example, he treated development as if it were solely equivalent to the systematic emergence of ideas. So the meaning of development here would indicate the emergence of ideas in a systematic context. This is a relatively abstract notion of development that, while it allows for the notion of time, context, and circumstances in which the ideas emerged, does not value prior stages so much in themselves as in their usefulness to generate later stages. It is particularly disconcerting for the interpreter of Lonergan's thought who is examining one pair of procedures (the way of historical development and the way of systematic presentation) to have another pair introduced in the way of systematic presentations that also speaks of development (*in fieri* and *in facto esse*).

Part of this first element of the problematic connected with the twofold way of ordering ideas, then, shows up as an insufficient attention to the way of historical discovery. While attention to historical procedures and to the findings of historical inquiries is not lacking, there seems to be a disproportionate weight given to the value of systematic presentations.

Likewise, there is an inadvertence to a possible confusion of terms. This confusion seems to stem from a preoccupation inherent in the medieval horizon and manualist tradition, a preoccupation with the systematic ordering of ideas in the speculative context with little regard for the problems raised by positive scholarship for the dogmatic context.

B. The Thomist Horizon of Wisdom

The second element in the problematic connected with Lonergan's development of the analytic/synthetic procedures stems from the thematic statement of the twofold way in the 1954 book review, "Theology and Understanding". The main influence in this thematizing was the horizon of St. Thomas, for whom wisdom was the correct ordering of all things.

The backdrop for Lonergan's thematizing the procedures by which theology achieved its aim was the First Vatican Council that emphasized the role of speculative theology and warned against abuses of historical scholarship, particularly the positive studies that would undermine a correct interpretation of scripture. While insisting that reason illumined by faith does reach some understanding of mysteries (DB 1796, DS 3016), the First Vatican Council did not fully appreciate the problems posed for theology by positive historical investigations of scripture and of other theological sources. As specialists in a host of varied fields (scriptural, patristic, conciliar) began to come between dogmatic theology and its sources, the dogmatic theologian not only was unable to organize the burgeoning material according to a unifying principle (as the "way of teaching" recommends), but as well was increasingly prevented from saying anything at all. The positive contributions of modern scholarship that drove a wedge between the dogmatic theologian and his sources was one of the key elements that led to the transposition of the twofold process in theology. The impetus of historical consciousness was central to the differentiation of the twofold way because it raised problems that could not be solved within the relatively ahistorical analytic/synthetic system.

THE ROAD TO LONERGAN'S *METHOD IN THEOLOGY*

Although Lonergan defended the Aristotelian and scholastic notions of science as adequate for elaborating the nature of speculative theology in 1954, he now realized better that these procedures were not adequate for all of theology's tasks. In fact, he described four contemporary methodological issues that needed attention, issues that strained the carrying capacity of the twofold process elaborated in the review article. The common thread running through these four issues was theology's need for history, for positive scholarship to recover theology's own prescientific evolution, and for adequate principles of hermenteutics. While he still felt that the Aristotelian notions of philosophy and science as used by St. Thomas were adequate for framing the procedures in speculative theology, he recognized that these four issues demanded the attention of critical history and hermeneutics. Yet even two years later in the 1956 text, *De constitutione Christi*, he felt that speculative theology -- with its task of understanding revealed truth in its *prius quoad se* expression in the "way of teaching" -- sought more adequately the intelligibility cited by the First Vatican Council as possible for the theologian than did positive scholarship in the "way of discovery". While he alluded here to the problem of the relationship between speculative theology and positive theology, he did not seem to realize yet how extensive for theology were the problems raised by the role of history in theological investigation.

An ambiguity of the medieval horizon that has a bearing on Lonergan's use of the twofold way of organizing theological ideas concerns theology's handmaid, philosophy, and its approach to the systems. For some medieval philosophers, as for example the disciples of Scotus, the method for doing systematic thinking was logical, that is, it was rooted in a set of basic terms and relations from which other derived terms and relations could be defined. Through the derived terms and relations, systematic thinking could relate to the whole range of human experience. These basic terms are metaphysical. So in the logical ideal, philosophy was the love of wisdom that ordered everything according to basic metaphysical principles. But this static notion of system was not capable of accommodating new questions that could not be answered by the terms and relations of the old system. This problem became acute when theology tried to account for its development of dogma in the movement for the "first-for-us" of scripture and the Fathers to the "first-in-itself" of conciliar definitions. In contrast to Scotus and his disciples, St. Thomas did not practice a systematic ideal based on logic that rendered thought immobile. St. Thomas did not practice theology as a conceptualist does, with logical consistency as his aim, but the way an intellectualist does, with understanding as the goal, and with terms sufficiently defined for that. The notion of wisdom as conceived by Aquinas insured that thought be dynamic precisely because it was based on the dynamism of intelligence answering its two fundamental questions, *quid sit* and *an sit*. In fact, he did not have the concerns of a systematic thinker -- to set down definitions, axioms, postulates, and then to make deductions. His method was not to formulate a cluster of insights so much as to engage in a "process of presentations, inquiry, insight, conception, and sufficient conception to deal with the question at hand".[2]

Following St. Thomas, Lonergan held that part of the role of wisdom is the correct arrangement of data. Since arranging ideas in theology is precisely what our topic is about, it is clear that what Lonergan thought about wisdom is significant.

After extensive reflection about wisdom in the *Verbum* articles, as the Index of the articles indicates, Lonergan wrote in the 1954 "Theology and Understanding" article that the role of wisdom was to control the selection and use of the theoretical elements of the "way of teaching". Again, understanding and science are subordinate to wisdom, a natural subordination of speculation to judgment, of *quid sit* to *an sit*.[3] In the *Divinarum personarum conceptio analogica* of 1957 , Lonergan said that only the wise can judge the value of the synthetic process, and so the Church proposes as a guide in our studies not every theologian but only St. Thomas.[4]

It is especially in the *"De intellectu et methodo"* of 1959 that Lonergan indicated in what wisdom consists.[5] The context of the discussion about wisdom centered around theology's foundations problem and how to order a whole series of questions and responses into a system, and how to move from one system to another. The main point was that wisdom has to do with judgment. The solution to the foundational problem can be posited in wisdom because the human mind is always the human mind. An explanation of the way wisdom functions in cognitional theory as the principle of judgment would take us beyond the scope of this thesis. But wisdom was treated one final time in "*De intellectu et methodo*" in method's fifth rule. The theologian is told to take responsibility for judging whether a new understanding of revealed truth is true or not. Since the only wisdom proportionate to judging about the understanding of faith is the divine wisdom, the theologian is exhorted to submit his judgment to the Church.[6]

In the *De Deo Trino : Pars Analytica* of 1961, the point is made that theology treats its historical development in a different manner from natural science. Because revealed truths contain something implicitly, no one can determine what is implicitly present except the one who has wisdom proportionate to this revelation, namely, God. And this divine judgment is not left to philosophers or exegetes, but to the Church magisterium whose job it is to judge about the true sense and interpretation of scripture (DB 1839, DS 3073).[7]

In the *De Deo Trino II: Pars Systematica* of 1964, the role of wisdom is to order the total series of questions and responses that compose a system.[8] It is wisdom's task to discover the problem that is first in the sense that (1) its solution does not presuppose the solution of other problems; (2) once it is solved, a second problem is quickly resolved; (3) the remaining problems and their solutions follow easily. Moreover, earlier and later stages of understanding can be compared by reason of the perfection attained on the basis of wisdom that more fully orders the totality of the subject matter than earlier orderings. Thus, while St. Augustine explored the trinitarian analogy psychologically, St. Thomas examined it both psychologically and metaphysically, creating the possibility of a wider ordering of wisdom.[9] In the section that explained how the systematic part of theology can be conceived according to a kind of analogous relation to the synthetic process, Lonergan elaborated in 1964 the "way of logical simultaneity" that corresponds with his earlier explanation of the way wisdom works. Once wisdom grasps the ordering of questions and once understanding has apprehended the principle, there follow simultaneously the conclusions and the applications of the systematic process.[10]

In the "*De methodo theologiae*" of 1962, the issue of wisdom was raised in the context of general responses to the theological problematic based in three antithetical worlds. When theology becomes methodical, the work of wisdom is done by dialectic -- which is the normative element in method. Since method's concern is for the subject in his operations as either converted or unconverted, dialectic shows the lack of moral, religious, or intellectual conversion. The use of dialectic in the analysis of a development reveals why some statements are set aside and others are accepted. Moreover, this introduction of a normative element is germane to the procedures of analysis and synthesis because it effects the transition from the history of doctrine to the doctrine itself, from understanding the history of the doctrine to understanding the doctrine. It builds the bridge from a positive theology that investigates what was said. The addition of the normative element brings us what is true.[11]

The issue of wisdom is raised in the methodical context, moreover, when there are sought general responses to the theological problematic based in the three antithetical worlds. The question regarding theology's theoretic element as modeled either on the Greek scientific ideal or on the modern empirical scientific ideal is a problem of judgment. There is a technical treatment of wisdom as judgment: it is an absolute positing, it is a rational act, it has to be preceded by a grasp of the sufficiency of evidence.[12]

Finally, in a section on the relationship between history and philosophy, Lonergan theorized that critical philosophy contributes to method its upper blade, the normative element that is implicit in such notions as horizon, authenticity, and conversion. Again, the way dialectic functions is through the subject's use of judgment. And it is likewise clear that wisdom transposes in the methodical context to the functional specialty, "foundations", in its concern for conversion. But this consideration takes us once again beyond the scope of this present study.

C. Theology as Analogously a Science

The third element of the problematic surrounding Lonergan's use of the twofold way comes from the investigation of the ways in which theology is analogously a science.

In the Halifax lectures of August, 1958, delivered as a guide and explanation of *Insight*, Lonergan observed that the scholastic notion of science as certain knowledge of things through their causes implied two directions of inquiry -- analysis and synthesis. Analysis starts from a commonsense knowledge of things as they appear and works to discover their causes. Synthesis starts from the discovered causes, and working backwards, checks out the causes until it constructs things out of them. But the scholastic notion of science gave way to Newton's scientific ideal of law and system, which in turn yielded to Einstein's ideal of states and probabilities. As the notion of science developed, some components of the earlier notions survived and others did not. For example, as science developed, analysis and synthesis survived but not the things and causes as understood by Aristotle. Using examples taken from trinitarian theory and from natural science, Lonergan showed that as knowledge developed, scientists moved away from the field of things in the Aristotelian sense of that which falls under one of the ten predicates (substance, quantity, quality, relation, action, passion, time, place, posture, habit) and from causes in the sense of end, agent, matter, and form. So science started off with an ideal in terms of things and causes and advanced to a practice that was a matter of analysis and synthesis. But then the twofold procedure gave way to laws and systems which then evolved to the ideal of states and probabilities. This steady advance in the ideal of knowledge and how to know what knowing is became a problem whose solution Lonergan posited in the self-appropriation of the subject -- a whole topic that takes us far afield of our present concern.[13] But what is important for our purpose is that Lonergan perceived clearly the starting point and direction of the analytic/synthetic movement even if at this time he had not worked out the implications of his awareness for the requirements of a theological method.

A weakness of the medieval world view was that the scientific model to which theology was analogous was the scientific ideal of Aristotle. He conceived science as a deduction from first principles that expressed objectivity necessity. As Lonergan wrote *Insight*, his appropriation of his own operations prompted him to shift from the medieval horizon's systematic context that was predominantly logical and metaphysical to the type of systematic context that is found in modern science. Modern science no longer derives its basic terms and relations from metaphysics but works out its own basic terms and relations. Modern science no longer seeks the intelligibility of what must be so, but more modestly aims at what can be so and happens in fact to be verified. Modern science no longer tries to present certain truth but works toward an understanding that reaches ever greater degrees of probability. These changes in the notions of science have a bearing as well on Lonergan's ordering of ideas in theological science.

In the 1957 Introduction to the *Divinarum personarum*, theology is analogous to *natural science*. Each has a prescientific grasp of things, an analytic process that seeks to discover the causes of things, a synthetic process that wants to understand the things themselves, and an evolution of understanding throughout history. "History" while here differentiated from what will become the functional specialties "research" and "interpretation" does not yet have the meaning developed later for the functional specialty, history, as "what was going forward". Earlier, Lonergan had turned to the method of the natural sciences in his *gratia operans* study. He saw that just as mathematics gives quantitative sciences an *a priori* scheme of such generality that there can be no manipulation of the data in order to maintain the scheme, so it is possible to construct the generic scheme of the historical process for speculative theology.[14] Of course, the analogous model from natural science as it is used in theology only works if we assume that historical development is equivalent to the evolution of systematically defined ideas. If we ask where these ideas arose, then the model from natural science is not adequate in theology for accounting for historical development. It is not adequate because natural science starts from data whereas theology begins from revealed truth. Who is going to control the correct interpretation of the revealed truth -- the positive scholars or the dogmatic theologians? As positive scholarship increasingly challenged the legitimacy of the dogmatic theologian's task, the analytic process in theology came under closer scrutiny as an analogously scientific procedure.

In addition to being analogous to natural science, theology is also analogous to *human* science where the notion of the *prius quoad nos* is ambiguous. Because theology's prescientific sources were uttered to particular peoples, classes, and cultures, there arises the transcultural problem of moving from one *prius quoad nos* expression to another. The problem with theology being analogous to scientific models is that assumes a closed system. When the issue is a problem of moving from one system to another, from one cultural expression to a catholic definition, then the question requires moving from a procedure that is static to one that is dynamic. This was the exigence created by the need to explain the development of dogma -- the need to move from a static, atemporal, logical procedure to one that is dynamic, historical, and methodical.

The procedures that Lonergan used in 1957 were the familiar process of analysis and synthesis derived from natural science. When he tried to introduce the historical process, it became a third process alongside the other two, a kind of appendage to an already integrated, closed system. It seems that the historical process did not fit with the other two because it was like asking a ballerina to dance with statues -- one was dynamic, the other static. And it appears that the twofold process did not sufficiently overcome the static because there had been neglect of the exigencies of the analytic part of theology.

D. The Role of History in Theology -- Accounting for the Development of Dogma

The fourth element of the problematic revolves around the need to account for development. Here we see the intra-Lonergan dialectic that moves from one notion of the "way of analysis" to a further differentiation of the tasks of positive and dogmatic theology. Beyond the logical ideal of coherence that the Middle Ages pursued methodically, theology needed to explain the ongoing process of development inherent in deeper understanding of the truths of faith.

The 1959 *"De intellectu et methodo"* continued the exploration explicitly begun in 1954 of the place of history in a theological work. Theological ordering still conformed to the model of wisdom outlined by St. Thomas. But the issue of history raised other questions about the method of positive theology and its relation to speculative theology. The issue of development was raised here in the threefold aspect -- foundations, chasm, historicity -- of the single methodical problem, and addressed by five rules for a general method that were then applied to theological illustrations. This led to a comparison between historical and speculative theology that spotlighted the need for a proper method for biblical theology. So it was that this fourth element in the problematic generated fruitful reflections on systems, on development, on stages of consciousness, on rules of method, and on wisdom as the source of what eventually became the functional specialties, dialectic and foundations.

The 1959 doctoral seminar *"De intellectu et methodo"* demonstrated that if we omit a consideration of history, then the "way of discovery" and the "way of teaching" give splendid results for theological understanding. But history shows that St. Thomas did not understand the divine missions in the same way as scripture or the Fathers understood them. So history raised problems for theology that did not occur in the natural sciences where the human person -- whose thought is always evolving -- does not enter constitutively among the objects of science. So the introduction of positive studies is a problem for speculative theology because all continuity between various concepts of dogma seems impossible.

The 1960 Thomas More Institute lecture, "The Philosophy of History", revealed a further unfolding of such terms as historicity, dialectic, and stages of consciousness. When history became an objectification of the existential memory of a people, then the emergence of historical conscious- ness required theology to account for its prescientific stage in a more methodical fashion.

The 1961 *De Deo Trino: Pars Analytica* focused on the troubled analytic part of theology. Before now, history was treated as a separate process apart from the analytic/synthetic procedures of speculative theol- ogy. Now the analytic part of theology is historical as well. It is historical both objectively and subjectively. The history treated in theology's analytic part was seen to be both doctrinal and sacred. In order to integrate biblical theology with doctrinal and sacred history, we must understand what constitutes a mentality that is differentiated or undifferentiated. Formerly, the analytic way was the accomplishment of a single theologian or school that moved from the revealed truths to the limited understanding that was available at the time. Here the analytic way was much more the movement of history itself. As a *via historica*, it reviewed the various specific and culturally conditioned usages of the magisterium in particular historical circumstances. While its task now was to discern "the same dogma, the same meaning and the same view" (DB 1800, DS 3020) inherent in the diverse cultural formulations of dogma, the earlier aim of the analytic process was not entirely left behind. So an ambiguity which remained in the 1961 formulation of the analytic way was historical since it still had not differentiated the positive part of theology from the dogmatic part.

In the 1964 *De Deo Trino I: Pars Dogmatica*, a major reformulation of the analytic way resolved the former ambiguity about its function as historical. Now there appeared the significant development of the analytic way that was expressed in its further designation, the *via dogmatica*. The development here is the differentiation between the aims and procedures of positive and dogmatic theology. The dogmatic aim is to demonstrate how Church dogmas are implicitly contained in the sources of revelation. Positive theology aims at discovering the intelligibility that is present in the data of specific historical events. Furthermore, the analytic way no longer was exclusively concerned about the transition of ideas from premises to conclusions. As the dogmatic way, it was concerned with viewing problems and solutions in their historical context, as well as with showing the historical evolution from one mode of thought to another that underpins the development of dogma.

In the new first chapter on dogmatic development in the 1964 *Pars Dogmatica*, Lonergan indicated that the development of dogma is a transition from undifferentiated common sense to the intellectual pattern or experience. The job of positive theology is to track down these transitions, but it cannot do its job without the support and performance of the dogmatic theologian whose task is to certify what the Church teaches. So Lonergan not only eliminated the possible confusion arising from the aim of analysis in meeting the exigencies of history, but he indicated functional connections that made possible more extensive collaboration between practitioners of positive and dogmatic theology.

When Lonergan revised the 1957 synthetic part of trinitarian theology in the 1964 *De Deo Trino II: Pars Systematica*, he focused on the ordering of questions into systems and indicated that the systematic theologian's task was to order a total series of questions and answers correctly. After showing that theological understanding relates both to the truth of revelation preceding it and to the theological truth that flows from it, he theorized that the systematic theologian basically obtains the expression of the mystery he seeks to understand from catholic categories rather than from biblical categories. He then distinguishes the aim and proper method of the systematic theologian and the biblical scholar. There were distinctions given about the solutions of biblical, dogmatic, or systematic problems. After discussing the problems for positive and systematic theologians who embrace the opinion of conclusions theology, namely, that there are no properly theological principles, he added two new terms to elaborate his maturing thought on the "systematic way". Here the systematic way of doing theology is not only synthetic, the way of composition and the way of teaching or learning, it is also the way of probability and the way of logical simultaneity. So systematics does not reach for the certitude of faith that is the expression of dogmatics, but it is satisfied with understanding that is merely probable. And systematics accomplishes its deductions rapidly because with the positing of its principles, the applications of these principles are clear and expeditiously reached. Finally, instead of referring to history as theology's "third process" as the 1957 version did, the revised *Pars Systematica* of 1964 considered the recurrence of the dogmatic and systematic movements throughout time to be a "prior historical process" that contains the transitions from one system to another, from one mode of thought to another -- but a process that functions within the ambit of dogmatics.

E. Methodical Theology's Shift to the Subject

The fifth and last element of the problematic revolved around methodical theology's shift to the subject. In the 1962 "*De methodo theologiae*", we saw several reasons why Lonergan eventually transposed the twofold ordering of ideas in theology according to analysis and synthesis.

The first reason is that medieval theology, which, as we saw, neglected the dimension of time, disregarded a consideration of historical context. An historical consideration of theology's context does not pertain merely to the objects under scrutiny such as credal formulas, patristic writings, conciliar documents. The focus of a theology that considers historical context is upon the subject who in his differentiated operations makes statements that belong to a dogmatic-theological context. Lonergan found that the chief problem of putting the dimensions of time into theology, of meeting the historical exigence of focusing on the subject in his dogmatic-theological context, was to work out some sort of classification of development. Analysis and synthesis were adequate as one classification of development, as long as the development did not require a shift from one historical context to another. But with the emergence of the historical exigence, a new, more flexible classification of development was needed to account for theology's procedures.

A second reason for Lonergan's shift in his view of methodical theology is that the task of accounting for a development required new reflections on the human good, value, and meaning. These in turn raised the requirement of a further consideration of the roles of positive and systematic theology, of the four types of meaning, of hermeneutics and of history.

A third reason for the shift is that there must be a resolution of the three antitheses in theology between the worlds of the sacred and the profane, of the subject and the object, and of common sense and theory. By introducing the notion of mediation, Lonergan showed that when the analysis of human development runs into the limits exemplified by these three antitheses, then the classification of development can be made in terms of the dynamism, structure, and specialization of human conscious-ness. This focus on the subject and his operations provided a whole new perspective for meeting the complex requirements of emerging theological specialization, but how this specialization took place is beyond the scope of our study. Suffice it to say that in order to round out his explanation of development, Lonergan introduced the notion of worlds of community, theory, and interiority. How to integrate the commonsense world and the world of theory was the fundamental problem created by the need to integrate the twofold way of analysis and synthesis with history. And the integration could not be accomplished by an immobile, ahistorical system, but only by method -- by the mediation of the world of community and the world of theory by the world of interiority, by reaching down to the fundamental operations involved in knowing anything.

THE ROAD TO LONERGAN'S *METHOD IN THEOLOGY*

Concluding Remarks

In his 1967 Introduction to the first collection of Lonergan's articles, Frederick Crowe wrote that insofar as the basic structure of the analytic and synthetic processes results from a kind of transcendental deduction, "they are not likely to be changed".

> That is, just as cognitional structure is a transcendental settling the way men have to know if they are going to know at all, so there are natural inevitabilities in the two orders of the historical growth of knowledge and of its systematic communication, and such a transcendental order seems to lie behind the sketch of theological method proposed here.[15]

After 1964, however, Lonergan gave only scant mention of the analytic and synthetic processes for arranging ideas in theology after the publication of his twin volumes on the Trinity. While the development of his thought moved into functional specialization, and that movement is beyond the scope of this study, it is curious that there is so little mention of analysis and synthesis in the definitive work on theological procedures, *Method in Theology*.[16]

It may seem that the twofold process was simply discarded because it was unable to respond to the emerging demands that theology required of its own procedures in meeting the aim of faith seeking understanding in the context of historical consciousness. The fact remains, however, that the analytic and synthetic movements are perennial because they reflect how the mind works. The mind starts from what is particular, concrete and obvious, then scrutinizes the particulars until general observations emerge, then thematizes these general observations in definitions, terms, principles (analysis). In light of these principles of intelligibility, the mind descends back to the particular elements with a unified and integrating understanding of the same realities (synthesis). In theology, we see analysis as the movement from a rather descriptive, culturally limited expression of a truth of revelation to its more objectified thematization and universal application.

Likewise, in theology we view synthesis as the systematic ordering of the whole truth that derives from a deeper understanding of the mystery as objectified on the theoretic level. So Crowe's observation of 1967 is correct that the historical growth of knowledge and its systematic communication mirror the way the mind works, hence that these two processes are still present in the changed context of methodical theology. In fact, Lonergan himself supports this conclusion. In the 1975 article, "Christology Today: Methodological Reflections", he referred once again to the twofold procedures:

> In theology, finally, one proceeds not only from the data of revelation to more comprehensive statements but also from an imperfect, analogous, yet most fruitful understanding of mystery to the syntheses that complement a *via inventionis* with a *via doctrinae*.[17]

In a footnote to this quotation, he said that the *via doctrinae* corresponds to the functional specialty, systematics, and that the *via inventionis* would cover the first four or perhaps five previous specialties (research, interpretation, history, dialectic, foundations). This means that the analytic and synthetic processes are still present, only now more distinctly differentiated and conceived in a new fashion. Another work that substantiates this assessment is the 1972 St. Michael's (Spokane) lectures on the integration of the philosophy of God and the theology of God. The presence of the old procedures, however, can only be properly understood in the context of the horizon of methodical theology and in light of the contemporary developments in the notions of science, philosophy, and critical history.[18]

A few observations remain. First, is there any value in trying to emulate the procedure recommended by the "way of composition", namely, to organize an entire course according to a single unifying idea? The functional specialty, systematics, of *Method in Theology* remains the "way of composition", and the prior functional specialties of dialectic and foundations are the derivation for the type of ordering of ideas that systematics accomplishes. So the "way of composition" is a recommended procedure, even if it is one that requires the collaboration of many specialists. While the learning theory is sound that says that students learn more effectively from a unifying insight than from an accumulation of examples, the task of presenting a course according to a unified, basic principle would require the synthesis not only of the ideas involved in the subject area, but an explanation of the context, the meaning, and the evolution of the ideas in the horizon of the thinkers who conceived them. Lonergan's explanation of the elements of the "way of composition" reveals just how cumulative is the task of systematics and how reliant upon the prior functional specialties.

A second observation relates to Lonergan's own use of the twofold procedures in arranging his theological writings. It seems that he was able to organize his trinitarian thought into two distinct treatments because this was the procedure he recognized as the culmination of Aquinas' trinitarian presentation. While Lonergan's contribution was to thematize what St. Thomas did, still he benefited enormously from the structuring of the trinitarian reflections he found in Aquinas, a benefit that shows up in his separate treatment of the speculative and dogmatic parts of trinitarian theology. Perhaps the reason he did not organize his Christological texts in a similar fashion is that without the massive groundwork done by a St. Thomas, such an effort at organization would be too demanding for one thinker. Clearly, Lonergan's own interests became less caught up with the particular theological issues of his day and more with the theoretic and methodical exigencies of theological procedures. This concern for the transcendent questions perhaps accounts as well for the infrequent use of the analytic/synthetic procedures in his own theological productivity.

A third observation relates to Lonergan's interest in the theoretic part of methodical development rather than in answering practical issues on various topics. His pervasive theoretic interest is clearly present in *Insight*, written as a general exploration of methods in order to provide foundation for a method in theology. While the intentionality analysis of *Insight* took him beyond the horizon of theology conceived in the manualist tradition, he seems only later (especially with the Introduction to the *Divinarum personarum* and with *"De intellectu et methodo"* as well as with *De Deo Trino: Pars Analytica* and the revision of the trinitarian volumes in 1964) to have understood all of the implications of the historical dimension for theology when he wrestled with the role of historical consciousness in the explanation of the development of dogma. Perhaps his almost exclusive interest in the cognitive side of methodological development has a bearing on the way his thinking about the analytic/synthetic procedures evolved. It might be argued that he continued to use them and theorize about them well after he first thematized them in 1954 -- and that this continued maintenance of the procedures stemmed from an exaggerated concern for theology as fundamentally a cognitive set of operations focusing on intellectual content. Historicity raised existential questions about the human good, value, meaning, about the subject as authentic, intellectually, morally, religiously converted. So increasingly Lonergan could not be content with a procedure that simply dealt with the arrangement of ideas, as if ideas were all that needed arranging or attending to in doing theology. With the need to differentiate and integrate theology's historical movement and its dogmatic and systematic parts, he had to make a shift from the analytic and synthetic procedure's focus on premise/conclusions and move to methodical theology's concern for problems and solutions of the subject. This shift he was able to accomplish later as he transposed analysis and synthesis through functional specialization in *Method in Theology*.

One final observation. In Lonergan's writings on theological method during 1940-1964, he seemed to be almost defensive in returning again and again to the topic of theology's procedures. It was almost as if he wanted to justify the legitimacy of calling theology a science. He borrowed the processes used by natural science and adjusted them to his needs, but not without the huge difference in theology -- that one begins not from data but from revealed truth. After 1964, he taught that even theology as a science begins from data -- the data on the conversion of the religious subject. And after 1964, he emerged from the theological horizon dominated by St. Thomas; after February, 1965, he entered the methodological context that grounded functional specialization in the levels of consciousness in human self-transcendence. Once he had seen for himself how theology is scientific, how its procedures need not be expressed in terms of the conspicuously successful processes of natural science, then he could leave behind the terminology of analysis and synthesis borrowed from an earlier scientific ideal but no longer adequate to express theology's scientific procedures in a theological milieu sensitive to historical consciousness.

NOTES

CHAPTER IX

[1]Bernard J.F. Lonergan, S.J., *Verbum: Word and Idea in Aquinas* (South Bend, Indiana: University of Notre Dame Press, 1967), p. 214.

[2]Bernard J.F. Lonergan, S.J., *Understanding and Being, An Introduction and Companion to Insight*, ed. Elizabeth A. Morelli and Mark D. Morelli (Toronto: The Edwin Mellen Press, 1980), p. 62.

[3]Bernard J.F. Lonergan, S.J., "Theology and Understanding", in *Collection*, ed. Frederick E. Crowe, S.J. (New York: Herder and Herder, 1967), p. 134.

[4]Bernard J.F. Lonergan, S.J., *Divinarum personarum conceptio analogica* (Rome: Gregorian University, 1957), p. 27.

[5]Bernard J.F. Lonergan, S.J., *"De intellectu et methodo"* (mimeographed student notes, Rome: St. Francis Xavier College, 1959), pp. 17-22.

[6]*Ibid.*, pp. 67-68.

[7]Bernard J.F. Lonergan, S.J., *De Deo Trino: Pars Analytica* (Rome: Gregorian University, 1961), p.7.

[8]Bernard J.F. Lonergan, S.J., *De Deo Trino II: Pars Systematica* (Rome: Gregorian University, 1964), p. 15.

[9]*Ibid.*, pp. 25-26.

[10]*Ibid.*, p. 35. See Bernard J.F. Lonergan, S.J., *Grace and Freedom* (New York: Herder and Herder, 1971), p. 116; see as well *De scientia atque voluntate Dei*, Vol. III of *The Early Latin Works of Bernard J.F. Lonergan,*

S.J., ed. Frederick E. Crowe, S.J. (Toronto: Regis College, 1973), the references to "*simul*".

[11]Bernard J.F. Lonergan, S.J., "The Method of Theology", (summer institute, Toronto: Regis College, 1962), transcribed from the tapes taken for the 1962 summer course at Regis College by John Brezovec, Vol. I, pp. 52-55.

[12]*Ibid.*, Vol. I, pp. 178-187. A shortcoming with the presentation of the notion of dialectic here was that its conception embodied a somewhat exaggerated emphasis upon dialectic's cognitive component. This almost exclusive concern for dialectic as operating in the realm of intellect contrasts with the fuller notion of the fourth level dialectic expressed in chapter ten of *Method in Theology*.

[13]Lonergan, *Understanding and Being*, pp. 6-10.

[14]Bernard J.F. Lonergan, S.J., *Gratia Operans: A Study of the Speculative Development in the Writings of St. Thomas of Aquin* (Rome: Dissertatio ad lauream in facultate theologica Pontificiae Universitatis Gregorianae, 1940), p. 4.

[15]Frederick E. Crowe, S.J., ed., "Introduction" in *Collection: Papers by Bernard Lonergan, S.J.* (New York: Herder and Herder, 1967), pp. xxv-xxvi.

[16]Bernard J.F. Lonergan, S.J., *Method in Theology* (London: Darton, Longman & Todd, 1972), p. 394. The reference to the twofold procedure occurs under the heading, "Order", in the Index. There is another reference, although oblique, on p. 136. Furthermore, the only allusion in the Index to "wisdom" is to wisdom literature as the beginning of philosophy, p. 275, although there are other references to wisdom not indicated in the Index, pp. 269 and 289.

A CRITICAL REVIEW

[17]Bernard J.F. Lonergan, S.J., "Christology Today: Methodological Reflections", *Le Christ Hier, Aujourd'hui et Demain* (Quebec: Laval University Press, 1976), pp. 45-65. Footnote 10 is on p. 50.

[18]Bernard J.F. Lonergan, S.J., *Philosophy of God, and Theology* (Philadelphia: The Westminster Press, 1973), p. 34. "The proposal, then, that philosophy of God be treated along with the functional specialty, systematics, does not stand alone.... There is supposed a notion of theology that integrates a religion with the culture in which it functions.... Textual criticism and the edition and indexing of texts used to be considered merely auxiliary disciplines, but in *Method in Theology* they are regarded as the functional specialty, research. Exegesis once was considered merely an auxiliary discipline, but in *Method in Theology* it is regarded as the functional specialty, interpretation. History once was considered an auxiliary discipline, but in *Method in Theology* it is regarded as the functional specialty, doctrines, while their foundational function has been handed over to the evaluations and decisions of the functional specialties, dialectic and foundations. Philosophy used to be regarded as the *ancilla theologiae*, the handmaid of theology; it happens however that the handmaid for some centuries has gone in for women's liberation, and so in *Method in Theology* the philosophy that the theologian needs is included in the first four chapters on Method, The Human Good, Meaning, and Religion. Finally, what in Aquinas were considered probable arguments for the truths of faith or reasons for confirming Christians in their faith, in a later age became proofs from theological reason. In *Method in Theology* they are placed in the functional specialty, systematics, and its function is not to prove but to endeavor to find some understanding of the propositions established as true in the preceding functional specialty, doctrines."

BIBLIOGRAPHY OF WORKS CITED

1. The Works of Bernard Lonergan

We list here in chronological order all the works of Lonergan that were cited. A complete bibliography is available at the Lonergan Research Institute of Regis College, Toronto.

"*Gratia Operans*: A Study of the Speculative Development in the Writings of St. Thomas of Aquinas", a thesis written under the direction of Rev. Charles Boyer, S.J., and submitted at the Pontifical Gregori an University, Rome, towards partial satisfaction of the conditions for Doctorate in Sacred Theology, 1940. The dissertation includes a 47-page Introduction which remains unpublished.

"St. Thomas' Thought on *Gratia Operans*", *Theological Studies*, II (1941). 289-324; III (1942), 69-88, 375-402, 533-578. Reprinted and edited by J. Patout Burns as *Grace and Freedom: Operative Grace in the Thought of St. Thomas Aquinas*. New York: Herder and Herder, 1971.

"*De sacramentis in genere: supplementum*". L'Immaculee-Conception, Montreal, 1940-1941.

"*De materia confirmationis: supplementum*". L'Immaculee-Conception, Montreal, 1943.

"*De notione sacrificii*". Notes for lectures at L'Immaculee-Conception, Montreal, 1943-1944.

De ente supernaturali: supplementum schematicum. 1946. Vol. II of Frederick E. Crowe, general editor, *The Early Latin Works of Bernard J.F. Lonergan*. Willowdale (Toronto): Regis College, 1973.

"The Assumption and Theology". First published, *"Vers le dogme de L'Assumption"*, *Journees d'etudes mariales*, Montreal, 1948, pp. 411-424. Reprinted in F. E. Crowe, S.J., ed., *Collection: Papers by Bernard Lonergan, S.J.* New York: Herder and Herder, 1967.

Verbum: Word and Idea in Aquinas, ed. David B. Burrell, C.S.C. Notre Dame: University of Notre Dame Press, 1967. This is a republication of articles originally published in *Theological Studies*, VII (1946), 349-392; VIII (1947), 35-79; 404-444; X (1949), 3-40, 359-393.

De scientia atque voluntate Dei: supplementum schematicum. 1950. Vol. III of *The Early Latin Works of Bernard J.F. Lonergan*.

De sanctissima Trinitate: supplementum quoddam. Rome: Gregorian University, 1955.

De constitutione Christi ontological et psychologica. Rome: Gregorian University, 1956. 2nd, 3rd, and 4th editions in 1958, 1961, and 1964 unchanged.

Insight: A Study of Human Understanding. London: Longmans, Green and Company, 1957.

"Existentialism: Lectures at Boston College, July 1957". Montreal: Thomas More Institute, 1957. (28 pp. mimeographed).

Divinarum personarum conceptio analogica. Rome: Pontifical Gregorian University, 1957.

Lectures on *Insight*. Tape recordings of lectures given at St. Mary's University, Halifax, 1958. Published as *Understanding and Being, An Introduction and Companion to Insight*, ed. Elizabeth A. Morelli and Mark D. Morelli, Toronto: The Edwin Mellen Press, 1980.

THE ROAD TO LONERGAN'S *METHOD IN THEOLOGY*

"De intellectu et methodo". *Reportatio* of the course at the Gregorian University. Rome: St. Francis Xavier College, 1959. (72 pp. mimeographed).

"The Philosophy of History". Montreal: Thomas More Institute, September 23, 1960. Tape recording and typescript, 14 pp.

De Verbo Incarnato. Rome: Gregorian University, 1960.

De Deo Trino: Pars Analytica. Rome: Gregorian University, 1961.

"De methodo theologiae". Notes from lectures at Gregorian University, Rome, 1962, 60 pp.

"Method of Theology" course. Tape recordings transcribed by John Brezovec and three sets of student notes (Crowe, Fallon, Martinez) from course given at Regis College, Toronto, July 9-20, 1962.

De Deo Trino I: Pars Dogmatica (Editio altera et recognita), *II: Pars Systematica* (Editio tertia et recognita). Rome: Gregorian University, 1964. 308 and 321 pp.

"The Dehellenization of Dogma", *Theological Studies*, 28 (1967), 336-351, reprinted in William Ryan, S.J. and Bernard Tyrrell, S.J. editors, *A Second Collection*. London: Darton, Longman & Todd, 1974.

"Philosophy and Theology", Medalist's Address in *Proceeding of the American Catholic Philosophical Association*, 46 (1970), 19-30. Reprinted in *A Second Collection*.

Method in Theology. New York: Herder and Herder, 1972.

"Insight Revisited", Milwaukee: Marquette University, 1972. 18 pp. Reprinted in *A Second Collection*.

A CRITICAL REVIEW

Philosophy of God and Theology. Philadelphia: The Westminster Press, 1973.

"Christology Today: Methodological Reflections". Lecture in *Colloque de Christologie* Laval University, Quebec, 1975, printed in *Le Christ Hier, Aujourd'huiet Demain.* Quebec: Laval University Press, 1976.

The Way to Nicea: The Dialectical Development of Trinitarian Theology. Translated by Conn O'Donovan from *De Deo Trino I: Pars Dogmatica,* 1964. London: Darton, Longman & Todd, 1976.

2. Secondary Bibliography

Aumonier, Eric. *"Traite de la Trinite et methode Theologique",* Science et Esprit, 25 (1975), 319-339.

Carmody, John. "Lonergan's Latin Theology: Resume and Critique", *The Princeton Seminary Bulletin,* 68 (Autumn, 1975), 81-89.

Collins, James. "Bridging the Chasm", review of *Collection in The Critic,* (August-September, 1967), 64-67.

Conley, Peter Vincent. "The Development of the Notion of Hermeneutics in the Works of B.J. Lonergan, S.J.". Thesis for S.T. D., The Catholic University of America, 1972.

Corcoran, Patrick E., S.M.,ed., *Looking at Lonergan's Method.* Dublin: The Talbot Press, 1975.

Crowe, Frederick E., S.J. "Bernard Lonergan", in Thomas E. Bird, ed., *Modern Theologian, Christians and Jews.* New York: Association Press, 1967, 126-151.

-------. *The Doctrine of the Most Holy Trinity.* Willowdale: Regis College, mimeographed for the use of students, 1965-1966, 198 pp.

THE ROAD TO LONERGAN'S *METHOD IN THEOLOGY*

-------. "Doctrines and Historicity in the Context of Lonergan's Method", *Theological Studies*, 38 (1977), 115-124.

INDEX

positive 2, 3, 9, 17-21, 43, 45, 46, 56, 58, 68, 69, 73, 76, 79, 81, 83, 84, 86, 98, 102, 105-108, 111, 115, 116, 124, 127, 128, 135, 140-142, 153, 154, 157, 158, 165, 170, 174-176, 182, 185, 187, 192, 196-198, 200-207, 209, 211-213, 217, 232-234, 239, 241, 249, 250, 253, 256-259, 261

speculative 2-4, 9, 16-20, 23-25, 27, 31, 33-35, 39-43, 48, 53, 55, 62-69, 71, 73, 77-79, 81, 83-85, 105-108, 111, 115, 116, 119, 127, 128, 130, 138, 140, 141, 148, 151, 152, 153-155, 157-159, 161, 165, 174, 185, 186, 196, 197, 211, 213, 217, 240, 242, 246-250, 255, 257, 258, 264, 268, 270

systematics 10, 175, 190, 234, 235, 238-241, 260, 263, 264, 269

teaching 3, 15-17, 19, 20, 24, 31, 33-42, 53, 57-68, 71, 74-80, 91, 104, 107, 120, 121, 125, 126, 163, 170, 174, 200, 231, 235, 237-239, 247, 249-251, 257, 260

theology 1-11, 13-15, 15-24, 27, 29, 34, 35, 37-42, 44-49, 51, 53-58, 60, 62-69, 71-73, 75-81, 83-86, 89-91, 98, 100, 101, 105-108, 110, 111, 114, 115-117, 120, 121, 125-129, 131, 132, 139-146, 148, 151, 152, 153-155, 157-162, 165, 169-183, 185, 187, 188, 190, 192, 195-207, 209, 211-214, 217-220, 223-225, 228, 231-234, 236-239, 241, 245, 246, 248-273

via analytica 3-5, 21, 84, 92-96, 99, 105, 158, 170, 186, 187, 190, 212, 218, 234, 236, 238, 241

via compositionis 7, 22, 31, 43, 50, 75, 121, 185, 195, 211, 238 *via dogmatica* 5, 212, 218, 258

via resolutionis 7, 31, 75, 185, 195, 211, 238

via synthetica 4, 5, 21, 84, 92, 93, 96, 99, 105, 158, 174, 190, 218, 234, 236, 238, 241, 237, 238, 240

way of analysis 257, 261

way of composition 16, 17, 19, 24, 25, 31-34, 39, 41-44, 46, 48, 49, 53, 74, 75, 87, 88, 89, 91, 174, 235, 237, 247, 248, 260, 263, 264

way of discovery 17, 32-34, 40-42, 53, 57-61, 63-67, 74, 77-80, 120, 124, 126, 163, 171, 236, 237, 250, 257

way of resolution 16, 17, 19, 24, 31-34, 39, 41, 44-46, 74 ,75, 87, 89, 91, 121, 171

way of synthesis 237, 238

AUTHOR INDEX

Abelard 141, 142, 219

Banez 30

Beumer 5, 54-57, 62, 65, 71, 72

Bleau 21

Brezovec 19, 28, 192, 242, 268, 272

Bultmann 135, 166

Burrell 26, 50, 271

Coreth 187

Crowe 3-6, 13-15, 50, 51, 21, 26-28, 50, 51, 54, 64, 80, 161, 193, 262, 263, 267, 268, 270-273

Dunne 15

Egan 15, 272

Euclid 131, 168, 208

Fallon 81

Fogliacco 5, 14

Jaspers 180

Kant 177

Lazarus 128

Lennerz 19, 42

Lombard 142

Lonergan 1-11, 13-15, 15-29, 31-35, 38-45, 47-51, 53-60, 62-66, 68, 69, 71-81, 83, 84, 86-92, 94-96, 98, 99, 102-104, 107-114, 165, 166, 168-178, 180, 183-193, 195-198, 203, 204, 207-214, 217, 218, 220, 222, 227, 231, 234, 236, 238-242, 245-251, 253-257, 259-265, 267-271, 273, 274

Morelli 267, 271

Mueller 41, 44

O'Donovan 14, 42, 51, 214, 273

Peckham 104

Ryan 15, 51, 272

Sartre 180

Thomas 10, 14, 15, 15, 16, 19, 20, 23, 24, 26, 27, 29, 33-35, 37-40, 42, 43, 48, 49, 53, 55-57, 59, 60, 62-64, 66, 71, 92, 94, 109, 114, 165, 166, 168, 177, 191, 204, 213, 219, 226, 227, 246, 249-252, 257, 258, 264, 265, 268, 270-273

Toynbee 167

Tracy 2-4, 7, 13-15,

Tyrrell 15, 51, 81, 272